THE PENNILESS BILLIONAIRES

MAX SHAPIRO

THE
PENNILESS
BILLIONAIRES

A Truman Talley Book

Times BOOKS
New York

Published by *Truman Talley Books* • *Times Books,* a division of
Quadrangle/The New York Times Book Co., Inc. Three Park
Avenue, New York, N.Y. 10016

Published simultaneously in Canada by
Fitzhenry & Whiteside, Ltd., Toronto

Library of Congress Cataloging in Publication Data

Shapiro, Max, 1909–
　　The penniless billionaires.

　　"A Truman Talley book."
　　Includes index.
　　1. Inflation, Finance—History. I. Title.
HG229.S434 1980　　　332.4′1′09　　　80-5131
ISBN 0-8129-0923-2

Manufactured in the United States of America

This book is dedicated
to my wife Hannah,
in appreciation of her help
and understanding.

CONTENTS

THE PENNILESS BILLIONAIRES

What Early Men Learned About Money

Despite the impression created by many economic historians, Adam Smith did not lead the human race out of a wilderness of monetary ignorance. Thousands of years before A.D. 1776, when Smith's book *Wealth of Nations* was published, primitive men and women had already acquired a vast store of information about the nature, function, and dynamics of money. In fact, such knowledge had been attained long before 700 B.C., when the first government-minted coin was put into circulation.

But for most economic historians the vast, dark terrain stretching back thousands of years prior to 700 B.C. remains uncharted domain. The tendency by modern observers to overlook the monetary lessons learned during prehistoric periods is pungently discussed by Paul Einzig, a perceptive economist, in his book *Primitive Money.* He says:

I consider primitive money to be a "terra incognita" in many respects. Monetary historians prefer to confine themselves largely, if not entirely, to the study of the evolution of money in comparatively recent periods. ... And the worst of it is that—even though most economists have spent very little time in investigating primitive money—textbooks on monetary history and on monetary or economic theory dutifully register in a few conventional paragraphs their author's views on the origin and early evolution of money.

Economists whose names are household words commit themselves unhesitatingly to views on primitive money without taking the trouble to study even such material on the subject as is easily accessible. Most of them still live on the few stimulating but casual remarks on the subject in Smith's *Wealth of Nations.* They take in one another's highly inadequate washing and do not even trouble to find original instances to illustrate the well-worn conventional theories which they put forward with an amazing degree of self-assurance.

What are some of the important insights primitive men and women obtained about money? To answer that question we need to take a backward look—however fleeting—into the prehistoric past.

For about a million years, the human race learned nothing about money simply because it had not yet been invented. There was no need for money because there was a chronic shortage of goods available for exchange. Existence in most areas of the world was a struggle to stave off starvation. Day after day, bands of women foraged in uncultivated fields and woodland underbrush for wild-growing fruits, roots, and hard-to-find grains, while the men of the tribe joined in a common hunt for meat-bearing animals. At the end of each day the slim pickings were pooled and doled out to each family. On the following day the procedure would begin again. Under such conditions there were no items available for trade.

Then, one day in the eighth millennium before Christ, an unknown person—probably a woman—planted some barley, tended it, and brought forth humanity's first cultivated food. This act—the birth of agriculture—proved to be one of the most important developments in mankind's existence. Society moved from food-gathering to food production, from a hazardous subsistence to a more secure and more abundant way of life. In the beginning the change was imperceptible, but as more crops were created and as more land was cultivated, the impact was unmistakable. The world did not suddenly become a cornucopia. (Despite all its technological improvements, today's advanced agriculture cannot adequately feed all of the world's population; the rudimentary farming of the prehistoric world was even more unavailing.) But the life span rose, population increased, and the living standard improved.

By 7000 B.C., agriculture had become the primary subsistence of village farmers in a number of areas in southwestern Asia. Until around 5000 B.C., farming and animal-raising remained tribal or collective enterprises. After that time, more and more farmland became privately owned.

This gradual shift brought about a division of labor and the beginning of trade. Farmers—freed from the task of hunting for food—could devote their full time to their own profession. They depended increasingly on toolmakers for agricultural implements. Toolmakers, who could now depend on farmers for food production, could devote all their efforts to their vocation. Archival evidence illuminates the great diversity of labor and output existing in ancient times after the rise of agriculture. Recorded material referring back to a civilization that existed in southern Mesopotamia in 4000 B.C. describes a community containing the following: "farmers, herdsmen, smiths, plow-makers, metalworkers, carpenters, basket-makers, masons, weavers, leather-workers, potters and merchants."

As production rose and became more diverse, barter developed. The toolmaker in need of flour attempted to exchange his product for the output of the miller. The pottery maker in need of barley looked about for a barley-raising farmer who was in the market for clay pots and jars. The trade of one commodity for another worked well when both parties in the transaction were readily joined. But it was a clumsy, difficult, and inefficient means of exchange in most instances. For example: winter is coming on and A, the pottery maker, is eager to get some flour before the bad weather sets in. He approaches B, the local miller, who promptly tells him he has lots of flour but doesn't need pots or jars or pans. He does need two new large milling stones, but unfortunately, C, the village stonemaker, doesn't need flour. So A, the pottery maker, goes to the stonemaker and tries to trade pots for milling stones. But as luck would have it, C already has enough pottery to last him several years. What he needs is some barley but lately he hasn't been able to interest a single farmer in stones of any kind. A, after much searching and trudging, finds a farmer in a nearby village who is willing to exchange barley for two large clay jars. He takes the barley to C, the stonemaker, trades it for two heavy milling stones. He now hauls the two stones to B, the miller, and trades them for the much needed flour. At last the circle of exchange has been closed, but in the process, the pottery maker has lost almost a full day and has plodded across eight miles of countryside.

Primitive men struggling against the intricacies of barter must have importuned the gods for a better answer. The solution came, not from the gods, but from the perceived effect of supply and demand in the marketplace.

As barter expanded with the increase in population, commodities maintained a relatively stable value to one another. If you exchanged a medium-sized ox for a young slave today, you would be able to trade a medium-sized ox for a young slave three months later. But soon people began to notice that on those rare occasions when there was an oversupply of some item, that item's trade value in relation to other goods began to decline. The maker of arrows who could not move his output because of a sudden drop in demand began to offer his wares at a discount from their former exchange value. Whereas he had been able to obtain a measure of flour for two arrowheads in the past, when demand was good, he was now willing to offer three arrowheads for the flour.

Conversely, it soon became evident that those basic goods which were in constant demand, and in limited supply, maintained a steady exchange value or rose in value against other products. Wheat—always in strong demand—was usually one of the consistent value items.

Gradually, primitive people began to save small quantities of wheat as a reserve asset to facilitate barter. The pottery maker attempting to exchange his output for tools no longer had to find a toolmaker who at that very moment needed pottery. He could offer him some of the hoarded wheat; in all likelihood the toolmaker, convinced of the durable trade value of the wheat, would be willing to exchange his tools for the grain. As more and more people accepted wheat as a reserve asset, the "staff of life" became a recognized medium of exchange—it became humanity's earliest form of money, the accepted measure of the value of other commodities. As a monetary medium, it possessed those three criteria which are required of modern money: (1) it was a recognized medium of exchange, (2) it was an effective store of worth, and (3) it was a measure by which other commodities were valued.

The earliest instance in which wheat was used as money is unknown. But a clue is furnished by pottery remains uncovered through archaeological digs in various areas bordering on the Mediterranean Sea. Dating back to the first half of the fifth millennium B.C., these fragments depict scenes of marketplaces where various items are being exchanged for uniform measures of wheat. On viewing these etchings, one can have little doubt that the wheat was being used as a medium of exchange and a measure of value.

Barley was another form of ancient money. For an estimated 1,500 years, probably as far back as 4500 B.C., it was the chief medium of exchange in the southern part of Mesopotamia, the Levant, Anatolia, and various areas of southwestern Asia.

A host of other commodities served as money in primitive times. Salt, for example, was used extensively in Asia, Africa, and Europe during early periods. The height of its popularity as a medium of exchange probably occurred during the Roman Empire. At that time it was used to settle accounts and pay the wages of workers and the salary of soldiers. The word "salary" comes from the Latin word *salarium,* meaning "salt." Salt continued as a medium of exchange into the twentieth century. Until World War II, road workers in the Congo were paid in salt. In New Guinea coarse salt remains, until this day, an important exchange medium. After the Russian Revolution of 1917, when paper money became discredited, salt became a leading barter item, and by 1920 it had become the chief standard of value in Moscow as well as an excellent store of wealth and medium of exchange—in short, for a brief period it had, once again, become money.

Oxen and cows served as an important money form in ancient times. Homer, the Greek poet, frequently refers to the ox as a means of exchange in both of his famous works, the *Iliad* and the *Odyssey.* He describes a competition in which the first prize is a tripod "that the Achaeans priced amongst themselves at the worth of twelve oxen." The second prize was "a woman of manifold skills, worth four oxen." A cauldron "that the fire hath not yet touched" was valued at one ox. A certain shield, "a rare work of art, all gold—a hundred oxen's price." In the *Iliad,* a son of King Priam upon being sold as a captive "fetched the price of a hundred oxen. Later he was redeemed for thrice that." In the *Odyssey,* Homer refers to the purchase of a slave girl by Laertes, "who gave for her the price of twenty oxen."

Oxen and cattle have served as money in such diverse places as Indochina, Kenya, Uganda, Zambia, Germany, Russia, southwest Asia, northern Africa, and the Mediterranean areas of Europe. In such areas the ox or cow was used as a monetary unit when large transactions were involved. For small transactions an ancillary exchange medium existed, such as stones, grains, or shells. The word "pecuniary" which the dictionary defines as "pertaining to money" comes from *pecunia,* the Latin term for "money," which in turn is based on the Latin word *pecus,* meaning "cattle."

Shells—primarily cowries or diwara (both of which are the products of snails)—have served as money in many areas of the world since prehistoric times. Brightly colored cowries, strung together into strands and predating 3000 B.C., have been unearthed in a number of graves in North Africa and Asia. Such strands have circulated as money in Micronesia, India, Indochina, Siam, Japan, Ghana, Guinea, the Sudan, the Ivory Coast, Egypt, the Congo, and various Pacific islands. The shells, obtained with great difficulty and considerable labor, are found off the east coast of Africa in waters around the island of Mafia and also off the Maldive Islands, near India. In most countries where cowries were once the principal medium of exchange, modern money now serves as a currency. However, in certain parts of Africa, the use of cowrie shell money prevailed until World War II among the more primitive tribes, its value increasing with the distance of the tribal territory from the source of supply, the island of Mafia. In many places in the interior, everything was paid for in cowries. Among the Buboka tribesmen, an ox sold for 250 cowries, a bolt of cotton had a value of 900 cowries, a bar of soap went for 200, and a bride was valued at 2,000 cowries. Among the Bassaris, who are farther removed from the source of supply, the price of a bride was 30,000 shells plus a cow.

Diwara shell money, once the leading exchange medium in Asia, has been replaced by other currencies. But it is still a medium of exchange in certain backward areas although it is being threatened daily by more modern money forms. It is used in the purchase of wives (a wife can be bought for 20 to 100 diwara strings). Fines, taxes, and contributions to secret societies are made in diwara. A man's rank in the community is largely determined by the number of fathoms of diwara he has on deposit in the community tambu house (the people's bank).

The list of primitive money forms is almost limitless: leather, beads, cloth, gongs, bells, tusks, dogs' teeth, goats, pigs, rice, sheep, and slaves. But with the passage of time, these archaic types of currencies were replaced with what each society in its time judged to be a more efficient money form. Gradually, oxen and grain were replaced by items made of metal. In the beginning of the fourth millennium B.C., the more advanced nations of that period replaced barley and wheat with copper forms and iron rings and other objects made of iron such as arrowheads and axes. Still later (between 2800 B.C. and 2700 B.C.), silver rings became a leading medium of exchange. Another step to modern currency took place in Crete around 1300 B.C., when an iron disc with the appearance of a coin, and a hole in its center, began circulating. One hundred years later, in China, discs of gold and silver became the medium of exchange. Finally, in Asia Minor, in the eighth or ninth century B.C., privately issued silver coins appeared. But the first coin minted by a government was struck in the province of Lydia around 700 years before the birth of Christ (the exact date is in dispute).

The "money road" traveled by ancient peoples, from the day the first measure of grain became an exchange medium until the time of the Lydian coinage, spanned almost 4,000 years. A four-millennium journey is more easily taken in the chapter of a book than in actuality. In reality the journey was tortuous, with some wrong turns taken and some steps retraced, but along the route, important insights about money were obtained.

The first of these is evidenced in the transition from agrarian monies to money made of base metals, such as copper, iron, and bronze. By 3000 B.C., many city-states and nations had already converted from wheat to copper forms (molds or rings). The wall paintings of the great pyramids at Gizeh, Egypt (most of which were executed before 3000 B.C.), depict market scenes in which a great deal of barter is being conducted and—more important—

payment for goods is being made in copper rings. But wheat, which was the leading medium of exchange in Egypt 500 to 1,000 years before the scenes were painted, is no longer in evidence. Other archaeological findings, particularly grave goods, attest to the widespread existence of base metal—especially copper—as the medium of exchange in areas where agricultural products were once the accepted money form.

Why did the change occur? It stemmed from the realization by various rulers that the hegemony they had once held over money supplies was at an end and that their nations would face upheavals unless they could restore the control they once possessed. Originally, when agricultural money first came into being, all farmland was owned by the secular ruler or by the priesthood. It was therefore possible for the government to regulate the flow of barley, wheat, cattle, or whatever agrarian money was used in a particular area. But as farmland increasingly fell into private hands (for example, in Sumer approximately 50 percent of existing farms were already privately operated by 2700 B.C.), individual farmers were able to create new money almost at will, simply by raising it. Cognizant of the inherently anarchic dangers, rulers of nations sought substitute money forms which they could once again regulate. Copper and iron appeared to be the answer to the problem since the base-metal mines then in existence were exclusively the property of kings. Moreover, copper ornaments of all sorts were prized by the population and were regarded as a store of wealth; in many areas, copper was already being used as "bride money" (for the purchase of wives) and as gifts to priests for favorable intercession with the gods. In short, the population was already prepared for the transition which rulers, in nation after nation, finally enforced.

The transition to base-metal money represented a preference by responsible leaders for established order which a controlled money supply would bring rather than the more rapid but anarchic growth which an open-ended, uncontrolled money supply might create. Agrarian money systems—despite their crudity— had brought about a very considerable expansion. Villages had grown into towns, towns into cities, and cities into nations. International trade had sprung up. Great armies had been established. Wastelands had been turned into productive farmlands and the living standard had been greatly improved. Undoubtedly, heads of government had realized that this growth—which enhanced their power—might be halted by the institution of a new, limitless money supply. However, prehistoric rulers (whom we frequently denigrate for their supposed backwardness) concluded correctly that humanity—given the opportunity—would go on creating an ever-expanding amount of new money in order to satisfy its proliferating needs and its greed, regardless of consequences. It was the responsibility of heads of state, therefore, to control the supply of money so that stability might be assured. This decision, made 5,000 years ago, may seem self-evident today. Five millennia ago, it was a primordial concept—original, daring, and important to the subsequent development of mankind.

Some economic historians have suggested that the shift from agricultural money to base-metal money which occurred early in the fourth millennium B.C. also reflected a keen insight on the part of early rulers and their advisers into what we now term "the quantity theory of money." It is possible that the kings and heads of city-states existing fifty centuries ago knew that the size of a money supply determined economic activity and growth and realized that an inordinately expanded money stock created inflation. But, unfortunately, we have no proof to substantiate what is probably a correct assessment. Writing had not yet been created and so we have no written evidence of such prescience, nor do we have any proof in wall paintings or pottery decorations. If the ancients possessed such insights, they were evidently too complex and too abstruse to record in painted images.

At any rate, the high resolve of fourth-millennium kings was not maintained by their successors. During the next thousand years (3000 B.C. to 2000 B.C.), endless hostilities broke out among city-states and war after war raged among the nations of Asia Minor, Mediterranean Europe, and northern Africa, depleting treasuries. To meet the expense of military activities, rulers expanded the quantity of new money by stepping up the output of base-metal mines and introduced silver forms into the money supply. This monetary expansion had the inevitable result: it created inflation. Prices shot upward in areas where, a millennium before, princes and kings had attempted to establish stability. An illuminating document from the period, revealing the extent of the inflation, has come down to us. It was written to the ruler of Sumer in 2022 B.C. by an enterprising mercenary, Ishba-erra.* In the letter, Ishba-erra informs the king that he has been able to buy 10,000 tons of grain at a price of a half-shekel per measure, but that the price has suddenly doubled to one shekel per measure.

In 2020 B.C., the situation became more disastrous. The price of barley and fish rose eightfold. Riots and rebellion erupted, and the king was subsequently deposed.

Other proof of soaring prices is reflected in thousands of cuneiform tablets recorded in Babylonia and Assyria. Available evidence indicates that the rulers of that era, caught up in endless hostilities and facing the greater danger of military defeat, disregarded the seeming lesser danger of enveloping inflation or desperately tried to fight fire with fire by adding new money as prices rose. The annals of the period are, perhaps, the first written evidence of monetary recklessness practiced by beleaguered heads of state—a recklessness which governments in difficulty were to manifest repeatedly throughout recorded history.

Although there is no recorded admission of the fact, the rulers who were in power during the third millennium must have come to the realization that a great deal of money begets a great deal of inflation. Written records were already being kept in many countries, revealing the rise in prices. Of course, these records were not kept as statistics, but they were maintained as legal and transactional documents. At any rate, they reflected the continuing inflation. In addition, officials in charge of mines and the smelting of metal money forms were aware of the steady creation of new money. They must have come to the inescapable conclusion that the increased money supply was responsible for the rise in prices.

Any remaining doubts on the subject can be resolved by a reading of the Code of Hammurabi, the Babylonian king who came to power in 1792 B.C. When Hammurabi took the throne, his nation was exhausted from long, intermittent wars, its economy and silver-based money weakened from heavy military expenditures. After instituting some administrative improvements and repulsing fresh attacks from rival nations, he annexed new territories and established the first Babylonian Empire. He now turned

*Cuneiform writing had begun in Egypt and Sumer around 3000 B.C.

his attention to civil and economic matters and, around 1745 B.C., promulgated his famous Code, a compendium of laws dealing with social justice, marriage, property, and commerce. Of particular interest are the sections covering money, wages, and prices.

The economic sections of the Code address themselves to two problems confronting the kingdom: a nagging chronic inflation and, simultaneously, a need for enormous amounts of money for rebuilding the nation. Hammurabi was faced with a seemingly insoluble dilemma. If he increased the amount of money in circulation, inflation would be accelerated. On the other hand, the vast expenditures he contemplated for reconstruction required a considerable expansion in the money supply. His solution of the problem is revealed in various decrees in the Code.

He ordered that barley, the agrarian money used in the area 2,000 years before his time, should be reinstated as the only medium of exchange in rural areas. However, silver—which had been the standard throughout the nation for almost a millennium—should now be used only in urban areas.

The Code specified that farm laborers, shepherds, and all persons selling their wares in rural areas "and the hire of animals shall all be paid in grain." A schedule of appropriate payments "to the scale fixed by the king" was then stipulated. The value of farm produce was also designated. In short, Hammurabi established a rigidly controlled money supply for rural areas and simultaneously invoked wage and price controls.

Loans collateralized by farmland must be repaid in barley. Interest on such loans also had to be paid in grain with the maximum yearly rate set at 33 percent.

If a debtor cannot repay a loan in silver if he resides in a city, the creditor must take payment in barley.

If a wine-seller insists that she be paid in silver instead of in grain, she shall be thrown into the water [presumably to drown].

The Code then set forth a scale of payments, or wage controls, to be made in silver to persons who were employed or offered services in cities, including tailors, carpenters, masons, artisans, bricklayers, and doctors (with specific fees designated for certain surgical services).

Although several of the remaining economic caveats in the

Code are vague, Hammurabi's intent is very plain. Since all payments for farm products and services were to be made in barley, there would be a decreased turnover in the use of the silver money supply (a step in the right direction in the struggle to check inflation). Moreover, a considerable portion of the silver money stock, which formerly would have been used for the purchase of farm products by city dwellers, was now available for reconstruction expenditures, obviating the need for additional, new money input (another important weapon in the fight against inflation).

In rural areas, the introduction of the new money supply (barley), under ordinary conditions, would have raised the price of farm products. But with the institution of wage and price controls, Hammurabi checkmated a possible increase in agricultural prices. In the cities, the wage and price controls enacted for urban areas had the same dampening effect on inflation.

This complex, highly sophisticated program—fashioned without the benefit of electronic computers, econometric models, and advice from prize-winning economists—enabled Hammurabi to achieve his two goals: the stemming of inflation and the reconstruction of his country.

The whole operation reveals a considerable insight into the interplay of economic forces, a keen understanding of the function of money, and—most important for our consideration here—a grasp of the dynamics of inflation, particularly the manner in which escalating money produces escalating prices.

Hammurabi concluded his Code with the following invocation: "The great gods proclaimed me. I am the guardian, the governor. My words are precious, my wisdom unrivaled. In the days that are yet to come for all future time may the king who is then in the land observe the words I have written."

Several years later, Hammurabi was dead and a long dynasty came to its end. The empire he had built was overrun and dismembered. Some of the moral and legal precepts outlined in the Code have survived. But the finely wrought economic plan was shattered and abandoned by the new conquerors of Babylonia.

About a millennium and a half later, a more famous king was involved in another incident which reveals the extensive monetary knowledge of antiquity. In 331 B.C., at the age of twenty-five, Alexander the Great, the king of Macedonia, rampaged through Asia. He invaded Persia's wealthiest city, Persepolis, stormed the palace of Darius the Great, captured it, looted it of its immense treasures, and burned it. The booty taken from the palace—consisting mostly of gold bullion, gold and silver coins, and precious artifacts—represented one of the largest single concentrations of wealth known in the world until that time. Its worth has been estimated at 180,000 gold talents, or about $360 million.

In terms of the bloated, debased money supplies existing today, this may seem like small potatoes; 2,300 years ago it was a staggering sum. It was 250 times the size of the entire national treasury of Macedonia when Alexander assumed power in 336 B.C. (In that year, the treasury amounted to only 700 talents, or $1.4 million, and the national debt was 1,300 talents, or $2.6 million.)

After his capture of Persepolis, Alexander decided to resume his long march to the Indian Ocean, sent messengers home with the news of his staggering booty, and pressed on to Ecbatana, another large Persian city, which he later captured. Fifteen thousand pack animals carried the spoils of war to Ecbatana. When the news of the treasure reached Macedonia, wild jubilation broke out and the long process of Alexander's deification began. The 600,000 inhabitants of that small country had suddenly become wealthy—or so they thought.

A few months later, Alexander's financial advisers and his royal treasurer who had been summoned to Persia held a turbulent meeting that lasted several days. The discussion concerned itself with the disposition of the new wealth now in their care.

The more astute men employed in the royal treasury maintained that the release of 180,000 talents into the small Macedonian economy would have a destructive effect. It would produce an initial improvement and then set off wild price rises, speculation, and instability (modern translation: it would create a chaotic hyperinflationary effect). Others at the meeting pressed for a partial release of the treasure and the creation of some new gold money. They maintained that there would be widespread discontent if the Macedonian people did not receive some tangible benefits from the extensive capture. The discussion then went on to deal with the financial needs of the nation, the current money requirements of the army, and the projected cost of Alexander's future operations.

At the end of the conference Alexander, who on numerous previous occasions had been forced to make intricate monetary decisions (including the setting of exchange ratios between newly minted gold and silver coins), took the matter under advisement.

A short time later he decided that none of the new wealth should be monetized. There would be no additions to the money supply because there was already a mild inflation and because economic needs were being adequately met with the amount of money in circulation. He concluded that a monetization of the "golden hoard" would injure his kingdom. There might be some discontent created by his decision but this would be blunted later by the news of fresh victories he foresaw. At some more appropriate time in the future, the subject could be taken up again. But for the time being, the treasure would be kept under heavy guard at Ecbatana, to be used only if military financing required sudden outlays. So ended one of the earliest reported deliberations involving a nation's money supply.

The deliberations and decision taken regarding the treasure at Ecbatana reveal that Alexander and some of his ministers possessed considerable economic sophistication, understood the mechanism of inflation, and recognized the effect of the quantity of money on demand and prices. And—what is equally relevant —faced with political and social risks (the resentment of a population denied the beckoning benefits of great, new wealth), they preferred stability to prestige and a temporary increase in their own power.

A postscript is appropriate. Fate disposed of the golden hoard with characteristic irony. Its value of 180,000 talents was immediately eroded because Alexander began dipping into it to fund his military campaign in Asia. Dissatisfied officers and soldiers guarding it reduced it further through pilferage. A considerable amount was misappropriated by Harpalus, the royal treasurer who became more interested in the service of prostitutes than in his own service to the kingdom. In the meanwhile discontent grew in Macedonia over the decision to "let the gold lie useless in a distant desert."

When news of the treasury's shrinkage and the population's mounting dissatisfaction reached him, Alexander—who had moved eastward with his army to conduct his campaign against India—ordered that the treasure should immediately be transferred to Macedonia.

The inevitable occurred. A wild inflation broke out. It was still raging when Alexander died of fever and exhaustion in 323 B.C. at the age of thirty-three. According to some historians, at the time of his death there were more than 50,000 talents circulating in his kingdom, most of them derived from the gold of Persepolis. But this figure must be regarded as an estimate rather than a reliable statistic.

In historic retrospective, the events surrounding the golden treasure of Persepolis are uniquely interesting. But the knowledge and sophistication possessed by Alexander and his advisers was in no way unique. Many leaders who preceded him and many who were his contemporaries were equally well informed.

Their knowledge had been acquired gradually over centuries and millennia, through trial and error, and had been transmitted by word of mouth from generation to generation. The tribal chief transmitted his hard-won expertise to his son or some other person next in line of succession. Kings instructed their heirs and financial advisers to kings enlightened their sons and successors about the arcane entity called money.

Evidence indicates that the accumulated wisdom was—by design—withheld from the general population. By the beginning of the second millennium B.C., universities in more advanced nations were already offering a wide curriculum, including courses in mathematics, astronomy, biology, religion, agriculture and husbandry, medicine and surgery, philosophy, art, engineering, and writing. But there was no course in finance or economics.

Nor did ancient rulers divulge figures about royal treasuries and governmental expenditures. And, of course, governments did not maintain economic statistics in the modern sense of the word. Heads of government issued proclamations and announcements on a wide variety of subjects ranging from executions to proscriptions against using chamber pots in certain sections of the royal palace. But there were no public communications of any kind about money except in times of emergency.

Money was a royal cabal. Recognizing that money was power —power in the hands of the people which some day might be used against the Crown—the princes of antiquity decided that secretiveness and silence were the best policy. The less said in public, the better—about a potential source of trouble.

It is this lack of published information that has led many mod-

ern economists to conclude—erroneously—that the leaders in the
ancient world were economic ignoramuses who knew next to
nothing about the functioning of money.

But they knew a great deal. They had discovered that anything
could serve as a medium of exchange if it had the approval of the
State and if it was accepted as a measure of worth and was regarded by the community as a reliable store of value. Long ago
they had learned that, no matter how much money was in existence, the needs and desires of people would outrun the supply of
money. More money would beget more aspirations. They had
found that a moderate amount of money created stability but an
abundance of money—although it produced a better living standard initially—soon created difficulties as prices rose. The more
rapid the pace of newly created money—whether it was barley,
stones, dogs' teeth, or gold—the more rapid was the increase in
prices. After a while, more and more people could afford less and
less. And finally disorder would break out.

Men in authority—even in early prehistoric periods—had discovered that the attitude of the population toward money and its
uses was predominantly determined by the attitude of the existing
authority (government). If the government approached money
cautiously in both its creation and its use, then the community's
response would be conservative. But if the government created
money in great volume, then the population would become reck-
less, would spend money without restraint, would demand a constantly greater amount of it from their government, and finally
would lose confidence in its purchasing power and in the authority
which had permitted purchasing power to erode.

All this was known by persons of high power before Jesus drove
the money changers from the temple. All this—and more—was
known by the perpetrators of the superinflation which shook
Rome in the fourth century A.D.

T W O

The Roman Road
to Ruin: In the Days
of the Empire

When Augustus was installed as the first ruler of the Roman Empire in 27 B.C., jubilation and a sense of destiny enveloped Rome. Poets composed odes to the Eternal City and most of its population (of around 1 million) believed that the capital would remain the center of the civilized world throughout all of time. A new coin—a denarius of pure silver—was struck to commemorate the occasion. On one side it contained a much idealized profile of the new Emperor; the other side was inscribed with the word *Aeternitas* ("Eternity"). The coin and the state which had issued it would remain constant and would last forever!

In less than 400 years, the coin disappeared, replaced by a copper imitation whose purchasing power shrank with the passing of each day.

In 700 years the Appian Way, where Roman legions had frequently paraded in celebration of victory, was clogged with rubble and weeds. Wild dogs roamed through the ruins of the Forum, in search of food. And the 60,000 souls who inhabited the desolate place which had once been called the Eternal City now referred to it as "the great cow pasture."

But when Augustus assumed power, optimism and expectation were in the air. The Empire under his control was the greatest the world had yet known and stretched from the western shores of Spain to the eastern rim of Asia Minor, a distance of 2,500 miles. It encompassed much of northern Africa and a considerable portion of Europe. A successful military campaign conducted by Augustus shortly before he was named Imperator had brought Egypt and its vast riches into the Empire. The spoils of war and the tribute collected from various provinces flooded into Rome, lifted the living standard of the expanding nouveau riche middle class, and made new fortunes for the already immensely wealthy landowners. Property values rose and trade quickened. Stores were crammed with a dazzling variety of goods: richly painted potteries from Arretium, olives and grapes from Italy's vineyards, ornamental tiles and silver amulets from Egypt, nuts and dates from Greece, figs from Smyrna, ornaments of gold, ebony, and ivory from Nubia, rouges and pomades from various areas of Asia Minor, silks from China, copper vessels from Spain, ceramics from Dalmatia, and textiles and laces from Gaul.

Of course, the buyers of these items were predominantly men and women of wealth and members of the rising bourgeoisie. But the lower classes of Rome and other cities—the menial laborers, the shopworkers, and the badly paid petty artisans who lived on less than the equivalent of $35 a year—could afford to buy only the cheapest of these wares, and only on very infrequent occasions. The benefits of the Empire trickled down to them very, very slowly. But—what was more important—with the advent of the new Emperor, they began to feel that some day they would be able to acquire more of the items now beyond their reach.

Even the lowest of the low among Rome's citizens—the 320,000 plebs on the dole—felt a surge of hope because of "the great plan" which Augustus had announced shortly before he was installed as emperor. He had proclaimed that he would donate 250 million denarii from his personal funds to the *aerarium* (the public treasury) to finance a vast construction program which would create work for the unemployed. Substantial sums would also be given to every person on the relief rolls and to soldiers and veterans.

When Augustus turned the promised money over to the treasury, his detractors secretly accused him of "buying his way into the palace." Although his plan enhanced his popularity and influence, bribery certainly was not on his mind. His donation was an act of high generosity and far-seeing statesmanship. The immensity of his grant and the potentially stimulative effect it could have on Rome's economy can be put into perspective by comparing it with the yearly expenditures for all governmental functions. Since government outlays were then running at an annual rate of about 100 million denarii, Augustus's gift could have met all of the State's expenses for a two-and-a-half-year period. In short, his donation was about equal to a gift made to the United States Treasury in the amount of $1 trillion. (The federal budget is now running at an annual rate of $500 billion, or at a rate of $1.25 trillion every two and a half years.)

The great reconstruction project—a forerunner of Franklin Roosevelt's W.P.A. of the 1930s and the world's first example of a massive governmental make-work program to reduce unemployment—got underway with fanfare and high hope. The plan, conceived jointly by Augustus and Maecenas (the shrewd capitalist who was the Emperor's unofficial economic adviser and the steward of his monetary and economic policies), was pushed vigorously with no expense spared. The sounds of hammers and axes rang out in Italy's towns, and especially in the Eternal City. New roads were built. They radiated out of Rome to all points in the Empire like spokes extending from the hub of a great wheel. Port facilities were enlarged; bridges and aqueducts were erected. Commercial vessels—constructed at an unprecedented rate—carried a rising volume of goods in and out of Italy. Scores of amphitheaters and forums were repaired. Eighty-five temples were rebuilt and a dozen new basilicas were erected. Years later, Augustus—remembering the period of reconstruction with a sense of longing and loss—remarked, "I found Rome a city of adobe, I made it one of marble."

As the plebs found work on the various projects, their number on the relief rolls fell from 320,000 to 250,000 and later to 150,000. The small shops which dotted Italy's cities turned out a mounting volume of items from togas to tables of imported teak. But, disappointingly, only the rich and the middle classes were buying them. Despite all the money which had been injected into the economy during several years, the living standard of the working class did not improve. The increase in the common man's wages was almost imperceptible, and for good reason: the presence of a great pool of slave labor. For centuries, Rome had been extending democracy to its citizens while it imported slaves from the entire Mediterranean area. Numbering in the hundreds of thousands, slaves worked without pay in the homes and the shops of the rich and the newly rich in cities and towns and on the vast farms—the latifundia owned by some of Rome's oldest and wealthiest families. Year after year, they were imported into the Italian peninsula at the cost of a handful of silver. After the third century B.C., the nonslave population of Italy grew very slowly but the birth-rate of slaves climbed sharply. With growing frequency, slaves displaced the citizen tenant-farmers who worked on the latifundia and the menial "free" workers in the cities. And—more important —they were used by employers as a convenient threat against workers who were demanding better wages. A lowly compensated pleb insisting on higher pay could always be told that if he didn't like what he was getting, he was free to leave; there was always a slave nearby willing (and, in many cases, able) to take his place. In this manner, employers were able to enforce a chronic poverty on the millions of nonslave workers while they skimmed off the great sums expended by the State on Augustus's reconstruction effort.

But with characteristic tenacity Augustus (whom Suetonius, the great Roman historian, described as "unyielding as a leech") stuck to his task. He swelled the money supply by bringing out coin issue after coin issue. In the first twenty years of his reign, he brought out eighty issues of aurei (the gold aureus, the standard coin of the realm, was used in large transactions and governmental payments). In addition, 400 different series of denarii spewed out of the mints at the unheard of rate of twenty per year. To obtain the metal for these coins, Augustus ordered that the government-owned mines in Spain and France should be worked around the clock. He enlarged the mint in Lyons and modernized the mint in Rome. Several times when a deficit loomed (due to unusually heavy military expenditures incurred by sudden invasions by enemy troops), he dipped into his still large but waning personal funds and bailed out the government. On other occasions when the State had run out of coin and metal, he decreed that the silver statues which had been erected to his memory in numerous cities of the Empire should be melted down and converted into denarii.

There are no figures available regarding the extent by which Augustus ballooned the supply of money. Monetary, fiscal, and other economic statistics as we know them were not kept by governments 2,000 years ago, or if kept were not released. Much of the information about economic developments in ancient Rome has come down to us in historical and literary works produced by such writers as Tacitus, Suetonius, Plutarch, Horace, Virgil, Seneca, Livy, Petronius, and the biographer-historian Cassius Dio (whose monumental eighty-volume *History of Rome,* now curiously neglected, sheds considerable light on Augustan affairs). Of course, none of these writers was an economist, and so the references to money matters contained in their works are entirely nontechnical and frequently vague. Other sources which shed light on Roman socioeconomic events are the ancient coins which have been retrieved through archaeological digs as well as gravestones and tablets which—unlike their modern, uncommunicative counterparts—frequently conveyed much social and historical data. Inscriptions on walls of temples and monuments dedicated to high-ranking government officials are also valuable sources but —once again—they do not contain economic statistics per se.

The most accurate information we have available regarding the increase in money supply under Augustus comes from the coins he issued (many of which have been found in graves throughout Europe, Asia, and Africa) and from the inscriptions on the walls of the magnificent mausoleum in which he was buried (used by modern Romans as a concert hall). From these sources, we learn that the volume of money he issued in the two decades between 27 B.C. and A.D. 6 was more than ten times the amount issued by his predecessors in the twenty years before his realm!

The literary works and archival evidence of the period reveal that the cumulative effect of this cascade of coins into the economy finally produced a business boom such as Rome had never seen, with production of all kinds of goods at an unprecedented rate. And at last even the common laborer and small artisan began to feel the benefits of the easy money policy. Their pay almost doubled; their employers, unable to keep output up to the level of demand, were willing to pay more in order to get the goods turned out fast enough. Some of the better-skilled workers were able to save enough money to set up small shops of their own and moved up into the prospering middle class. Others not so enterprising chose to put aside something for a rainy day. Roman graves dating back to around 10 B.C. show evidence of this temporary prosperity. In one grave some denarii are found in an iron box. In another a vase of fairly good pottery is encountered. Burial places dating back a century prior to this period are either empty or contain some nearly worthless trifle, such as a pewter spoon—probably the sole possession of the deceased that was considered worth burying. Epitaphal evidence also attests to improved conditions. A tombstone of the early Augustan period informs the world that the deceased—a member of the leather-workers' guild—has donated 300 denarii to his association, with the stipulation that each year on his birthday "several members shall meet for a commemorative supper in my memory and eat good food so that my life will be remembered with satisfaction." Another tablet on the grave of a carpenter proclaims that the deceased has set aside 500 denarii "to have the lamp on my grave filled with oil and burn forever brightly so that I will not be forgotten." Such bequests by ordinary persons would not have been possible before Augustus's "twenty years of reconstruction." A lack of money would have precluded them.

Unfortunately, however, inflation began to wipe out these gains. The price of all kinds of goods and farm produce rose. It is estimated that between 27 B.C. and A.D. 6, the cost of wheat (the index used most frequently for the Roman Empire to reflect prices) about doubled. Pork (eaten by the plebs only on holidays and other celebrations because it was too expensive for everyday consumption) also rose by 100 percent. Real estate prices near Rome climbed by 150 percent. Interest rates which had been running at 12 percent when Augustus took power in 27 B.C. declined to 4 percent by 5 B.C.—another reflection of easier money conditions.

Apparently both Maecenas and Augustus were upset by the escalation in prices and they began cutting back the rate of coinage. Except in periods of drought and drawn-out wars, Romans did not experience inflation. Only once—in the latter part of the fourth century B.C., when Rome resorted to an abortive experiment with money debasement—did prices climb rapidly. Cicero's speeches contain many references to the steady price at which wheat could usually be bought throughout the Italian peninsula.

And so, when the cost of wheat and other goods doubled, Augustus was taken aback. In retrospect his surprise seems totally unwarranted. After all, a rise of 100 percent in twenty years represents a compounded rate of inflation amounting to only 4 percent per year, a pace we would gladly accept today. And—considering the surge of money which had flooded into Rome's economic mainstream during a comparatively short period—the resulting 4 percent inflation was almost absurdly low.

After 6 B.C., prices stabilized and finally declined moderately as Augustus throttled the creation of new money. It is estimated that in the second half of his reign (6 B.C. to A.D. 14), new coinage amounted to only 5 percent of the rate of the first half. Here was restrictive monetary policy with a vengeance! The sudden shift had a positive effect on living costs for those who could afford to live. But the poor—by far the greatest part of the population of the Empire—were pushed back into their former grinding poverty. The number of persons on the dole climbed back first to around 200,000, then gradually to 250,000, and by A.D. 14 the total reverted to more than 300,000.

A few historians have attributed the abrupt shift in Augustus's economic policies to a sudden personality change, brought on by the onset of paresis. But, although the Emperor was plagued by a variety of illnesses as he grew older, and although he was not prone to renounce an available object of lechery, there is no evidence that he ever suffered from a sexual disease. He did, however, change drastically in his last twenty years. From the optimistic, forward-looking man of action of earlier days, he became somber, irritable, and introspective. In the past he had spent fourteen to sixteen hours a day on the affairs of government, with scores of people filing steadily in and out of the modest two-room suite in the palace reserved for "work of the realm." As he grew older, he worked fewer hours, the number of people with whom he conferred dwindled, and he was frequently found in silence and alone.

Undoubtedly, a series of tragic events within his family affected him profoundly, and although no one recognized it at the time, they also shaped the future economic policy of the Empire.

At the age of twenty-five, Augustus had married his third wife,

Livia (each of his two previous marriages had lasted only several years and had ended in divorce). To all but Augustus, Livia must have seemed like a most unlikely mate for the rising general and future Emperor. She was already married when Augustus took a fancy to her, had already borne a son, Tiberius (who later became the second ruler of the Empire), and was five months pregnant with her second child when Augustus convinced her to marry him. With customary persuasiveness, he convinced her husband to assent to a divorce.

The new household consisted of Augustus and his daughter Julia by his second wife, and Livia, his new wife, as well as her two sons—Tiberius and the newly born Drusus. Although he adopted both boys, Augustus never had any affection for the older, but began to regard the younger as his possible heir when the years went by and Livia—who proved to be a little cold, ostentatiously virtuous, and a constant performer of good deeds—did not perform the one deed sought most by the Emperor: the delivery of a male heir.

The first real storm cloud showed itself several years later when Julia, his flighty and vivacious daughter, reached adolescence and began celebrating her womanhood in one sexual encounter after another. Alternating punishments and pleadings by Augustus (who adored her and was devastated by her behavior) availed nothing.

In desperation, Augustus married her off at the age of fourteen in the hope that a husband could control her. But the new groom had the good sense to die shortly afterward and Julia promptly showed all of Rome how merry widowhood could be. Her father —who was now beginning to proclaim his famous marriage laws which affirmed the moral aspects of marriage—was mortified. Again he married her off, this time to a man of forty-two, his trusted friend and collaborator Marcus Agrippa (who had to divorce his own wife before marrying Julia). Within eight years, Julia produced five children by him and boasted that in the same period she had been careful in her extramarital relationships "so as not to add to my brood."

The next blow hit Augustus when his stepson Drusus—whom the Emperor loved for his bravery, high spirits, and attractiveness —was killed in battle. Against the advice of his counselors, Augustus had elevated him to the rank of general at the age of twenty and had sent him into the battle that resulted in his death.

This was followed by the death of Marcus Agrippa eight years after his marriage to Julia. Again Julia became Rome's merriest widow. Again Augustus married her off. The unlucky choice this time was Tiberius, who had to divorce a wife he loved deeply in order to carry out the Emperor's wishes. During her third marriage Julia pursued her career of nymphomania until Tiberius, fearing that he might kill her in a fit of anger, left her and retired to a self-imposed exile in Rhodes. Another reason that might have motivated him was Augustus's hesitation to name him as his heir. During his seven-year exile, Tiberius passed the days cursing himself, Augustus, and "the Emperor's strumpet daughter." To the few visitors he received, he repeated one sentence over and over: "I sit facing the East; I have turned my back on Rome."

For seven years he seethed while the details of Julia's escapades reached him at Rhodes. Then Augustus, unable to bear the gossip and the ridicule any longer, banished Julia, forever, to an island where "no man was to reach her." Soon afterward, the only direct male heirs the Emperor had—his two grandsons, Julia's sons—died suddenly: one of typhoid and the other in battle.

Broken by these events, now in his sixties and riddled with chronic illnesses, Augustus grew progressively more morose. He began to find conspiracies where none existed. (It was in this period that he created the Praetorian Guard, the private army of the Emperor, which was to shield him from what proved to be nonexistent plots.) His enthusiasm and his belief that he could shape the course of events dwindled. And that is why the creation of new money dwindled as his reign drew to a close.

After years of hesitation, he finally asked Tiberius to end his exile in Rhodes, made him his heir, arranged to have the proconsular imperium (the control of the armed forces) pass to him, and asked the Senate to declare him his successor when the time arrived.

The time arrived in A.D. 14 when Augustus was seventy-seven. Colitis, a chronic bronchial condition, and a never-ending eczema which covered his entire body finally took their toll. There was long and genuine mourning, and a group of senators bore his coffin for hours through the silent streets of Rome. After his ashes were deposited in his mausoleum, he was deified by the Senate. He had united the Empire, quickened its commerce, strengthened various departments in the government, and had left it with a stable, highly regarded currency.

When Tiberius was installed as emperor in A.D. 14, at the age of fifty-five, he was a spent man. He had fought for almost forty years in long and difficult campaigns, having risen to the rank of general at the age of twenty. Gossip had it that Augustus would hurry him off to any distant point where a battle was raging because he disliked him and wanted him out of the way. Tiberius's problems with Julia and Augustus's refusal, for a long time, to acknowledge him as his heir and successor until there were no other "candidates" available had left him in a state of morbid anxiety.

From the moment of his installation he began fearing plots against his life and looked for plotters but—for a long time— found none. He beefed up the Praetorian Guard for protection and soon came under the influence of the commander of the Guard, a certain Sejanus. Ambitious, shrewd, ruthless, Sejanus soon concluded that the Emperor was somewhat mentally unbalanced, could be easily influenced by the proper man for the job, and could be overthrown. He fed Tiberius every comment directed against him and manufactured a steady stream of nonexistent conspiracies. As time went on, Sejanus became his only trusted adviser.

Tiberius's growing paranoia had a profound effect on the money supply and the economic life of the Empire. As he grew more fearful, he reduced the coinage of new money to a mere trickle. At the same time—mainly through a series of seizures—he accumulated a great deal of money into his *fiscus,* the royal treasury which was the property of each emperor while he was in office. Simultaneously, he added substantially to his own wealth.* But despite growing opposition, he refused to issue new money to meet the pressing needs of the public treasury. In short, he became a hoarder, a miser who piled up his money around him protectively against a threatening world.

As money dried up, commerce also shriveled. Some of the small shops in the cities failed, throwing more persons onto the relief

---

*Although the monies in the *fiscus* were supposed to be kept separate from an emperor's private funds (the *arca*), rulers intermittently treated the *fiscus* as if it were their own and "dipped" into it for their own benefit. Actually, the monies in the *fiscus* were intended for "expenditures of state," such as for games, gifts, feasts, ceremonial donations, and so forth.

rolls. In the rural areas the effect was even more serious. The price of farm produce fell and the owners of small farms could not meet their mortgage payments. They were refused credit extension by the lenders: the banks, individual professional moneylenders, and the owners of latifundia who had advanced money not only for the fat return but also in the hope that they could acquire more properties at bargain prices through foreclosure. Many small farmers gave up their holdings and fled into the cities to avoid persecution (a defaulter could be jailed until he made payment). Others turned their farms over to the big farm operators and became their serfs as land values collapsed. Then, a group of senators (who were property owners) appealed to the Emperor. Tiberius (who was a substantial holder of land throughout the Empire) promulgated an edict requiring the moneylenders to invest two-thirds of their capital in Italian farmland. This gambit miscarried when the lenders failed to comply. Finally the Senate, with Tiberius's approval, set up what was probably the world's first farmland bank, appropriating the equivalent of several million dollars for the bank's treasury. Farmers threatened by foreclosure could borrow from the farm bank, interest free, for a period of three years, by putting their farms up as collateral. In this way, the crisis was finally met.

But money continued scarce as Tiberius held coinage down. Food riots broke out in several cities. Finally—but only briefly—Tiberius relented. He brought treason charges against Sextus Marius, an owner of large silver mines in Spain. The Emperor—invoking a law newly enacted at his request which made "plotting against the Imperator" punishable by death—had Marius executed and ordered that his mines should be turned over to the State. From this source, Tiberius permitted the minting of new coins.

But the easing of money supply was short-lived. Tiberius continued his hoarding while resentment mounted against him. (Some historians have suggested Sejanus goaded the Emperor on, influencing him to pursue his restrictive monetary policy so that his reputation would be further undermined.)

In his reign of twenty-three years, Tiberius issued new money at a rate which was less than 10 percent of that of his predecessor. Moreover, most of the new money supply—consisting of aurei— had only a very marginal effect on the economy since most of the newly minted gold coins were sequestered by the government for international use. The amount of newly struck denarii for everyday use remained minuscule to the very end of his reign.

As resentment and the number of plots fabricated by Sejanus grew, Tiberius left Rome and settled in Capri, surrounded by large numbers of military guards and guard dogs. There, in his second self-imposed exile, he spent his last twelve years, leaving the field open for Sejanus, who suddenly came up with a new conspiracy against the life of the Emperor.

This one involved Tiberius's niece, Agrippina, her son, and a certain Titus Sabinus. All were found guilty. The first was banished to the same island where Julia spent her years in exile. The second committed suicide. The third was mutilated and executed.

One day in A.D. 31 his sister-in-law, Antonia, sent Tiberius a note, telling him Sejanus was plotting his assassination. The Emperor, now seventy-three, rushed to Rome, investigated, arrested the inventor of other men's plots, and handed him over to the Senate for trial. The Senate was waiting eagerly for its opportunity: Sejanus had intermittently threatened many senators and his noxious influence on the Emperor had long been resented by them.

Sejanus, as well as all of his relatives and his friends, was executed. Before being killed, his adolescent daughter was ceremonially raped before her trial because the execution of virgins was prohibited by law. His wife committed suicide, but only after writing Tiberius a letter in which she accused the daughter of Antonia of being one of Sejanus's coconspirators. She was arrested and starved herself to death in prison. Finally, Agrippina shortened her exile by killing herself.

Tiberius, now deranged to the point of incoherence, suffered a heart attack in A.D. 37. When it appeared that he was about to recover, members of the royal guard put a pillow over his head and suffocated him.

He left an empire riven with violence and 700 million denarii in the royal treasury (the *fiscus*). This was a staggering sum for those days, an amount almost thirty times the 20-odd million denarii Augustus had left. In contrast, the public treasury, the *aerarium,* had no surplus.

The hoard piled up by Tiberius, and a great deal more, was wasted during the next thirty-one years when the throne of the Empire was occupied, successively, by three lunatic autocrats.

The insane and bloody exploits of Caligula, Claudius, and Nero —chronicled in many good histories and some bad Hollywood films—are too well known to require repetition. When the three madmen were not occupied with incest, matricide, and the imprisonment and murder of thousands of innocent victims, they were busy squandering the coin of the realm. Within two years, Caligula completely dissipated the 700 million denarii amassed by Tiberius.

He wasted them on splendid religious and court ceremonies, feasts lasting several days which hundreds of thousands of Rome's citizens attended, the erection of many palatial villas for his own use, the building of marble temples where people could worship him and his proclaimed "brother," Jupiter. A great deal of money was consumed on the payment of lavish gifts to officers of the army and the Praetorian Guard whom he feared with good reason.

When Tiberius's treasure was exhausted, Caligula systematically seized the wealth of many rich families he had falsely accused of plotting against him. And he began coining money at a pace matched only by Augustus in his reconstruction period. The rate at which new money was minted in his and his successor's reign was approximately eight times that of Tiberius.

Despite Caligula's frequent payoffs to Praetorian officers, he was knifed to death one evening by the commander of the Praetorian Guard, Cassius Chaerea. For good measure, Chaerea also killed Caligula's wife and shattered his baby daughter's head against the wall.

The Guard then put forward Caligula's fifty-year-old uncle, Claudius, as the next ruler. Claudius, who had probably contracted syphilis (common in Rome at that time), had all the delusions of grandeur which accompany paresis. If Caligula's outlays were lavish, those of Claudius were grandiose. On one project alone—the draining of Lake Fucine—he spent 100 million denarii. Thirty thousand laborers and engineers worked for eleven years on the scheme. Munificent gifts were bestowed on the Praetorian cohorts at every opportunity. The poor of Rome got double rations and were entertained by races and games such as they had never witnessed.

As expenditures mounted, Claudius increased the supply of new money and killed off a rising number of wealthy men to get at their fortunes. During his thirteen-year reign, he slaughtered 35 sena-

tors and over 300 members of the equestrian class (the men engaged in banking and moneylending, officers of building corporations, officials of tax-gathering companies, and retired, moneyed
aristocrats). His atrocities and frenzied expenditures ended when
he was poisoned.

Nero, who succeeded him, at first gave no sign that he would
follow the route of his two predecessors. But in the fifth year of
his reign the first real indication of instability showed itself when
he forced some aged and unwilling senators to join him in combat
against heavily armed gladiators. A little later—when he imprisoned his mother on a sudden whim and then had her executed—
it became perfectly clear that the throne of Rome was once again
held by a madman.

Once again, the delusional expenditures were made on mass
feasts, week-long games that caught the adulation of the plebs, and
the building of bathhouses that could have passed for palaces.
Proclaiming himself a god, he erected silver statues of himself,
twenty feet high, in various cities of the Empire. But the most
exorbitant outlays were his gifts to his friends. When an accounting was taken by his successor, it was found that Nero had bestowed 800 million denarii on his cronies—enough to meet the
regular expenses of government during eight years.

Such lunatic largesse, of course, drained the treasury. Nero
decided to remedy the situation by taxation that threatened to
become confiscatory. Gaius Suetonius relates in his *De Vitae Cae-
sarum* that one day the psychopathic Emperor suddenly rubbed
his hands together and said, "Let us tax and tax again! Let us see
to it that no one owns anything!" He then reinvoked Caligula's
short-lived program which had levied a tax on "all eatables sold
in any part of the city: a fixed and definite charge; on law suits
begun anywhere: a fortieth part of the sum involved; on the daily
wages of porters: an eighth; on the earnings of prostitutes: as much
as each received for one embrace."

The burden fell on those least able to pay; as usual there was
no tax on accumulated wealth, large incomes, or vast landholdings. Not only were the taxes poorly conceived, they probably
failed also because the Empire had no effective tax-gathering system. Privately run corporations (stock companies) were engaged
by the government to collect the levies. Rival organizations would
submit sealed bids, specifying the amount each would guarantee

to collect. The highest bidder got the contract. Any monies collected over the guaranteed amount could be retained by the winning corporation and would be distributed to its shareholders. By using draconian methods in the provinces, the tax-collecting companies could sweep up a considerable amount, but in the cities of Italy where such an approach would meet with more resistance, the results usually were poor.

When taxation failed to keep up with his expenditures, Nero was forced into a fatal error: he debased the currency. The event produced consternation in Rome and a loss of confidence throughout the Empire.

Two thousand years ago, currency devaluation produced a sense of danger we cannot readily appreciate. Today, we regard the cheapening of currency almost as inevitable. We accept it as a perennial and regrettable nuisance, like crime in the streets, icy weather in winter, and infirmity in old age. We have come to believe that the deterioration of money (and accompanying inflation) will go on forever; it is our fate.

Ancient societies, however, pursued conservative monetary policies and ancient governments—particularly those of the world's more powerful nations—traditionally opposed the adulteration of money. Ever since the province of Lydia struck the first coin in the eighth century B.C., responsible governments placed great stress on the reliability, genuineness, and stability of their currency. A coin remained reliable if it remained unalloyed and maintained its original weight and size. If it remained unchanged, it—and the government which issued it—could be trusted. Those governments that (in their efforts to boost a dwindling monetary supply) tried to fob off adulterated, "clipped," or lighter coins were regarded as inferior and lacking in power.

The great value which ancient societies placed on the purity and constancy of coined money is illuminated in an edict promulgated by Solon, the archon of Athens, shortly after he assumed power in 594 B.C. To celebrate his ascension he struck a new coin and announced that from then on anyone who debased the coin would have his hands chopped off. He stipulated that the new edict would be applied to every person regardless of rank—including himself.

The reluctance of ancient governments to debase their coins was one of the primary causes of the constant state of war between nations. Since precious metals used in coinage were scarce, nations frequently ran out of money. The common way out of the dilemma was to capture the money supply of a defeated adversary. Rather than issue adulterated coins (and run the risks of inflation and loss of prestige), kingdoms and city-states preferred to run the risks inherent in warfare.

The Romans—although latecomers in the development of coinage (they used agrarian money until the fourth century B.C.)—scrupulously avoided alloying their coins. Their rulers and other leading figures frequently spoke with pride of the immutability of their gold and silver money. The inscription of the word *Aeternitas* on the coin struck by Augustus was not an empty gesture. It was the reaffirmation of a pledge and a prediction made by the Roman State for several centuries. The coin and the power of the government which had issued it would remain constant forever.

It is against this background that Nero's debasement of the gold aurei and the silver denarii must be viewed. In A.D. 64 he suddenly proclaimed that he was issuing a small supply of aurei which were 10 percent lighter in weight (forty-one aurei were until then struck from one pound of gold; forty-five aurei would henceforth be minted from one pound). The new denarius would be 12 percent lighter than the existing silver coin but—very significantly—it would be further cheapened by the addition of about 10 percent of base metal. The new denarius would therefore contain almost 25 percent less silver.

Events proceeded as one might expect. The new coins began selling at a discount from their old counterparts to the extent of their debasement, and the price of goods immediately rose. We have no exact statistics on the extent of inflation, but based on the reaction of the Roman economy in later episodes of money adulteration, the rise in the cost of living must have exceeded the 25 percent by which silver money had been devalued. But this was only the beginning of complications.

Nero, acting on the advice of his finance minister, also ordered that all old coins should be called in, melted down, reminted in debased form, and then returned to their owners. The new coins would be smaller and lighter, and the denarii would be adulterated with copper alloy. In keeping with Nero's plan, the reissued aurei would be debased by 10 percent and the denarii by 25 percent. The unreturned gold and silver that the government had extracted from the original, unadulterated coins would then be used for the minting of new coins. Nero hoped, through this stratagem, to add a considerable amount of newly minted money to the depleted public treasury and to his own *fiscus.* Gresham's law then began operating.

People concealed their old coins and began a run on the banks where they had stored their money for safekeeping or had deposited it for the interest it could bring. Not only did money go into hiding, but the owners of the money sometimes disappeared along with their coins—they emigrated—so intent were they on avoiding the debased money. Nero met this by sending his quaestors (public service employees in the financial administration) into homes to ferret out withheld coins. When this failed, he ordered small contingents of the Praetorian Guard to "search and seize." This brought some results, but rage against the Emperor mounted, and from that point on his assassination was a foregone conclusion. Finally, pressure against his program of search and seizure of undebased coins mounted and he was forced to abandon it. However, newly struck coins continued to be issued in debased form.

After a while the storm blew itself out. The rise in prices came to a halt as people, finally accommodating to the new, adulterated money, stopped chasing after goods and property to hedge themselves against inflation. Once this occurred, costs began a gradual descent; several years later they were no higher than they had been prior to the devaluation. Although the government had been able to issue a larger-than-average amount of coins (because of the amount of silver supposedly saved in each new denarius), the increase in coinage was not sufficient to maintain a stimulative effect on trade and commerce. Debasement had slightly alleviated, but had not overcome, a persistent problem of the Roman economy: a chronic shortage of gold and silver for the minting of new money.

Another factor had also aborted the initial stimulus Nero had secured from increased coinage—and, again, it reflected a deep flaw in the Empire's economy. The increase in the money supply had not produced a widespread rise in purchasing power. The newly created money had negotiated its usual ineffectual, short circuit: coins had gone out of the government mints into the treasury and out of the treasury into the strongboxes of the rich and the pockets of the middle class. But the vast majority of the people—perhaps 97 percent—received none of the money. The purchasing power of the great masses of poor people was not lifted. The common worker in Rome and other cities continued to live on about $35 a year, bought his one or two togas a year, subsisted almost entirely on bread and wine, lived in a basement or behind the shop in which he worked, and when he died his widow considered herself lucky if she could afford the $3.60 his funeral would cost. Of course, as the wealthy and increasingly opulent middle class acquired the newly minted money, they increased their buying—usually of luxury goods. But they were few in numbers and their purchases were not sufficient to raise the living standard of the seventy million common people of the Empire. Time and again newly minted money proceeded along this abortive circuit; time after time economic recovery was—literally—short-circuited.

In time Nero's treasury and the *aerarium* were—once again—in dire straits. In the end, his attempts to increase the money supply achieved no single constructive result. They had produced only a highly unsettling effect: faith in the government had for a while been badly shaken. And equally important, a dangerous precedent had been set: subsequent rulers, faced with monetary problems, would attempt to extricate themselves through money adulteration by fiat.

After his unsuccessful experiment at money manipulation Nero's influence declined rapidly. During his several remaining years he killed off thousands of Christians in mass spectacles and executed friends and purported enemies on the slightest pretext. But he overreached himself when he killed several highly regarded generals. Suddenly, in A.D. 68, Julius Vindex, an official stationed in Gaul, and Galba, the proconsul in Spain, raised an army against him and announced they would march on Rome to depose him. Nero's first reaction was to resist. He proclaimed that he would meet the traitors head on; in fact, he would lead an army against them. He promptly ordered several wagonloads of stage scenery. Between battles he would entertain his troops by acting, singing, and reciting his original poetry written for the occasion.

But the Senate had other plans. It was time to get rid of this deranged despot. After obtaining the "benevolent neutrality" of the Praetorian Guard, they met in secret session and declared Galba the new emperor.

Nero—alone and completely destabilized by the sudden events —tried to commit suicide but could not manage the act. A member of his retinue came to his assistance by slitting his throat.

There is no historical evidence of any major monetary developments in the seventy-year period which followed Nero's death. If any did occur, they have not been recorded. One interesting episode took place in the reign of Trajan (A.D. 98 to A.D. 117). After that Emperor captured and annexed the kingdom of Dacia (modern Rumania), the scene of Alexander at Persepolis was replayed. Trajan seized an enormous amount of gold coins, bullion, and gold artifacts as well as the country's gold mines. But unlike Alexander, he decided to monetize the booty. Gold suddenly poured out of the mints of Rome. The rise in the volume of newly coined gold was so great that it drove down the exchange value of the gold aureus against the silver denarius. To restore the balance, Trajan debased the silver denarius by slightly decreasing its base-metal content. The Neronian denarius had contained 10-percent alloy; the new denarius of Trajan was adulterated with a 15-percent alloy. The denarius promptly declined in exchange value vis-à-vis the aureus and the Emperor's purpose was accomplished.

Trajan might have followed Alexander's example by deferring the monetization of his Dacian treasure, but he had other designs. He was an expansive man, restless, optimistic, with visions of glory and a hunger for applause. He spent money as quickly as he coined—on buildings, the temporary tripling of the dole, and the staging of elaborate shows during holidays which he declared frequently and with much fanfare. He also spent considerable sums on two favorite projects. Implementing the plans of his predecessor, Nerva, he developed two government agencies: one was for "rural credits for farmers in difficulties" (a forerunner of our Bank for Co-operatives); the other was "for aid to indigent and widowed mothers" (a precursor to our Aid to Dependent Children program). Approximately 200 million denarii were appropriated for the two agencies.

There is no indication that prices rose during Trajan's time despite the input of a large amount of new denarii into the economy. The cost of wheat remained stable; in fact, it sold at the same price it had reached a full century earlier, at the end of Augustus's so-called period of reconstruction.

Another currency debasement of limited extent in the reign of Marcus Aurelius (A.D. 161–180) also had no visible impact on prices. Nor did the rather extensive devaluations introduced by Commodus (A.D. 180–192) and by Septimius Severus (A.D. 193–211) exercise any inflationary effect. Septimius reduced the silver content of the denarius to 50 percent, but prices remained stationary. As a matter of fact, real estate and farm values dropped sharply when he seized many of the large farms and appropriated them into his own estate.

Septimius and his predecessors who had adulterated the currency had attempted to create a money supply adequate to meet the proliferating expenses of the State. They had failed and the public treasury, with rare exceptions, remained under pressure. Although each successive debasement had reduced the amount of silver required for minting, a dwindling supply of the metal had canceled out the "savings." The shortage of coinable silver had produced one unintentionally beneficial effect—for two centuries it had forestalled the usual by-product of successive devaluations: inflation.

All this changed drastically in the third century.

Before his death, Septimius had recommended that the army should choose one of his two sons as his successor. Caracalla, the older son, made sure that the dilemma of choice should not weigh too heavily on the army; he had his brother, Geta, assassinated while his mother looked on in unbelieving horror. He then was made emperor. As soon as he was installed, he killed off everyone remotely connected with Geta. The historian Cassius Dio, who lived through the massacre, claimed that 20,000 were murdered.

Caracalla's next act—while not as bloody—proved even more destructive in the long run. Suddenly and (to quote Cassius Dio again) "in a stroke of stealth" he debased the currency. Proscribing further minting of the denarius he put a new coin, the antoninianus, into circulation. This coin was one and a half times as heavy as the displaced denarius and maintained a copper alloy content of 50 percent. But instead of being coined at one and a half denarii, it was tariffed at two denarii. This was debasement by concealment, by trickery. Resentment grew—not so much against another adulteration that brought the silver content down to

37-1/2 percent—but against the deceitful manner in which the devaluation had been carried out. Again—as in Nero's time—destabilizing fear took hold. People felt that a dangerous precedent had been set. What would prevent this Emperor or any other ruler in the future from issuing another new coin and surreptitiously debasing it further simply by assigning a larger denomination to it without increasing its silver content?

Confusion set in as the people refused to exchange two denarii for the antoninianus. They began to hoard whatever denarii they owned. Producers hiked their prices as soon as they realized that the buyer was about to make payment with the new coin. Cassius Dio aptly described the situation. "No one," he wrote, "wanted the spurious silver." As economic disorder grew, items of all sorts were withheld from the market. Goods were suddenly preferred to money and prices soared. In this way, for the first time in the history of the Roman Empire, a long-run inflation was induced. Within ten years, the price of bread doubled.

Later events proved that Caracalla had, in fact, started a dangerous precedent. In the sixty-seven years of spreading military anarchy that followed his assassination, twenty-seven brigands adorned with the title of emperor came and went. Each was shoved onto the bloody throne of Rome by some army corps that had achieved a transient ascendancy, only to be flung aside a little later to make room for the next puppet designated by a rival military clique newly come to power. The army raised them and the army cut them down—some by stabbing in the dead of night, some by garroting in broad daylight before a full palace retinue, and others by poisoning, deftly administered by hired experts. Some reigned for several months, others for several years.

But each remained on the throne long enough to adulterate the currency further and to issue a mounting volume of new coins in varying weights and denominations. Fifty years after Caracalla had issued the antoninianus, its silver content had been reduced to 5 percent and it was possible to mint the coin—now 95 percent copper—in almost limitless quantities. Each new emperor faced an empty treasury and the need to pay for rapidly rising government expenses. Government costs were ballooning not only because of inflationary pressures but also because of the drain from interminable hostilities among rival military factions. Each successive thug on the throne tried to cope with the problem in the manner of his predecessor—by turning out an ever-escalating amount of new money. But this only produced more inflation and —once again—a depleted treasury.

To make matters worse, new difficulties arose, requiring more outlays. Enemy barbarians smashed into the Empire from every border. When it wasn't the Parthians, it was the Goths, and when not the Goths, it was the Quadi or the Alemanni or the Ostrogoths. Contending factions within the Roman army stopped their internecine rivalries long enough to engage the enemy in many blood battles, but much territory was lost. At the same time army revolts in the provinces broke out; the Roman forces, occupied elsewhere, could not be diverted in time and foreign mercenaries had to be hired to put down the uprisings.

By A.D. 270, when Aurelian was installed, the economy of Rome was in a bad way. Inflation was soaring. The currency was in chaos, with billions of coins of varying silver and copper content, sizes, weights, and denominations creating confusion. Gradually—because of the monetary mess—barter was developing. Dissatisfaction was increasing in the army; the traditional annual salary of 225 denarii, by that time, had been so eroded by inflation as to be almost meaningless. Finally revolts broke out for higher pay. When this was not forthcoming, soldiers demanded a return to payment in commodities. Steadily Roman society was reverting to an agrarian economy and the price of farm produce continued to climb day by day. When the Emperor's representatives tried to work out contracts with the owners of large farms for "victuals at fair prices," the agri-business interests of that time refused. Finally, the State seized many of the farms from which it expropriated food for its troops.

Aurelian, in an attempt to restore some order in monetary matters, issued two coins to replace the welter of old coins (how he hoped to accomplish this has never been made clear). The smaller coin was tariffed at 1 denarius and the larger at 20. But neither contained an iota of silver. They were made entirely of copper and were "washed" during minting in a light, silverlike solution, which gave them a silvery finish.

The 20-denarii piece was similar to our half-dollar in appearance and size and was intrinsically as worthless. Two hundred and seventy years before Aurelian had struck the coin, 20 denarii of pure silver would have kept a man alive in Rome for almost eight months. In Aurelian's day it would be used up in about a week. The 150 denarii paid yearly to an indigent mother for her dependent child under Nerva's scheme now had a purchasing power of around 3 denarii.

Of course, Aurelian's attempted reform accomplished nothing; it merely abetted inflation. Now that no silver was required in coinage, money roared out of the mints in a greater flood. Prices leaped upward anew as people tried to convert increasingly worthless coins into goods.

The situation became even worse by the time Diocletian arrived on the scene in A.D. 285. Son of a Dalmatian slave, he had risen through the ranks of the Praetorian Guard to the position of commander. But he was hardly the common cutthroat the Praetorians usually put forward as emperor. Gibbon, in his monumental work *The Decline and Fall of the Roman Empire,* describes his reign as "more illustrious than any of his predecessors."

As soon as he took office he divided the Empire into two sections (so that each could be more effectively administered), taking the eastern portion for himself, and assigning the western part to Maximianus, an old-time associate. Each of the two Caesars would be assisted for twenty years by an Augustus (a kind of vice-emperor). After twenty years each would resign and the two Augusti would become Caesars. He then moved the capital to Nicomedia (in modern Turkey) and left Rome, the scene of assassination of twenty of the last twenty-one rulers.

He instituted many military and civilian reforms (including the imposition of some taxes which became confiscatory) and staffed expanded government bureaus with men he could trust. He made four partially successful attempts to overhaul the currency. He tried to reinstate the old silver denarius, which he called the "denarius argentium," as the common coin. But, according to the slender evidence that has come down to us, he failed because he could not obtain enough silver for an adequate money supply. After several years of experimentation the denarius communis— made entirely of copper—became, once again, the common coin. But by that time its purchasing power was so insignificant that it became very cumbersome to count out the large number of coins required in each transaction. As a remedy, Diocletian introduced *folles*—sealed bags containing copper coins of uniform size. The number of pounds of copper was designated on each bag, the largest weighing over 300 pounds and having a value (in relation to gold or silver) of about $4.00. Transactions were quoted in varying weights.

His most famous reform—and one that has elicited an outburst of vituperation from "free-market" economists—was his Code, proclaimed in 301. Modeled on Hammurabi's Code of 1792 B.C.—but much more extensive—Diocletian's Code established a rigid system of wage and price controls. Although only fragments of the edict have survived, hundreds of price and wage schedules are specified in them. No item is too insignificant to escape the purview of the controller and the gamut of the items covered is almost as wide as human existence. Prices are set for a single peacock feather, for a suckling pig, for a measure of truffles, for a liter of wine, and for "a container holding five reed pens." And there are prices for gradations in quality: "For one loin cloth of first quality, 1,000 denarii; same of second quality, 800 denarii; same of third quality, 600 denarii"; "for a shirt of pure soft, finished wool (new), 50 denarii; for shirt, part silk (new), 200 denarii; for shirt, all silk (new), 600 denarii."

Wages are set for "a notary for writing a petition of one hundred lines, 10 denarii; a tailor for cutting and finishing a hooded cloak, 60 denarii; a tailor for cutting and finishing a pair of breeches, 20 denarii; a tailor for sewing a fine garment, 6 denarii; a tailor for sewing a coarse garment, 4 denarii; for a teacher of Greek or Latin literature—each pupil per month, 200 denarii; for an advocate for pleading a case, 1,000 denarii; and for a keeper of a private bathhouse—each bather, 2 denarii."

The Code is an illuminating document of a vanished civilization. However, as a source of reference for students of inflation and economic historians, its value has been somewhat undercut by the absence of comparable prices charged for identical items during the first and second centuries. It does, nevertheless, contain two statistics that clearly reveal the sweep of inflation during the third century. The first concerns itself with the cost of an army uniform. In the Code, the designated price is 166 times the price at which a similar uniform sold during the first century and throughout the second century until A.D. 190. The second figure —and by far the more important—is the cost of wheat. Until A.D. 190 (the beginning of the reign of Caracalla and the inception of chronic inflation in the Roman Empire), wheat had traditionally sold at one-half denarius per modius (about nine-tenths of a peck). The price designated in the Code is 100 denarii for each modius, or 200 times the price prevailing during the previous two centuries! The significance of such an increase can be put into perspective by a simple comparison. During the past 100 years the price of wheat in the United States has risen from around 80 cents per bushel to $3.75 a bushel—or less than five times.

Moreover, according to Lactantius, a religious historian of that period, the going price for most items was substantially higher than the level set by Diocletian. His assessment is probably correct; a reading of the preamble to the Code will show that Diocletian's purpose in setting price levels was clearly deflationary. Undoubtedly, living costs had risen by more than 200 times during the century preceding the publication of the Code.

By the time Diocletian came to power, however, the last reliable historian of the Roman Empire—Cassius Dio—was dead. And so we do not have any narrative or description of day-to-day events during the third-century inflation (nor, for that matter, of the superinflation of the fourth century). We can only imagine the misery: the deepening starvation of the poor, the aged, and those who were living on small, fixed incomes; the apprehension of the middle class as they saw the purchasing power of their savings evaporate; the small storekeepers and few remaining owners of small farms giving up and joining the constantly swelling dole lines, the rich emigrating or scurrying about in an attempt to find a safe investment, and—over all—a mood of gathering desperation.

Although Diocletian pushed hard to have his Code succeed—hiring thousands of bureaucrats and spies to enforce the controls, and finally instituting an edict to prevent workers from changing jobs to circumvent the freeze on their wages—there is no evidence as to whether he succeeded in stabilizing costs. In 305—four years after the promulgation of the Code—he declared a "triumph" and, in keeping with his promise, gave up his position as emperor and retired to Dalmatia, where he died ten years later.

As soon as his successor took over, the Code was abolished. The cyclonic superinflation of the fourth century was now unleashed. Although Constantine (306–337) established a gold and silver standard (used almost entirely for government transactions and tax collection), copper coins—used in day-to-day transactions—

roared out of the mints in prodigious amounts. In the third century there had been a flood of new money; in the fourth, the flood was transformed into a thundering torrent. No records exist of the exact number of new mintings or, of course, of the amount of coins put out in each issue. We can rely only on the archaeological finds dating back to this period. These indicate that the Roman Empire was inundated by successive tidal waves of new copper denarii during the fourth century. Each of the twenty successors of Diocletian who ruled in that century repeated the same routine. He would begin with extensive issues of medium-sized copper coins. Succeeding issues would then be made in smaller coins. As the increased amount of new money proved inadequate because of the surge in costs, Caracalla's device would take over: the smaller the coins became, the larger was the denomination assigned to them. Then, as the purchasing power of these coins was eroded by soaring prices, still higher denominations were assigned to succeeding coin issues.

Ruler after ruler went through the useless, destructive charade. Even though he recognized that his predecessor had produced nothing but inflation in pursuing such a policy, each emperor persisted in it.

Of course, the inevitable happened. Prices vaulted day after day.

The surge in the cost of living became terrifying, almost incomprehensible. Again, we lack historical accounts or descriptions of the human condition, but the havoc which must have existed is adumbrated in the few price indexes which have survived. These come from Egypt where the destruction of records was far less extensive than in the European cities of the Empire. During the period of Diocletian's Code (301–305) wheat sold for 330 denarii per artaba, the common measure for wheat in Egypt. Since the artaba had a content which was 3.3 times the content of the Roman modius, the price of 330 Egyptian denarii was equal to the 100 denarii the Romans were paying for a modius of wheat at that time. But by A.D. 335 (thirty years after the Code) the price of wheat in Egypt had skyrocketed to 21,000 denarii and by A.D. 338 to 36,000 denarii. In short, within a period of thirty-three years, the cost of the basic, life-sustaining food had risen by more than 1,000 times.

But that was only the beginning. By A.D. 342 the price climbed to 75,000 denarii, and by A.D. 350 it had vaulted to 500,000 denarii, a rise of more than 150,000 percent in forty-five years! Although no later figures for wheat are available, the price must have gone much higher in the second half of the century. We can assume this from several figures quoted for pork. A document dated A.D. 362 indicates a price of 14,400 denarii for a pound of pork (this, by the way, compares with a price of 10 denarii during the reign of Augustus), but another document dated A.D. 390 shows that pork was then selling at 30,000 denarii, or twice the price prevailing in A.D. 362. The continued sweep of inflation during the second half of the fourth century is also evident in the deteriorating position of the denarius in relation to the solidus, a coin of pure gold struck by Constantine and used almost exclusively for transactions of the government. A document of A.D. 350 states that a solidus was exchanged for 576,000 denarii, but in a papyrus dated several years later, the writer exclaims: "The solidus now stands at 2,020,000 denarii; it has gone down!" Another papyrus dated around A.D. 390 indicates that the solidus was being exchanged for 4,500,000 denarii. In other words, the denarius had undergone an eightfold depreciation in relation to gold in the latter half of the century. With pork rising by 100 percent and gold by 800 percent, it is logical to assume that wheat during the second part of the century must have at least doubled in price from a mid-century level of 500,000 denarii to a level of at least 1 million denarii per artaba. It had sold at under 2 denarii per artaba at the time of Augustus . . . at 330 denarii in the reign of Diocletian . . . and at least 1 million denarii before the cyclonic fourth century came to an end! Not only do these figures reflect the most virulent inflation the world had experienced until that date, but they mirror also the disintegration and the coming end of the Roman Empire.

The end, of course, was not far off. During the fifth century incursions by barbarian tribes into the Empire became more frequent. One after another, parts of the Empire fell into their hands. Frequently whole Roman armies—demoralized and long ridden with corruption—joined the enemy to destroy what was once their own land. When the sacking of Rome took place in A.D. 476, many rival enemy nations were already fighting one another for control of dismembered segments of the once invincible Roman Empire.

Slender evidence indicates that the rate of inflation abated during the fifth century. Italy and the provinces, evidently, had been transformed almost completely to a barter economy by the time Rome fell and the minting of new money had been reduced to a trickle. Military events finally put an end to the purblind monetary policies that had been carried out for almost three centuries, policies which substantially contributed to the final collapse.

The Roman inflation—like so many other important historical events—has left a legacy of myths. One of the more frequently repeated fictions maintains that the Roman Empire's monetary problems were caused by the economic incompetence of its leaders. Ancient rulers and their finance officers—the theory goes— simply lacked the required economic expertise. Ignorance led them to adopt the measures that started the inflation, and ignorance (notably evidenced in the constant repetition of the same monetary blunders by successive rulers) perpetuated the inflation. A corollary inference put forward by holders of this theory suggests that the Roman disaster would not have occurred if the heads of state in the ancient world had possessed the fund of economic knowledge we have today.

The proponents of this theory have misread the evidence. For those who have the will and the patience to dig it out, ample proof of the economic expertise of the Romans can be found. Take the matter of banking. For a long time certain economic historians have circulated the notion that the Roman banking system was undeveloped. As evidence they have cited the frequent slurs made by Roman leaders against moneylending and banking. This attitude—supposedly—prevented the establishment of an adequate banking system. But, to get at the truth, one should examine what the Romans did rather than what they said. And what the Romans did in banking has been revealed in archaeological digs.

Excavations conducted during the late part of the nineteenth century uncovered the remains of certain banking establishments that had existed in Rome over 2,000 years ago (at around 200–300 B.C.). In his illuminating book *Banking Through the Ages,* Noble H. Hoggson describes what the archaeologists found and what they deduced about the Roman banking system:

The well-worn marble floors of these banking offices were found covered with loose coins which must have been scattered during a great fire, as many coins were melted and welded together and cemented to the slab of the pavement. . . . The ancient bank consisted of a large, solidly constructed, though sparsely furnished and badly lighted, apartment in which the money changer sat on a high stool with the coins spread out before him behind a bronze mesh screen. . . . A part of the ancient banker's daily routine included the opening of accounts, the receipt of deposits, the furnishing of letters of credit, the making of loans, the purchase of mortgages; in fact, most of the transactions performed by a bank-cashier today. Interest was paid on time deposits being termed *creditum* (credits)—as distinguished from those which were subject to call, on which no interest was paid. . . . When money was deposited as a *creditum,* that is, for a specified period of time, at interest, the banker was allowed to use and invest it to the best of his judgment.

So there we have it. Not only had the Romans developed an intricate, sophisticated banking system rivaling ours in scope, but they had actually gone as far as creating certificates of deposit, a money instrument most bankers believe to be a modern American innovation.

Another indication of the monetary expertise of the early Romans—and again it relates to banking—can be found in a plan put forward by Maecenas in 12 B.C. He recommended that the Empire establish a central bank that would lend money to other government agencies, channel funds into building programs and other public projects, and lend funds to regional government banks set up in each province. In short, it would have some of the functions now carried out by the Federal Reserve Board. Why this plan—the first recorded proposal for a centralized government bank—was not carried out has never been explained. More than 1,700 years would pass before Maecenas's scheme would be adopted. In 1694 the Bank of England was established, the first central bank in the world's history.

The grasp of economic dynamics possessed by Roman officials is evident, as well, in areas unrelated to banking. Several examples have already been mentioned: the first recorded instance involving the planned use of governmental fiscal stimulus to reduce unemployment (Augustus's "great reconstruction program"); the creation by Nerva of the Fund for Rural Credits, and his establishment of an agency "for aid to indigent and widowed mothers"; Trajan's adjustment of the denarius to bring gold-and-silver-exchange values into line; Diocletian's extensive wage and price controls; and the creation in the reign of Tiberius of a government-financed fund to rescue farmers from mortgage foreclosure (forerunner of our Federal Land Bank). Except for Diocletian's Code (which was patterned on Hammurabi's Code), each of these represented an original contribution in the development of economic planning and thought.

In analyzing why Roman leaders unleashed a devastating super-inflation, we must assume that they were fully cognizant of the consequences of their acts. Realizing that the creation of prodigious amounts of money might eventually produce a destabilizing rise in prices, ruler after ruler, nevertheless, swelled the money supply. Why did they pursue such a program? Because their aspirations—their drive for power, for privilege, and for inordinate wealth—required a continual creation of great amounts of new money.

Even when Rome was a mere village, the distinction between rich and poor was, of course, clearly demarcated in living style, privilege, and political power. The distinction continued as Rome progressed from a city-state to a kingdom, to a republic, and finally to a great empire. During its early history, however, when individual families had not yet acquired vast wealth, the gulf between rich and poor was not nearly as great as it later became. During the time of the Kingdom and the early Republic the Roman economy was largely agrarian, consisting of many small farms worked by their owners and by free, hired farm laborers. Although cities were increasing, their role was, as yet, secondary. Since the wealthier landholders had managed to enact laws that gave them sole representation in the Senate, they held the balance of power. (Even later—when pressure from the common people led to the formation of a supposedly more representative assembly —persons of wealth succeeded in extending their influence into that body through skillful gerrymandering.) But the exercise of power was, on the whole, fairly even-handed. Although wealth was protected and fostered by the State, the poor were not routinely victimized by the economic and political policies adopted by the government (as they were during the Empire). As a result, the distinction between the comparatively few well-off and the many poor was not nearly as glaring as it later became.

But the development of slave labor brought an important change. Large farms manned by hundreds of slaves could now turn out produce with virtually no expense. Year after year the latifundia were expanded as more slaves were imported, and year after year the number of small, independently run farms decreased as their owners—unable to compete against the large slave-worked farms—abandoned their land to become serfs of the prospering latifundia owners or migrated to the dole-ridden cities. Proliferating slavery—as we have seen—decimated the living standard of the working class in the cities. Owners of small factories, stores, or other commercial establishments used slave labor whenever they could. When it was necessary to hire a freedman (a former slave who had won his freedom) or a citizen, the amount paid for labor was abysmally small. During the first and second centuries A.D. the average wage in Rome of an unskilled worker was around one-half denarius per day (about 10 cents) plus a small food allowance. Ten cents a day worked out to around $35 a year. This pittance, however, was more than some workers got. Dacian tablets of the second century A.D. reveal that a miner's salary for a year's work came to $12.60 plus bread and lodgings. The average worker in Rome earned less than a total of $750 in his lifetime.

Meanwhile, with labor costs extremely low on farms and in factories, profits became enormous. The chronic underpayment of the millions of rural and urban workers in the Empire produced great wealth for the upper and middle classes.

But—as might be expected—the maldistribution of income created monetary difficulties. Newly minted money quickly left the economic mainstream. Almost none of it was retained by the millions of working poor. Almost as soon as it moved out of the mints, it disappeared from circulation into the strongboxes or the newly erected, palatial villas of the rich. Then the minting of new money was again required. Modern, developed economies (if they are well run) do not experience similar difficulties. In present-day industrial economies, the preponderant part of the money supply is used in the payment of wages. Only a very small fraction of it is skimmed off into profits, leaving great amounts free to circulate continuously through the economy. When new money is created, it is automatically reflected in higher salaries; demand is raised and the increased demand in turn creates new jobs, which in turn create new purchasing power. This constant recirculation of large amounts of money through the economy was almost totally absent in the Roman Empire; it was circumvented by the owners of great farms and the proprietors of shops who preferred the large profits they could make immediately to the long-run but smaller profits they might make in the future.

The rulers of the State—and their associates who influenced them—abetted the aspirations of the rich, since they had the same economic interests. The largest owners of land were the emperors, the relatives of emperors, and the intimate associates of emperors. Livia, wife of Augustus and mother of Tiberius, became the largest property holder in the Roman Empire. It is said that in terms of acreage owned, she was the largest private landowner in the history of the world. Every ruler was the proprietor of vast tracts situated in various sections of the Empire, many of which were manned by slave labor. Pliny (A.D. 62–113), a Roman author, in discussing the immense landholdings of the royal families said that six men owned half the land in Africa.

Relatives and close associates of emperors also made their money in commercial enterprises which produced or dealt in goods made with cheap labor. Rulers, therefore, had an abiding proprietary interest in keeping wages as low as possible. They perpetuated the system which routed new money out of the mints into the hands of relatives, friends, associates, and people they favored.

The maintenance of this type of economy required frequent coinage of new money for another reason. Since the under-developed economy produced chronic unemployment, rulers felt impelled to spend great sums on "bread and circuses." Year after year millions of denarii were spent for relief and on games. Since the public treasury was frequently empty, new coins had to be struck to take care of these expenses. In essence, public funds were being used to augment the low wages of the workers. In the end, of course, everyone was disadvantaged by the process since it contributed to the exhaustion of coinable metals.

New money to fill the chronically empty public treasury became a constant necessity also because an insufficient and inequitable taxing policy failed to raise enough revenue. Despite the existence within the Empire of a self-sufficient economy, yearly outlays by the government exceeded income. We know from proclamations made by Augustus that the annual costs of running the State came to around 100 million denarii, whereas income—largely from value-added taxes—amounted to only 70 million denarii. The difference was made up by tribute exacted from Gaul, Spain, and Egypt.

The outlay of 100 million denarii represented only 1-1/2 denarii per person—hardly an inordinate amount. The deficit resulted from an inadequate taxing system which permitted the owners of great wealth to escape their proper burden. There was no tax of any kind on incomes and no tax—with rare exceptions—on profits made on the sale of assets. During many years there was no inheritance tax; in periods when an inheritance levy was in force, it came to only 2 or 3 percent. Augustus had once suggested that it be raised to 5 percent, but the Senate—reflecting its class bias—turned the proposal down.

In this way the sources from which the greatest amount of taxes could be easily raised were left untapped, while an insufficient amount was extracted from those who could least afford to pay. (Nero was only sounding off when he said, "Let us see to it that no one owns anything." He proceeded to tax porters, pimps, prostitutes, and the bathers in public bathhouses. The latifundia owners and other owners of great wealth were untouched. His family owned some of the largest farms in the Empire.)

In the early days of the Empire, while Roman arms could still exact tribute from the conquered provinces, the budgetary gap could be closed by "tribute." But later it had to be filled by successive coinage. One of the perennial depleters of the public treasury was the military establishment. Year after year during the first century, close to 68 million denarii was spent on the army, the navy, and the Praetorian Guard. This represented more than two-thirds of all government outlays. In later periods when the armed services became riddled with graft and dissension and when they were suffering repeated defeats, expenditures climbed sharply. Of course, during the inflation-inflamed fourth century they rose exponentially, requiring mounds of newly minted money.

The drain which these continuing expenditures created on the Roman monetary system needs no elucidation. But an equally adverse long-term effect on the Empire's finances was created by the army's wealth-stripping operations. In the heyday of victories, when Rome's legions were overrunning other nations, it was not the annual stipend of 225 denarii that attracted the common foot soldier; it was the promise of lucrative bonuses and the lure of booty and plunder. When there were spoils of war, the Roman soldier was richly compensated. Rewards of 500 denarii were frequent. But more important were the divisions of property seized, especially land. At times the properties of entire communities were handed over to the army, with each soldier receiving a sizable tract, which he could sell or on which he could settle. In some cases a major portion of a defeated country was turned over for colonization. And, of course, there was always the attraction of the petty plunder of the household effects of defeated peoples. Septimius Severus, who had risen through the ranks of the army, summarized the situation in a piece of advice to his son: "Take care of the soldiers, and never mind the rest. That is the way to rule an empire."

But the major rewards fell to the victorious commanders and generals. Officers who brought about the annexation of a new nation into the Empire became wealthy overnight. They were frequently paid hundreds of thousands of denarii by the Emperor. Sometimes a general who had achieved a signal triumph—and had the additional good fortune to be a member of the reigning emperor's family—was allowed to exact tribute for a long time from the defeated nation and could retain the spoils for his own use. Pompey (one of Caesar's rivals) attained an estate worth around $4 million from his military operations. Several of his army associates amassed smaller fortunes, each amounting to more than $1 million. Crassus, reputed to be the richest private citizen in the Empire, made most of his money from the resale of properties he had purchased from generals (who had acquired them as booty). Jewels, coins, gold and silver plate, villas, houses, and palaces fell into the hands of generals and emperors. After a while, when a considerable amount of assets had been "appropriated," the seized province was turned over to the government. The prime examples of the wealth-stripping process are Julius Caesar and Augustus. Caesar secured a great fortune from the plunder he took for his own use when he conquered Spain and Gaul. He willed most of his estate to his grand-nephew, Augustus, who then overran Egypt in 31 B.C., appropriated the spoils of victory from that province during a period of eight years, and piled the riches acquired on top of the fortune he had inherited. The combined value of the two estates exceeded a half-billion denarii.

It is difficult to estimate the aggregate value of the spoils of war which were channeled into private hands. The total must have run into many billions of denarii. The public treasury was deprived of this income although booty seized was considered public domain.

The immense, self-glorifying expenditures of emperors also created the need for constant infusions of newly coined money. The grandiose disbursements of the three madmen—Caligula, Claudius, and Nero—were by no means exceptional. Essentially stable and prudent men like Nerva, Trajan, Hadrian, Vespasian, and Marcus Aurelius spent lavishly from a bulging *fiscus* on games, mass feasts, the erection of monuments to themselves, the construction of great palaces, and repeated ostentatious gifts to the plebs. Even Diocletian—who imposed burdensome taxes to meet skyrocketing military expenses and evidenced his concern over the sorry state of Rome's economy by enacting his much resented Edict—wasted many millions of denarii on splendid palaces, shows, and elaborate celebrations—all designed to enhance his prestige and assure his place in history.

An anonymous second-century author had a remarkably clear vision of the situation. He wrote, "The aerarium is denuded while the wealthy and the powerful are adorned in rich raiments." During the first two centuries the establishment forces of the Empire (the landowners-military-emperor complex) had engineered the rapid delivery of the Roman Empire's wealth into their own hands. These riches—acquired by the State predominantly through extensive conquest—were transferred into the holdings of the power structure at a highly accelerated rate through the implementation of certain economic, fiscal, taxing, and monetary policies that favored a minority and disadvantaged the majority. (Today the process would be euphemistically called rapid growth.) During the transfer process the State's gold and silver mines had been almost completely exhausted by repeated minting.

Looking back, we can see that the policies pursued by the establishment during the disastrous third, fourth, and fifth centuries represented a desperate but unsuccessful holding maneuver, designed to maintain wealth and hegemony until a return to the highly favorable status quo ante could be accomplished. The executors of power (from the third century forward, the army and its chief officer, the emperor, were the focal point of executive power, the Senate having been reduced to a ceremonial role) refused to introduce changed policies to meet changed conditions. Vespasian, an emperor who was a hard-headed businessman, and Diocletian, who was the ancient world's most persistent bureaucrat, attempted fiscal, economic, and monetary reforms but were promptly excoriated as traitors and enemies of established order.

But they were exceptions. During the last three centuries before Rome's destruction, ruler after ruler purblindly clung to the past and wasted his brief tenure and his energies in dealing with the exigencies of the moment and propping up the tottering structure.

In the monetary area a number of remedies were available. Instead of steadily throwing many billions of increasingly depreciating copper coins into the money supply, the Empire could have restored a stable and viable gold and silver standard through various approaches. In private vaults, in bank strongboxes, and in vaults provided by the State, there were hundreds of millions of undebased aurei and denarii which had been removed from circulation by their original owners and had been willed to their descendants. The Roman government could have made an effort to borrow a considerable amount of these coins. Borrowing by nations was infrequent in antiquity but it was an accepted modus operandi. Philip of Macedonia (father of Alexander the Great) had floated a considerable national debt. Pompey had made a sizable private loan at a fat rate of interest to the kingdom of Syria. Caesar had borrowed money to finance some of his early campaigns. In all likelihood, the Empire could have borrowed a substantial amount of money if it had guaranteed a high rate of interest. If this method failed, it could have imposed a tax, payable in gold or silver, on the hoarders of old gold and silver coins. Another means of raising gold and silver money was the sale of valuable government properties, especially extensive tracts of land and buildings. The numerous monuments scattered throughout the Empire and containing much mintable gold and silver plate were another lucrative source. (The invaders of Rome stripped these bare when they sacked the city in 476 and carried off precious metals whose value must have run into many millions of denarii.) As a last resort there were the splendid temples that graced many of the Empire's cities and contained a vast store of precious metals, jewels, and valuable artifacts made of gold and silver. These could have been sold for gold and silver coins or used directly in minting.

Strangely enough, it was only the last resort which was attempted. Constantine, who favored Christianity, removed a good measure of gold and silver from the pagan temples and had it converted into gold and silver coins of varying denominations. But he must have run into resistance since he did not secure enough to return the economy completely to a gold and silver standard. The copper *denarius communis* remained the chief exchange medium; gold and silver coins were reserved for government transactions and—whenever possible—taxes were collected in gold and silver. There is no existing evidence that any of the other alternatives were attempted.

Why were they not attempted? Perhaps it was because each emperor—even though he recognized that his repetition of the failed monetary policies of the past was producing an increasing destabilization—somehow believed that the worst would soon be over and that normal conditions would soon be restored. Perhaps the wealthy and the powerful, protected by their gold and silver plate, their hoarded coins, their palatial houses, their large landholdings, their factories, and their shops, felt that they could ride out the storm and saw no reason for radical experiments.

Or possibly the answer can be found in hubris—in the arrogance which so often warps the judgment of men and nations when they achieve the apex of power. Perhaps the powerful leaders of Rome—the rulers of the world's greatest empire—felt that they could defeat any force arrayed against them, even an inimical economy.

The French Connection: The Assignat Era

Following the path taken by the rulers of the failing Roman Empire, the leaders of the French Revolution also attempted to retain power by the obsessive fabrication of new money. The Romans had favored copper; the French were partial to paper, in the form of assignats or government notes.

Had Louis XVI been willing to devote less time to fox-hunting and more to the study of history, he could have discovered an ominous comparison. He would have perceived that the monetary problems confronting his realm during the 1780s were dangerously similar to the difficulties which had beset Roman kings at the beginning of the Empire's decline.

France's treasury, like Rome's, was chronically empty, having been denuded by huge military expenditures and inordinate outlays for the aggrandizement of royalty. In 1787, the financially beleaguered Crown suddenly proclaimed that "there will be a temporary suspension of interest payments" on outstanding notes issued by the government.

In the beginning of 1788, the treasury announced the flotation of a sizable new debt issue. But it became obvious several weeks later that the attempt would fail. Outstanding government obligations were selling at 50 percent of their original issue price; there was no need for anyone with capital to buy the new notes despite a slightly higher yield. Then, rumors suddenly swept Paris that the treasury would fail to redeem those notes which were soon maturing and that it was about to announce the bankruptcy of the government.

To scotch these rumors, Brienne, the incumbent Minister of Finance, advised the King to make a forthright publication of the government's true financial condition. Louis, who had a natural aversion to meeting problems head on, hesitated. Like every French king who had preceded him, he had—with but one regrettable exception—invoked the age-old right of "royal cabal" over state finances and had refused to divulge figures on budgets, income, expenditures, and deficits.

Back in 1781, Jacques Necker, the successful Swiss-born banker who then served as chief finance minister, had issued an "accounting of state finances," the first ever published in the long history of the French nation. His accounting covered the six-year period from 1776 through 1781 when he had served as financial adviser to the King. Describing his attainments in grandiloquent, self-serving language, Necker claimed that he had been able to show a slight surplus "despite the expenditure of almost a half-billion livres* for the War of the American Revolution." France had contributed and loaned these sums to the American colonists to weaken her chief enemy, the British. Necker had not bothered, however, to explain that outlays amounting to about 50 million livres annually had been made to cover the expenses of the royal family and that these had piled up into a large accumulated debt.

---

*The coinage of the period is somewhat complex. The common copper coin was the sou (equal to about 1 cent). Twenty sous equaled 1 livre. Silver coins consisted of pieces denominated at 12 sous, 15 sous, 24 sous, and 30 sous. There were also the 3-livre piece called the ecu and the 6-livre piece, the gros ecu. Both were of silver. The louis d'or, a gold piece equal to 24 livres in silver, was used in large trade transactions, in government transactions, and as a store of value.

In a final surge of ringing rhetoric, he had attributed the soundness of French finances to his ability to borrow large sums for the nation's treasury.

About his ability to find buyers for the government's notes, there was no question. For a short while after his presentation, Necker was able to raise more funds for the sorely pressed treasury —until it was discovered that he had manipulated his accounting. Instead of the small claimed surplus, there was a massive deficit. Long resented by the nobility and certain factions in the court— primarily because of his attempts to make the tax system more equitable—Necker was forced from office. During the episode, the King's influence was undercut and the government's reputation in monetary matters was badly damaged.

And so, in the bleak winter of 1788, when Brienne suggested another accounting, Louis wanted no part of it. But with the financial crisis mounting and disorders breaking out in several areas of the kingdom, and with subscriptions to the new debt issue lagging, the King finally consented to the publication of the Budget of 1788.

While the Budget of 1788 could not have been construed as a forecast of immediate insolvency, it was a shocking documentation of a government in dire financial straits. Expenses for 1788 were estimated at 629 million livres and revenues at only 503 million leaving a projected deficit of 126 million livres. A deficit amounting to 25 percent of revenues was bad enough but more disturbing was the revelation that debt service for the year (repayment of debt falling due plus the interest on the debt) amounted to 318 million livres or 63 percent of total anticipated revenues! (Present annual debt service of the United States government amounts to only 20 percent of annual revenues.) With deficits mounting* the sum required for debt service, in several years, would outrun annual income; a declaration of bankruptcy by the government would then be inescapable.

The budget had a few other points of interest. Expenses of the court were carried at 35 million livres, or 6 percent of total expenditures. This is a staggering figure; the cost of maintaining the British monarchy today comes to a small fraction of 1 percent. In

---

*Annual deficits had risen from 37 million livres in 1774 to 80 million in 1783, to 112 million livres in 1787, and to 126 million livres projected for 1788.

the time of George III (Louis' contemporary), Britain's monarchic costs also amounted to less than 1 percent of the kingdom's outlays.

Over 164 million livres was budgeted for "army, navy, and diplomatic services." The total for debt service, expenses of the court, defense, and diplomacy came to 517 million livres. This figure exceeded total anticipated revenues and provided no funds for conducting the civilian affairs of a nation of 24 million people. Such expenditures could be met only through the incurrence of an ever-mounting debt.

As might have been expected, Brienne's Budget of 1788, instead of attracting investors, frightened them away. The debt issue he had attempted was called off. A week later, the King—desperate for funds—published an edict in which he proclaimed that the government would soon issue paper money which was already being engraved.

The proclamation evoked a storm of objections. The French people, the King was advised, wanted no part of paper money. The prevailing opinion was recorded in a memorandum sent to the King: "Above all we (the French people) will not countenance the introduction of a paper money or a national bank, either of which can only produce a great evil and of which the memories alone are capable of frightening us because of the abuse and speculation they occasioned in the past."

The signers of the memorandum (an entire parish) were referring to the chaotic events of 1716–1720 during which John Law had introduced paper money into France for the first time and had set off a period of wild speculation and inflation that brought ruin to thousands of Frenchmen and foreigners. Since that episode, France had adhered strictly to a metallic standard and had shunned paper money.

With protests mounting against his newly issued edict, Louis did not release any of the printed notes. In the following month he canceled his order.

Unable to extricate himself from the financial impasse, Brienne resigned. Necker's recall was demanded, especially by the increasingly influential bourgeoisie—the lawyers, economists, writers, bankers, manufacturers, merchants, and professional civil servants. His manipulation of figures was forgotten and, if remembered, forgiven.

Reluctantly, the King called the master fund-raiser back into office in August 1788. Necker accepted, but with conditions. A foreigner and a Protestant, he had been deprived of his proper title during his former term in office. He had been referred to as the Comptroller of Finances. Now he insisted that the Catholic King of Catholic France should address him correctly with the title of Director-General of Finances. And—more important—he demanded the title of Minister of State (that title would raise him above all other ministers).

This time the King did not quibble about nomenclature. Necker got his titles, and—upon being installed—advised Louis that the nation's monetary problems would soon be brought under control.

At first, Necker's fund-raising campaign had little success. The rentiers of the bourgeoisie and the nobles living on pensions were fearful of entrusting more money to a government that had already suspended payments on some of its debt issues. But finally —despite the near insolvency of the government—he worked his magic, extracting large loans from the coterie of wealthy Protestant bankers who had emigrated to Paris from Switzerland, Norway, and England, as well as from the owners of "tax-farming" corporations and the contractors and merchants who had grown rich doing business with the Crown. His ability to entice these funds was all the more remarkable because it was accomplished in an atmosphere of growing unrest.

The year had begun with one of the worst winters on record, with dead sparrows covering the snow-drifted roads and fields and even owls freezing to death. Industry had ground to a halt; almost one-half of the nation's manufacturing work force was idled. In city after city, bread riots erupted (the average person—unable to earn enough in normal times to provide for an adequate diet— depended almost totally on bread, consuming 2-1/2 to 3 pounds per day).

Then came one of the worst crop failures in years, during which many families went hungry in rural areas and in the cities. Again bread riots erupted, with demonstrators demanding "bread at 2 sous." During the several months of crop failure, the price of bread had doubled from 2 sous to 4; for the majority of the French population, the increase raised the threat of starvation.

As these disturbances were nearing their peak, political agitation came from all segments of society. Certain members of the nobility who had been ousted from their former position of high influence in the court (probably at the instigation of the Queen, Marie Antoinette, who had her own faction) fomented demonstrations against the monarchy. The Duke of Orléans, who believed he could overthrow Louis, hired bands of vandals to pillage and destroy property. He was joined by scores of impoverished nobles, who, having sold off their lands to meet extravagant expenditures, now had no income and subsisted by sending their daughters out to work as common laborers on nearby farms. These ruined noblemen sent deputations to Louis, demanding pensions or suitable positions at court.

The hierarchy of the clergy also confronted the King regarding the threatened confiscation of Church lands. For almost two years leading members of the bourgeoisie had been waging an increasingly popular campaign for the nationalization and sale of Church properties—a plan that held forth two highly desirable results: (1) by making more agricultural land available to the 20 million persons living on farms (over 80 percent of the population), the economy of France would be quickly improved. The average farmer now owned less than a hectare (2-1/2 acres) of land and the limited yield he could coax from this marginal area kept him in a state of chronic poverty. By enlarging the area under cultivation, he could earn an adequate income; and (2) the hard-pressed national treasury would be aided by the money taken in from the sale of the confiscated properties.

Time after time, delegations of prelates descended upon Versailles to extract a royal denunciation against the proposed confiscation. On Sundays, rude churches in the countryside and the grand cathedrals in the cities reverberated with entreaties and prayers in which Church dignitaries exhorted the monarch "to thwart those who seek the destruction of religion and God's servants."

And in the increasingly militant Parisian press, articles appeared demanding a restructuring of the tax system that now permitted the rich to escape payment while it victimized the poor. Week after week, in pamphlets and in newspapers, well-known members of the bourgeoisie demanded the reconvening of the parliament, which had been closed down by royal decree in 1614, 175 years before.

The beleaguered King finally capitulated, issuing a decree for

the reopening of the Estates General (the parliament) in May of
the following year. At the time, the King's concession was regarded as a development of primal importance. The ground of
France had been shaken and a deep fissure had at last appeared
in the monolith of the Bourbon dynasty.

It was a development that heightened the sense of growing
destabilization, an episode hardly conducive to the raising of large
sums of money for a destitute government. But Necker was able
to bring off his promised miracle and, by the end of the year, had
secured enough funds to meet the needs of state and to avoid a
declaration of bankruptcy.

The first four months of 1789 proved to be a rerun of 1788 with
flour shortages recurring, increasing agitation in the cities as
crowds demanded "bread for the poor, hunger for the rich," and
the looting of bakeries and grain warehouses by organized mobs.
Throughout the days of escalating disorder, Necker pressed on
with his unending task of money-raising. Occasionally on a free
evening, he would hurry back from Versailles to attend one of the
invariably brilliant soirees graced by his wife in their palatial home
in Paris. There, lionized by some of the most famous intellectuals
of France, and the center of attention, he would be plied with
questions about the great event which the whole nation now
awaited with a mixture of hope and anxiety: the convening of
parliament. He would assure his audience that the King—having
at last seen the light—was prepared, within proper limits, to "aid
in the process of change."

The long-awaited first session of the Estates General took place
on May 5, 1789, in Versailles. The delegates of the Third Estate
(representing the "common people" but comprised mostly of
members of the bourgeoisie) were soon put in their proper place.
Instructed to arrive at eight in the morning, they were kept standing outdoors for five hours until the 300 delegates of the First
Estate (the clergy) and the 300 delegates of the Second Estate (the
nobles) arrived shortly before one o'clock in the afternoon. After
the First and Second Estates were seated, the 600 members of "the
commons" were allowed to enter the hall.

Louis, flanked by his ministers, entered after one o'clock. He
had balked at a morning meeting; he refused to give up a half-day's
hunting.

Reading his prepared speech the King began on an assuring

note, telling his listeners of the fatherly regard he held for all his subjects and of his desire for a satisfied and tranquil kingdom. But, unfortunately, all was not tranquil. Almost sadly he demurred about "a general state of unrest and an exaggerated desire for change, which might completely pervert opinion if not dealt with at once by a conference of wise and moderate men" (the assembled delegates). After a few additional generalities, he concluded his presentation by expressing his confidence that the "gathering of national representatives would, no doubt, pay attention to wise and prudent advice" (obviously his prudent advice).

Perfunctory applause followed but the members of the Third Estate felt a sobering chill. They had come to hear about change, but the King had stressed moderation and prudence. And there was nothing specific in his speech. This, obviously, was left by the King to be discussed by the next two speakers. The first was the Lord Privy Seal. After some obligatory generalities of his own, he told his audience that they were free to debate a number of subjects: "freedom of the press, maintenance of order, reform of criminal laws and of the system of taxation." But all such deliberations must be directed to the securing of "the internal quiet of the realm, the glory of the throne, and the happiness of the King's subjects," and there should be no "dangerous innovations which enemies of the State would like to introduce along with the welcome changes His Majesty desires." Stripped of its high-flown rhetoric, the speech meant only that they could talk and debate; for appearance sake they could pass lofty resolutions, but they could not bring about basic change.

When the Lord Privy Seal stepped down, most of the delegates in the two "higher orders" rose and clapped loudly and the "commons" merely sat, stiffly silent.

Then up came Necker, the hope of the bourgeoisie. Succumbing to his desire to hold the center of any stage for the longest time possible, the Minister of State had prepared an interminably long oration—a speech so lengthy that his voice gave way before it was half over and a stand-in reader was required.

It did not take the deputies of the Third Estate long to realize the melancholy implications of Necker's message. The remedy for the kingdom's disastrous fiscal and financial situation was to be found—not in a revision, by the parliament, of the discriminatory tax system—but in a voluntary surrender by the nobility and the clergy of their age-old preferential status. The parliament would not be given the power to enact legislation which would bring about a change in the nation's intolerable economic conditions. The rich manorial lords and wealthy hierarchs would go on paying no taxes. But the millions of small farmers who were able to eke out an annual income of less than 600 livres ($120) from their minuscule properties would go on paying about $45 a year for a bedeviling array of taxes and thereby would continue to be hostage to an endless poverty. And in the cities—where the highest paid workers earned only 40 sous a day and a textile worker was paid half that rate, and where a female spinner got 6 sous daily, and a general laborer earned 15 sous per day—the urban rich would escape taxation but the 4 million laboring poor would go on being deprived of about 30 percent of their income by the King's tax agents and the "leeches" of the tax-gathering corporations.

Instead of tax reform and the establishment of budgetary controls by a democratically elected parliament, Necker—to the delight of the First and Second Estates and the dismay of the Third Estate—recommended only a continuation of past practices. The remedy for national bankruptcy could be achieved by the floating of additional loans in the open market. The Minister then embarked on the reading of a long financial statement which included a deficit of 56 million livres for the past year (later finance officials found that the shortfall was closer to 160 million; Necker, evidently, had once again faked the figures to put himself in a better light).

When the Minister's stand-in took over there was a change of voice, but not of content. After another hour of wearying financial detail, fiscal forecasting, and reassurances, the peroration was concluded with a spate of patriotic exhortation. "The King," the 1,200 delegates were informed, "who has been enlightened by a long course of obstruction and by recent crises, has acquired the experience of a man twice his age. As soon as the dominant view of the assembly reveals itself, His Majesty will be able to judge the character of your deliberations. If it is such as he hopes and has a right to expect . . . then the King will support your wishes and your acts; he will think it an honor to approve them and from this cooperation of the best of princes with the most loyal of peoples will spring unshakable power, and benefits beyond compare." The message was clear: despite all the posturings and the trappings, the

King would remain the sole arbiter; the parliament would be only a rubber stamp.

Later that evening after the jubilant First and Second Estates and the depressed Third had filed from the meeting hall, Mirabeau (a count whose family had fallen from the King's grace and who sat with the Third Estate) said, "Let us hope that the Finance Minister will understand before it is too late that the time for shilly-shallying is over, that it is no longer possible to resist the tide of public opinion: one must swim with it or be drowned. And let us hope that the representatives of the nation will realize the dignity of their function, their mission, and their character."

During the next two tumultuous months, the Third Estate did "realize their mission" and brought constitutional rule to a nation that had been held in the grip of an autocracy for centuries.

It had been the King's scheme to render the Third Estate harmless by having the Estates General vote by sections; the two upper sections (nobles and clergy) could then outvote the reform-minded lower section by a margin of two to one. In time the disheartened representatives of the lower classes would give up the fight and the parliament would be closed down. The Third Estate, however, continued to insist on per capita voting. The subject was debated day after day, without being resolved. Demonstrations backing the Third Estate erupted in Paris. Thwarted, Louis had the doors of the meeting hall locked one night. On the following morning the barred delegation of the bourgeoisie assembled nearby and passed a resolution exhorting the French people to stop the payment of all taxes until their rightful representatives were allowed to resume their deliberations. Newspapers and pamphlets in Paris and other cities took up the call of "No parliament, no taxes!" Disorders increased. Louis then ordered parliament reopened and requested the Third Estate to return.

At this point some of the more forward-looking noblemen, including Lafayette, seated themselves among the delegates of the lower section. They were followed several days later by 150 members of the clergy. Now comprising a majority, the Third Estate declared itself to be the Assembly, the sole legislative voice of the nation.

But the King continued to balk. He asked Necker to intercede with the leaders of the bourgeoisie. The Minister of State—in what was probably his finest hour—refused and resigned.

Louis then had the meeting hall barred by soldiers. Members of the Assembly, now enlarged to more than 800 loyal adherents of all classes, surged against the guards, shouting that only bayonets would prevent their entry. Simultaneously, hordes of citizens from Paris were bearing down on Versailles. The King, fearing a general uprising, caved in, announced on June 27, 1789, that voting could proceed on a per capita basis, and acknowledged the hegemony of the Assembly in legislative matters.

The jubilant 800 delegates of the Third—with 400 defeated members of the upper orders straggling in after them—rushed into the meeting hall and declared the first meeting of the Constituent Assembly to be in session. The meaning of their announcement was unmistakable: the era of constitutional reform had begun in France.

On the night of June 30, 1789, at the request of the Constituent Assembly, all of Versailles was illuminated. Thousands of visitors were on hand to celebrate the victory of the people. Necker, who had been reinstated (the treasury was again empty), was cheered and cheered again for his refusal to knuckle under to the King. Time and again, in probably the most memorable evening of his life, he heard the repeated cry of "Long live Necker!" At one point during the festivities, Louis and other members of the royal family made a fleeting appearance on a balcony. The crowd roared, "Long live the King!" The Queen looked away; she was weeping.

Hardly anyone who had witnessed the tableaulike balcony scene could have guessed that Louis—just ten days later—would be sending a contingent of 50,000 troups against the citizens of Paris. Subsequently, the King stated that his action was taken because riots had created a condition of near anarchy in the capital. Strikes and demonstrations had erupted—as one might expect at a time when almost half the work force was unemployed and 120,000 persons (out of a population of 600,000) were begging for food or were listed as receiving alms—but the local police could easily have contained the situation. Louis's real motive was political: he wanted to prove to the nation that he—and not the Assembly—was the ruler of France.

On the following day, he dismissed Necker, at the insistence of the Queen. It was Saturday, July 11; the Assembly was not in session and so could not offer any resistance to the dismissal. The banks and the bourse, the stock exchange of Paris, were closed and would remain closed on the following day, Sunday, and so there would not be an instantaneous adverse financial reaction. Necker, fearing that he was in physical danger, left that evening for the Swiss border.

On Monday, July 13, the governors of the bourse decided to keep it closed for twenty-four additional hours. Rumors swept the country that the government was about to proclaim its insolvency. A shooting flurry broke out between the royal troops and the newly armed citizens' militia. Crowds milled in the city, shouting, "Bring back Necker!"

On July 14, bands of armed men, searching for gunpowder and having learned there was a considerable amount stored in a medieval fortress, laid siege to the building. After two and a half hours of cannonading and exchange of musket fire during which ninety-eight of the attackers were killed, the Bastille fell before the onslaught of the citizens of Paris. The victorious invaders seized several of the officials in charge—officers and symbols of the King —decapitated them, and paraded their heads through the cheering crowds of the city.

While these history-making events were shaking Paris, the Assembly was meeting in urgent session at Versailles. It demanded that troops be withdrawn from the capital, Necker should be recalled, and under no condition should the government repudiate its loans or announce its bankruptcy. For two days the King hesitated, but as news of spreading riots in Paris reached him, he again capitulated. On July 16, Necker was recalled. Louis agreed that there would be no announcement of debt repudiation. The Queen, who in preparation of flight had been burning some of her private correspondence, put back the fifteen jewel boxes she had packed.

Late that night the King found enough time to bring up-to-date his usually promptly kept diary. It was a journal in which he meticulously recorded his hunting activities, and on rare occasions included some important personal event. During the seven years from 1774 to 1781, there were itemized 1,274 stags brought down and 189,251 other hunting trophies captured or killed. He recorded two words for the events of July 14, 1789, the day of the beginning of the French Revolution: "Today—nothing." Not a single animal bagged, a day of no consequence.

The members of the Assembly, however, had a more realistic

view of events. They realized that the entire nation would soon be convulsed unless corrective measures were taken. They gave urgent priority to the government's precarious financial situation.

After two weeks of intensive deliberation, the Finance Committee of the Assembly recommended that the full Assembly—as a stop gap measure—should accept Necker's advice to float a loan at 5 percent (a high rate of interest for that period). The Assembly assented in August but foolishly reduced the interest rate to 4-1/2 percent. Although the amount to be raised was limited to 4 million livres (enough to meet urgent expenses until, they hoped, "more permanent solutions are available"), only about 2 million livres were raised. In September Necker secured a substantial amount of money from banks (the exact amount is in dispute).

In October the government was again without funds. The Assembly, with great reluctance, raised the salt tax. It passed a decree instituting the payment (spread over a three-year period) by all income-earning citizens of a tax amounting to 25 percent. It also called upon all "those patriots who can afford to do so to make voluntary contributions to their government." All three attempts failed to produce meaningful income for the State: people refused to buy salt causing revenues from the salt tax to fall. The rich resisted the novel experience of paying a levy on their income. The income tax produced less than the equivalent of $500,000 a month. In the subsequent six months the "patriotic donation" came to a total which was less than the equivalent of $1.5 million (the actors of the Comédie Française contributed $5,000; the mounted officers gave $1,300; the Irish College sent its silver plate; instructors at the Royal Fencing School donated their rapiers; and a group of students sent $200, along with their silver buckles). The combined yield from all these money-raising efforts was not even enough to meet the monthly interest on the government debt.

The Assembly continued to labor with the financial problem as the end of the year approached. Its deliberations returned again and again to the regrettable necessity of nationalizing and selling off the valuable Church lands (estimated to be worth over 2 billion livres).

Simultaneously the Finance Committee became preoccupied with the issuance of assignats (government-guaranteed, interest-bearing notes) which would be backed by the security of the nationalized Church properties. As discussion proceeded, the legislators adopted a scheme in which the buyers of Church lands would present assignats in payment for their purchase. To make the ownership of assignats more attractive, the holder was given the privilege of spreading payments over a five-year period. Individual farmers would have a convenient method to enlarge their woefully inadequate landholdings and members of the bourgeoisie would be in a position to buy—on highly favorable terms—some of the valuable properties now held by the Church in urban areas. The more the scheme was debated, the more attractive it became. Here was a way to satisfy everyone except the Church hierarchy. By issuing and selling substantial amounts of assignats (400 million was finally suggested), the government would take in a considerable amount of money quickly and so would avert bankruptcy. Many individuals who were now hoarding money (Necker estimated that about 20 percent of the nation's money supply of gold louis d'or and silver livres had gone into hiding) would be willing to exchange it for assignats with which they could buy properties offered at bargain prices.

When the Assembly dealt with the issue in plenary session, the Finance Committee's proposal obtained considerable support. There were, of course, objections. While many of the priests and others of the lower clergy were in favor of nationalization of Church property, most of the prelates opposed it bitterly, asserting that it would "destroy the Church and all its works." To counter these objections, the Assembly guaranteed to pay the salaries of all priests and dignitaries and to provide an annual income (to be raised by a specific "religious" tax) for the maintenance of all necessary Church activities. These assurances finally satisfied most clerics.

But the most vehement dissent came from those deputies who denounced the assignats as a reversion to paper money and "all its known evils." These men rose in the Assembly Hall to wave some of the confiscated bank notes that had been issued by John Law in 1720, at the time of the Mississippi Scheme. Some of these speakers, reviewing the wild inflation and financial disaster that had overtaken their parents during the "great paper money flood" of that period, shouted, "We want no blood on our hands. Paper money begets ruin and blood."

These outcries were rebutted by one of the supporters of assignats in the following statement:

Paper money is without inherent value unless it represents some special property [such as the yet-to-be-confiscated Church lands]. Without representing some special property it is inadmissable in trade (as an exchange medium) to compete with a metallic currency. Paper money which has only the public authority as its basis has always caused ruin where it has been established; that is the reason why the bank notes of 1720 issued by John Law, after having caused terrible evils, have left only frightful memories. The National Assembly does not expose you to this danger, but has given this new paper money not only a value derived from the national authority, but a value real and immutable, a value which permits it to sustain [through its backing of valuable lands] a competition with the precious metals themselves.

Other speakers favoring assignats urged the delegates to nationalize the Church lands and "issue notes backed by the rich confiscated properties as a means of saving the Revolution."

On November 2, 1789, the National Assembly took the first momentous step; it ordered the confiscation and nationalization of Church properties. A few days later, D'Arcy, a member of the Assembly, proposed a sale of property worth 472 million livres "to help liquidate part of the debt and meet immediate charges." In the midst of the debate on the resolution, Necker voiced criticism against paper money in general, but he did not voice outright opposition "to a limited issue of assignats" and implied that at some future date the government might require—and welcome—further issues of assignats. The Minister's implied position was: do not issue the assignats as legal tender, but consider them a means of raising (indirectly) money to repay the royal debt and expenses.

On December 19, 1789, after a wearying, all-day debate and the newspapers of Paris headlining the question ASSIGNATS OR INSOLVENCY?, the Assembly passed a resolution authorizing the immediate creation of 400 million livres of assignats which were to be supported by set-aside confiscated Church properties valued at 400 million livres (actually the stipulated property was worth much more). The assignats, bearing interest of 5 percent, were to be redeemed serially over a five-year period. They were to be used for the purchase of the confiscated properties (on the installment basis, if so desired) but were not to be used as legal tender in normal transactions. In order to insure against their use as legal tender, they were to be issued in large denominations only, in the form of 1,000-, 500-, and 200-livre notes.

A final self-congratulatory note was struck in the proceedings after the resolution was overwhelmingly adopted. "These assignats," the Assembly announced, "bearing interest as they do, will soon be considered better than the coin now hoarded and will bring it out again into circulation."

The King (whose likeness and signature were engraved on the notes) was induced to issue a proclamation in which he heartily supported the action of the Assembly and asked the populace to "welcome the notes without objection." Soon pamphlets in Paris announced, "The government is saved. The representatives of the French people have acted with wisdom and statesmanship!"

The government was actually saved, at least temporarily. The entire issue of assignats was quickly sold out and the Crown took in 400 million livres in coin with which it met its outstanding bills, redeemed the notes then falling due, and paid up whatever interest was in arrears on its obligations. But only time would tell whether the Assembly had acted with "wisdom and statesmanship."

As might have been expected, the benefits obtained from the issuance of assignats proved temporary. Tax legislation put through by the Assembly made the new tax system more egalitarian but not more effective; the wealthy—despite the efforts of many newly installed tax collectors—were still able to slip through the net. Simultaneously, the salaries of the extensive, newly created civil service staff caused a large drain on the treasury as did the considerable "expenditures for the Church" which the government had agreed to meet when it nationalized Church properties. The upkeep of the royal court still exceeded 35 million livres per year, and the payment of interest on the mountainous national debt (estimated at 4 billion livres in late 1790) continually emptied the treasury. In March 1790, Necker reported that the government's deficit during the previous two months had run at an annual rate of 360 million livres, a new high.

In August 1790, Mirabeau urged the creation of assignats to be used by the government solely for the redemption of its debt, as it fell due. Simultaneously, D'Arcy, a frequent collaborator of Mirabeau, stressed the need for new money since a considerable part of the nation's money supply "had gone into hiding." Anson, another Assembly member, linked assignats with money by asserting, "The government badly requires new funds, and every nation has the right to manufacture money, whether in the form of assignats or in some other form."

Ringing applause greeted this dictum. The euphoria was heightened when another delegate, Gouy, proclaimed, "It is the solemn duty of this gathering to liquidate the near-term debt by one single operation through the creation of 2 billion and 400 million of legal tender notes." He demanded that a law be passed prohibiting the payment—in coin—for any purchase of nationalized properties. Reporting his speech, newspapers indicated that "his address was loudly and repeatedly applauded."

A few delegates did not join the rush for paper money. Du Pont de Nemours, the Physiocrat economist, issued a pamphlet maintaining that "doubling the quantity of money or of a money substitute simply increases prices, disturbs values, alarms capital, diminishes legitimate enterprise, and so decreases the demand for products and for labor. The only persons to be helped by it [the rapid print-up of new money] are the rich who have large debts to pay." Repeatedly Du Pont de Nemours rose to tell the Assembly that he "would always vote against the emission of irredeemable paper."

Necker was, perhaps, the severest critic of paper money. Repeatedly, he attacked the proposal to create new assignats in the form of legal tender. With considerable eloquence, he stressed the inflationary dangers inherent in the "printing press operation." A handful of others joined him, but as the debate grew more acrimonious and ground on for months, he was increasingly isolated. In September the Paris press, which a year before had heaped praise on him, now called him "traitor to the Revolution." Gradually the celebrities who formerly flocked to the salon conducted by his wife began sending apologies and stayed away. Never a favorite at the royal court, he was now ostentatiously cold-shouldered. Worn out, increasingly abused on the Assembly floor for his bitter opposition to paper money, and deprived of the adulation he required for survival, he sent the King his resignation and left France forever.

On the last day of September 1790, the Assembly created 800 million new assignats. They bore no interest and were issued in both large and small denominations. There was no stipulation against their use as legal tender. The Assembly had started up the paper-money printing presses and, in one stroke, had increased the monetary supply by 50 percent.

At the time, its action brought exuberant acclaim from the Paris press and from influential pamphleteers. The sense of jubilation is caught in one of the publications, *The Friend of the Revolution:* "Citizens, the deed is done! The assignats are the keystone to the arch! Now I can announce to you that the Revolution is finished and there only remain one or two important questions. The provinces and the commercial cities which were at first alarmed at the proposal to issue so much paper money now send expression of their thanks. . . . Soon France, enriched by her new prosperity and by the national industry which is preparing for fruitfulness, will demand still another creation of paper money."

As might have been expected, the initial, deceptively beneficial effects usually produced during the early stages of a massive monetary expansion soon appeared. The tempo of industry rose; goods —produced by workers who were increasingly paid in assignats— became more abundant. More plentiful money induced stepped-up purchases by the bourgeoisie and the rich, particularly of property, which rose in price. In a position to undercut their foreign competitors because they could pay their workers in cheap paper, French producers increased their exports (they promptly hoarded the foreign coins they received for their goods). Farmers—relieved of some of their more onerous taxes through legislation passed by the Assembly in 1790, and benefited by increased income from the properties they had acquired through the expropriation of Church lands—were lifted temporarily from the poverty they had endured for centuries.

The chief beneficiary of the outpouring of paper money was the government. It paid salaries with assignats and used them for the purchase of commodities. Interest on its debt and debt redemptions were discharged with assignats.

But the assignats had not produced any tangible benefits for the proletariat of Paris and other cities. Employment had been somewhat increased but wages remained at their near-starvation level. Begging had become so commonplace that the Assembly created a Committee on Beggary with instructions to "examine the problem and make urgent recommendations." Several months later the committee announced that there were over 3 million beggars in France (or more than 12 percent of the population) and that over 125,000 adults and children (almost 20 percent of the city's population) "were regularly begging in the streets of Paris". The committee's "recommendations" turned out to be platitudinous pieties, and no action was taken. The desperation of chronic starvation—despite the print-up of paper money—continued in the capital; it nurtured a seething anger which intermittently erupted into looting, arson, and mob-perpetrated murders of suspected royalists, shopkeepers, and "refractory" clerics.

Many of the Paris newspapers, however, held forth the prospect of a better life—one that might be secured by the issuance of more assignats. Early in 1791 *The Journal of the Revolution* editorialized:

The assignats have accomplished much and can accomplish more in the future. Only good has flowed from them and none of the evils we were promised have transpired. Months ago we were told prices would rise and assignats would fall in value. Neither has occurred. Coal and wood have not risen in price. The cost of subsistence in the provinces has not risen. Bread in Paris still is selling at 2-1/2 to 3 sous a pound. Grains sold in the public and private markets have not advanced. And what is more, everyone knows that assignats of small denominations are selling at a premium over gold and silver coins, and are being hoarded. We may comfort ourselves with the assurance that one day metal money will be outlawed and we will have only the most beneficial of all monies: paper!

In the middle of 1791, the Assembly authorized the third issue of assignats in the amount of 600 million livres. These, like all subsequent issues, were emitted as legal tender, bringing the paper money supply to 1 billion 400 million livres. Evidence indicates two reasons for the new issue: (1) taxes continued to lag behind expectations forcing the government to fill the budgetary gap with newly created paper money, and (2) there was considerable pressure exerted on certain delegates to create more assignats for the perpetuation of a speculative craze that was sweeping the nation. Early in 1791 the stock manipulators of Paris had successfully hiked the prices of many equities on the bourse. The fever spread to the wealthy nobles, members of the royal family, and the upper bourgeoisie. Finally the shopkeepers, merchants, and some of the better-off farmers joined the stampede. Since a considerable part of the metal money supply had now gone into hiding, the momentum of speculation had to be maintained by an increasing supply of paper money. Throughout the spring of 1791, a number of the delegates who were heavily involved in the stock market (Mirabeau made and lost fortunes in stock issues he helped to rig) exhorted the Assembly to create additional assignats. Jullien, Delaunay, and Falre d'Eglantine, all of whom professed the most fervent patriotic zeal on the Assembly floor while continually thumping for more paper, were found, in subsequent investigations, to have "accepted bribes totaling 500,000 livres for aiding legislation calculated to promote the purpose of stockjobbers."* They and others finally had their way in the Assembly.

Shortly after the latest issue of assignats was announced, the first disturbing sign of value depreciation—little noticed at the time—showed itself. The assignat, which had been quoted at a one-to-one exchange ratio with the silver livre, declined by 10 percent; an assignat note of 100 livres suddenly brought only 90 livres in silver. Supporters of the assignat attributed the decline to "the work of foreign agents who were causing disaffection among the people."

The 10 percent decline, however, was suddenly overshadowed on June 21 (two days after the newest issue of assignats) by the incident that has become known as the Flight to Varennes.

After August 27, 1789, the date when the Assembly passed the Declaration of the Rights of Man (the legislative cornerstone of the French Revolution), the King regarded himself as a powerless "hostage of the new nation." The Declaration affirmed that "all men are born and remain free and equal in rights" and these rights are "liberty, property, security, and resistance to oppression," that "all men are innocent until proved guilty," that "society has the right to hold accountable every public agent of administration," and that "all sovereignty rests essentially in the nation and no individual may exercise authority which does not emanate from the nation."

For Louis the message was unmistakable: he was no longer the sovereign; the people were sovereign and could hold him accountable. From the day this act was passed, Louis and Marie An-

---

*From *History of the French Revolution* by Louis A. Thiers.

toinette had planned an escape from France. Once on foreign soil he hoped to raise a loyal army with the aid of friendly rulers who were alarmed by the Revolution. He would launch an attack from his foreign haven and then reenter France after his forces had smashed "the revolutionaries."

After making elaborate arrangements with loyal officers and sympathizers, the royal family began their escape in the dead of night on August 21, 1791. Louis, disguised as a footman, Marie Antoinette, disguised as a governess, their children, and two female servants set out from the palace in the Tuileries in a heavily curtained coach. They sped, undetected, under a moonless sky, through the dark streets of Paris and raced northeastward toward the border of what is present-day Luxembourg. Then came a series of unbelievable mishaps. But despite these, on the next day the fugitives finally approached a town called Varennes, situated a half-day's ride from the border. Here they stopped for a prearranged change of horses and a planned link-up with friendly troops clandestinely stationed in the area. The horses did not arrive on time. While the apprehensive occupants waited, a worker on his way home passed by, looked into the coach, and recognized Louis "from his likeness on the assignats." He summoned help; the royal family was taken into custody. Several days later the fugitives were returned to virtual "house arrest" in the Tuileries. The population, apprised of the flight, was in a turmoil. Rumors flew that Louis had attempted to engineer an overthrow of the Assembly and had tried to bring on a foreign invasion. The threat of war filled the Paris air.

It was amplified during the next few days by the steady exit of royalist refugees who were seen leaving the country, loaded down with their possessions. These wealthy émigrés, it was believed, were leaving French soil while there was still time.

The Assembly, of course, was fully cognizant of the population's apprehension, but its attention was elsewhere. The delegates were racing against a deadline. They were occupied with the completion of the Constitution of 1791 before their term expired in September, a task with which they had been struggling for almost two years. The Constitution was finally enacted early in September. Under it, France—despite Louis' attempts to revert to an autocracy—was to remain a constitutional monarchy, but the reforms fashioned in the Declaration of the Rights of Man were broadened and concretized. The nation was not yet ready for a republic although republicanism was on the rise. The "hostage" in the Tuileries palace would still be the titular head of the nation, but his powers would be restrained by the nation and would be predominantly cosmetic. And at any time these powers could be abrogated by the Assembly. Since he had no viable alternative, the King signed the document.

De facto control of the newly elected Legislative Assembly which came into power on September 30, 1791, was vested in the bourgeoisie, whose 486 delegates (most of whom were lawyers and other professionals, owners of small farms, and shopkeepers) by far outnumbered 200 royalists, holders of large landed estates, the high clergy, and other reactionaries. The bourgeois representatives were split into two factions: the first consisted of 350 centrist moderates whom history has come to know as Girondists, and the second contained 136 so-called revolutionary adherents of the Jacobin left who possessed zeal, a driving purpose, and the support of an increasingly seething capital city.

The new Assembly was immediately involved in debate on war; the King's attempted flight had pushed the matter to the center of the stage. Various delegates from all factions voiced their apprehensions over the possibility of an attack upon France, especially one launched from the Austrian Netherlands, territories (now corresponding to Belgium and Holland) which were part of the Austrian Empire. Marie Antoinette had been in constant touch with her brother Leopold, the ruler of the Empire, regarding a possible attack on France by Austrian forces. In August 1791, he had issued the Manifesto of Pillnitz in which he openly promised "assistance when the time was propitious."

The prowar forces in the new Assembly were spearheaded by a Girondist adventurer, Jean-Jacques Brissot. A man of elastic morality, a restless schemer, he had—after a career of varying loyalties—achieved a reputation as an inflammatory speaker and a revolutionary editor. He—and other "Brissotins," who were hungry for power—worked incessantly to have France launch a "preventive strike" against the Austrian forces in the Netherlands. As the year 1791 closed, their mission was aided by mobs of Parisians armed with pikes who occupied the Assembly's gallery and roared for "war to save the Revolution." At the same time bread riots broke out in the city and refractory clerics were run down by roving bands, their heads decapitated and paraded at the ends of pikes before the Assembly Hall.

As turmoil rose, more émigrés fled the country, disposing of all assignats in their possession and converting them into silver money or jewels. Paper money began to depreciate visibly against the silver livre. This, however, did not prevent the Legislative Assembly from going down the paper road its predecessor (the Constitutional Assembly) had elected to travel; it created 300 million new assignats just before the year 1791 closed. By year-end the assignats had fallen to 77 percent vis-à-vis the silver livre and living costs had risen by about 15 percent.

By March 1792, the assignat had plummeted to 47 percent and the price of bread (the best index of the cost of living for the period) had risen by 50 percent in Paris and other cities. The customary phenomenon of a gathering superinflation began to appear—the race to exchange depreciating "paper" money into possessions. Clavière, who became Finance Minister in March 1792, described the trend in his memoirs, as a "sudden rush to build new houses, to furnish them with an unaccustomed lavishness, to purchase jewels and trinkets without a second thought as to price, and to start new enterprises of all sorts."

As the economic deterioration worsened, the drive for war gathered greater force. Recurring and heated debate on the subject rang through the Assembly Hall for more than six months. Then, on April 20, 1792, in a paroxysm of appropriate patriotism—with the galleries howling approval—the Assembly declared war on Austria, which then fielded the strongest army on the continent of Europe. Only 7 of more than 700 delegates opposed the resolution. When the war declaration carried the day, the nobles and landed gentry exulted. They were convinced that France and the Revolution would be crushed and that they would be restored to their former privileged status. Louis and Antoinette rejoiced, certain that the coming debacle would save them. The poor and the miserable of Paris hoped that the war would somehow attain for them what other recent events had failed to secure: improved living conditions. And members of the bourgeoisie believed that war would solidify their newly secured power in the legislature and would bring them the financial benefits that the inception of military hostilities usually confers upon the entrepreneurial class.

Rarely had a nation entered into a war with as much optimism about its outcome. The annals of the Legislative Assembly show that early in May—despite several weeks of military reversals—army procurement officers indicated that "there is a half-year's supply of grain available, which should be sufficient." Obviously, the war would be over in six months (it raged for almost twenty-five years).

The deliberation of the Assembly delegates regarding the advisability of issuing more assignats—conducted in almost leisurely fashion during a four-month period of mounting military disasters —gave virtually no consideration to the probable economic impact of the war. But the majority, as usual, favored the emission of more paper money despite its continuing decline against gold and silver (many farmers were already refusing to sell grain unless half of the payment was made in specie). The "expansionist"-minded deputies who favored "more stimulus to increase employment" (140 years before Maynard Keynes!) insisted on "more circulating medium," maintaining that the assignat would soon be stabilized. They were countered by a small stubborn minority who emphasized the foolhardiness of "throwing more coal into a fire which is already raging." Boislandry—evidently of the "monetarist" school—insisted that there was "far too much money in circulation" and read an erudite paper in which he demonstrated that the velocity of circulation had increased substantially and had outrun "the needs of trade." Excessive money, he asserted, was being used for speculative ventures and the purchase of "unrequired objects at unnecessarily high prices."

The expansionist deputies prevailed; the Assembly ordered 700 million more assignats, raising the total outstanding to 2 billion 400 million by August 1792.

By that time the enemy had already driven past Metz and Longwy. The war that had been entered into so lightly now posed a dark threat, especially to Paris where the course of hostilities was reported daily in the press. Panic swept the city when the Duke of Brunswick, commander of the Prussian forces, issued a manifesto warning the capital's inhabitants that he would be in Paris within a month and would burn it to the ground if he found that the King had been molested. Armed mobs roamed the city in search for enemy agents, killing suspects on sight. It was during this period of growing terror that the guillotine began lopping heads with an increased tempo.

The King with characteristic obtuseness aggravated the situation by augmenting the Royal Guard customarily stationed before the palace with several hundred men of the royalist-leaning Swiss Guard. He then announced that on the morning of August 10 he planned to review a newly arrived unit of the National Guard in the square adjacent to the palace. On the appointed morning, 20,000 armed citizens descended on the square motivated by a desire to demonstrate that the people were capable of meeting the King's show of force with their own show of force. As Louis emerged from the palace to perform the ceremonial charade, the crowd surging forward, yelled, "Long live the nation! Down with the King!" Louis, realizing the danger of the situation, turned quickly and reentered the palace. He, Marie Antoinette, and their children then fled into the Assembly Hall, where the deputies were in session. At the same time shots rang out from the windows of the palace. The screaming mob and the National Guard returned fire. When the confrontation was over, 383 Parisians and National Guardsmen lay dead and about 800 of the nobles in the palace and members of the Swiss Guard had been killed on the spot or later massacred.

A wild rage surged through the city. Mobs besieged the Assembly Hall. They were finally persuaded to disband only after extracting a promise that the King would be put on trial. Louis was suspended from all his functions and the royal family was imprisoned in the Temple. With the removal of the King from office, the monarchical constitution was dead and a new legislative body was required.

A new election was held in haste. The Convention, which replaced the Legislative Assembly, was—as the two predecessor parliaments had been—a body predominantly representative of the bourgeoisie. Of the 900 deputies who sat in the Convention at one time or another from 1792 to 1795, there were only 2 members of the proletariat. They were more than offset by 7 marquises and a "prince of royal blood." Businessmen, merchants, manufacturers, and tradesmen constituted 10 percent. Lawyers made up 47 percent. The professions (literature, art, medicine, and teaching) were represented by 12 percent. The Church and landed interests commanded a combined total of 12 percent. The remaining 12 percent were a miscellany of the middle class. The center of power of the nation and of the Revolution was to be found—as it had been in the Constitutional and Legislative assemblies—in the bourgeoisie.

September 20, 1792—when the Convention met for the first time —was a grim day of forebodings and alarms. Lafayette, having suffered a series of military defeats, had given up his post and had deserted to the Austrians. Verdun had fallen; the newspapers of Paris were exhorting, "The road to Paris is open to the enemy. To arms! To arms!" But when the delegates reassembled on September 21, news suddenly arrived that the enemy had been routed at Valmy on the previous day by Dumouriez's forces and were streaming eastward toward their own borders. In a burst of exultation the deputies announced the abolition of monarchy and the establishment of the French Republic. At that moment they did not realize that they had arrived at the high point of the Revolution, and that from then on—in the political sphere—it would be downhill all the way.

Short-lived military successes, however, came quickly; before the year was over the French army had overrun Belgium and was marching into the Rhineland, Savoy, and Nice. Carried away by these victories, the French bourgeois government announced to the world in November 1792 that it would "grant fraternity and aid to all people who want to attain their liberty." In December there came another manifesto that France would "treat as enemies" those countries which supported "princes or privileged orders," and would "guarantee the independence" of those countries which "establish free and popular governments." Alarmed by these threats, almost all the monarchies of the continent sent their armies against France. England—France's powerful archrival— and Spain came into the war early in 1793 when France declared war on them.

The Convention—unlike its predecessor—now began draconian preparations for a long war. It organized itself into commissions, tribunals, and committees. The notorious committees run by dictum and star-chamber tyranny would gradually bypass the Convention, arrogate its power to themselves, and would finally subvert the Revolution and bring on its demise.

One of the special commissions was given the task, in January 1793, of sifting the evidence obtained during the recent trial of the

King. In November 1792, a locksmith had found a safe in Louis' former apartment in the Tuileries (next to hunting, his two leading passions were carpentry and locksmithery). The safe was opened and in it was found enough damaging evidence to fill two large cartons. Among the documents were letters received from Leopold in response to Louis' request for an attack on France and correspondence with other heads of state about possible intervention as well as several letters dealing with a plan to escape via a town named Varennes.

The special commission found the King guilty, as did the Convention. He was led to the guillotine on January 21, 1793. When he reached it he said in a loud voice, "I die an innocent man. I hope that my blood may secure the happiness of the French people." The blade screeched as it fell. The executioner held up the severed head and the crowd screamed, "Long live the nation!" Louis' three-cornered hat was auctioned from the platform, as were locks of his hair and buttons from his coat. Men and women dipped handkerchiefs and swords into his blood. Dancing and singing ended the ceremony. Then the crowd drifted away; there were no other executions scheduled. Some of the singers and the dancers were to return, however, on October 16, when Marie Antoinette was brought to the festivities, holding her head high —until she lost it.

The terror that raged during the tenancy of the Convention has been repeatedly and effectively portrayed by writers and historians, and requires no detailed treatment here. Unfortunately, however, there has been created an impression in some quarters that the gruesome events—particularly of 1793 and 1794—were the very epitome of the Revolution. In actuality they were its antithesis. Almost all the liberties won by the struggles of 1789–1791 were subverted by the oppressive edicts of the committees and by the wholesale guillotinings not only of royalists, refractory clerics, and suspected would-be émigrés, but also of thousands of common people accused of petty violations (such as carrying forged assignats) whose real guilt was that of being alive in a time of mass bloodletting. Almost every prominent revolutionary leader also died by the knife, having been brought to the guillotine by internecine factional strife. In the long-running vendetta, death-producing charges were leveled against opponents so that the accuser might prove his allegiance to the Revolution and thereby assure his own survival. The Brissotins and other leaders of the Girondists were beheaded by the charges of the Jacobins, the Hérbertists by the Enragés, and the Dantonists by the Montagnards. Finally, the Thermidorians rallied the Convention against the increasingly tyranical Robespierrists, to bring the reign of blood to a close. Robespierre and twenty-one of his associates were dragged to the guillotine on July 28, 1794. Robespierre—the most fervent advocate of liberty before he assumed leadership and its persistent perverter after coming to power—had on a sky-blue coat he had recently bought in anticipation of attending a patriotic celebration. He also wore a bandage on his jaw which had been shattered at the time of his arrest. He had resolved to show no emotion during his execution, but when the headsman suddenly ripped the bandage from his jaw he let out a wild yelp. After that he was quiet. A few months after his execution the Reign of Terror, which he symbolized, came to an end.

But the story of the assignats was far from its conclusion.

During the three-year existence of the Convention (September 1792 to September 1795) the nation's finances came under the stewardship of Joseph Cambon, head of the Committee of Finance, member of the dreaded Committee of Public Safety, and member of both the Committee of War and the Committee of Diplomacy. A tough, shrewd, and successful capitalist, he had those qualities that would have produced a brilliant career for him as a member of our Federal Reserve Board: he had a keen perception of the functioning of money, he was a trustworthy "team man" who was capable of carrying out the most prodigious assignments, and, most importantly, he was an expert in public deception—the deception which enables a bureaucrat to lure people into thinking that their government is taking steps to control inflation when—in reality—it is engaging in acts that abet inflation.

Saddled with the task of funding the equipment and the provisioning of a military establishment that in time encompassed fourteen armies, almost 1.2 million soldiers, and a sizable navy, he had to rely increasingly on the print-up of additional assignats. The staggering sum of 3 billion livres was authorized by the Convention during 1793; 1 billion 200 million would find their way into the money stream during the first nine months of the year, raising the amount in circulation to 3 billion 600 million.

Aware of the potential inflationary effects of so massive an increase in money supply, Cambon went through the motions of several fiscal reforms. A graduated income tax was proposed (the first in France's history); a "forced loan" was instituted against the rich (later abandoned as unproductive); a plan was promulgated whereby the government would pay for goods and services by issuing short-term notes instead of assignats (this, too, was soon abandoned when resistance developed); an attempt was evolved to consolidate the yet-considerable government debt and to make the purchase of new government debt issues more attractive.

As might have been expected, all of these measures proved unavailing after a time. In retrospect, it becomes evident that—although he hoped for beneficial results—Cambon must have realized that they would not be secured. He must have known that his efforts to reduce the government's requirements for additional assignats in the conduct of civilian affairs would be overwhelmed by the constant emission of large quantities of new paper notes to meet the expenses of an expanding war.

It is apparent, too, that Cambon's insistence—in the face of failure—that his program would succeed was an obvious psychological ploy calculated to shore up the value of the plummeting assignat. This conclusion is sustained by some of the events that occurred in Belgium.

When Belgium fell to French forces in November 1792, Cambon stressed the monetary benefits that would flow from the victory. Belgium's metallic money stock would be "appropriated" by the French army. Only the money of the rich and the coins and bullion owned by the Belgian treasury and by the nation's banks would be taken. But the Belgian people would be enriched with assignats brought into the country by their "liberating" comrades-in-arms, the "soldiers of the people's revolution." In that way—according to Cambon—there would be an inflow of metal money into the French treasury and a simultaneous decrease of assignats circulating in France, brought about by their export into Belgium. All in all, a tidy plan that should have reassured the advocates of "hard money."

But the anticipated did not occur. After several weeks of France's reversion to the ancient custom of "stripping" occupied territories, the effort yielded the equivalent of $28 million—all secured from the plundering of religious artifacts contained in Belgian churches. Almost no other form of treasure was seized.

The common people of Belgium resented their would-be liberators with a passion. They refused to sell wheat and other provisions to "Catholic destroyers of Catholic churches" in exchange for assignats. Even the small minority of Belgians who still believed in "revolutionary humanism" told their French brothers that they had no confidence in foreign paper and would much prefer a manifestation of solidarity in the form of coins.

The failure of Cambon's plan became evident to government officials by December 1792, but he continued to speak (at least in public) of its possible success until—after a sudden military reversal—French forces had to flee Belgium in February 1793. His continued insistence on the likely success of a plan that had already failed was an act of legerdemain during which his right hand was ostentatiously engaged in issuing statements designed to maintain confidence in the assignat while his left hand was furtively throwing prodigious amounts of paper money into circulation.

But illusion was soon overtaken by reality. In the middle of March 1793, insurgency broke out in the Vendée, Brittany, and Anjou; wheat crops were burned and army provisioning agents had their throats slit. The assignat plunged to 30 percent of value against the silver livre and the price of grain doubled. The cost of bread leaped from its normal price of 2-1/2 to 3 sous per pound to 5 sous per pound, and the price of meat tripled. The laboring poor and the beggars of Paris and other cities had long ago proved to themselves that they could do without meat during long periods and so the rise of veal from 6 sous a pound to 18 sous was not a calamity, but bread at 5 sous a pound meant near starvation. The average laborer's daily wage was now sufficient to buy only 3 pounds of bread, leaving no money for all the other necessities. To meet other expenses each person in the average family of four had to reduce his daily intake of bread to 4 ounces. He could also have one bowl of meatless soup a day, but nothing else.

People in Paris responded to the situation by looting and recurring invasions of the Convention Hall.

In April, after a crushing defeat suffered in Holland by Dumouriez and his subsequent desertion to the Austrians, the situation worsened. The assignat plunged to 22 percent. The price of bread now surged to 12 sous a pound. The insurgent commune of Paris agitated for "punishment of the victimizers of the nation." Properties of bakers were set afire. In the midst of the turmoil the Convention—which had been holding intermittent deliberations as far back as the autumn of 1792 regarding the advisability of putting a control on rising grain prices—now resumed its debate in a more urgent mood. The advocates of free trade continued to resist "anything that trammels up the flow of commerce," insisting that there was already a law in existence which made "the hampering of the movement of wheat a capital offense." Other members of the Convention asserted that controls were a "tyranny on the part of a government which believes itself to be above the forces of nature" and "nothing but evil can come from such restraints." The writings of the Physiocrat economists—some of whom still were among the delegates—and the theories of Adam Smith were cited. (Anyone who doubts the bourgeois base of the Revolution needs only to reread these debates to appreciate how devoted most of elected officials were to "the freedom of the marketplace.")

But while argument mounted in the Convention, the price of bread also mounted, reaching 15 sous per pound, or six times its 1790 price. With rioting increasing and with shouts of "To the guillotine!" increasingly raised by demonstrators in the Assembly Hall, the opposition to price-fixing was worn away, and a control on grain was finally passed on May 3, 1793.

The decree was met with considerable resistance by many farmers. Wheat was hidden, destroyed, or sold to bakers surreptitiously at prices higher than the set maximum.

With rumors flying that other commodities were soon to be controlled, a rush began to stock up on other necessities such as coal, wood, candles, and clothing. The price of these items soared: candles—formerly selling at 13 sous—rose to 44 sous by midsummer 1793; eggs went from 10 sous to 50 sous; wool from 20 sous a measure to 65; coffee, wine, and tobacco sold at four times their 1790 price.

Agitation mounted for the extension of controls to items other than grain. Robespierre and his lieutenants on the Revolutionary Tribunal and the all-powerful Committee of Public Safety, who were now in their ascendancy, blunted all opposition to new controls.

On September 29, 1793, a comprehensive price-control system covering forty items of "basic necessity" was enacted. Because of a rising tide of opposition, it was modified and then remodified during its fifteen-month existence. Historians are at odds about its efficacy. A considerable amount of evidence indicates that it was subverted and rendered inoperable in many rural areas of France. It may have been partially effective in Paris and a few other cities but the harsh measures enacted to insure its enforcement suggest that even in these "left-oriented" strongholds it was sabotaged by bourgeois merchants and manufacturers at every opportunity. As a result, numerous transactions took place in the black market at higher than mandated prices. It is not possible to determine the extent of illegal transactions. Some of the decrees issued to secure compliance included: an order by the Tribunal of Strasbourg "to destroy the dwelling of anyone found guilty of selling goods at a price higher than set by the Maximum"; a dictum by the Committee of Public Safety that a farmer who refused to sell produce or livestock at prices fixed by law would have his property confiscated if his refusal constituted a first offense, but he would be imprisoned on a second offense and put to death on a third offense; and an order by the Revolutionary Tribunal of Paris that merchants refusing to sell goods at controlled prices or unwilling to accept payment in assignats should be put to death by the guillotine.

Gradually the repressive measures mandated to achieve the control of living costs became associated with strictures against nonacceptance of assignats for goods purchased. The Convention ruled that a person who dealt in silver or gold coins should be "imprisoned in irons for at least six years." A similar sentence was leveled against anyone who—in a first offense—accepted assignats at a discount from coins; a second offense drew a sentence of twenty years in prison, and a third offense would be punishable by death. But in May 1794, the Convention outdid itself: it ruled that the death sentence should be imposed on any person "convicted of having asked before a transaction is concluded in what money the payment was to be made."

In December 1794—less than twenty weeks after its two leading proponents (Saint-Just and Robespierre) had been carted off to the guillotine in the same tumbril—the Maximum was completely repealed.

Le Moniteur, one of the more responsible publications of the period, noted the passing of controls with this observation: "Most farmers, merchants, and processors were at all times opposed to it; they refused to consider its necessity even in a time of war. In the cities and towns, particularly the buyers of little means approved of it because it brought the rise in prices under control. True, the lines before bakeries and coal sellers' establishments were long and goods were frequently not available. Let us hope the demise of the Maximum will produce benefits for all."

That hope was not realized. Instead, there now got underway a hyperinflation comparable to that experienced during the fall of the Roman Empire. At the end of 1793 the assignats in circulation came to approximately 4 billion livres. They had been printed up during a four-year period. But in the next twelve months an additional 4 billion were flung into the already swollen money supply, bringing the total to 8 billion by the end of 1794. The inflationary effect of the massive input of 1794 was suppressed by price controls, which were in effect all year.

With the lid blown off by the repeal of controls, prices surged wildly in 1795. Cold statistics show the decline of the assignat's value vis-à-vis silver coin as follows: in January 1795 it had a value of 22 percent which declined in February to 17 percent, to 7-1/2 percent in May, to 3 percent in August, and eight-tenths of 1 percent in December. By the end of the year it was almost worthless as a purchasing medium; whereas one could have exchanged 100 livres in assignats for 100 livres in coin early in 1790, it now required 12,500 in assignats ($2,500) to get 100 livres in silver ($20). But the people of France were not interested in exchange ratios of paper to coin, since silver coins had all but disappeared from circulation. Their concern—and their horror—stemmed from the almost incomprehensible leap in prices. In May the price of wheat vaulted to a level six times the level of December 1794, or thirty times the normal level that had been maintained until 1791. A measure of flour that cost 6 livres during the Maximum suddenly went to 100 livres in June 1795. A hat bought for 14 livres in 1790 commanded 500 livres in mid-1795 (an amount equal to two years of wages earned by a laborer in 1789–1790). A pound of butter skyrocketed to 560 livres, an amount equal to five years of income for the average farmer before 1790.

A pound of sugar streaked upward from 2-1/2 livres in 1794 to 62 livres by mid-1795, coffee from 4 livres to 62, a pound of soap from 3-1/2 to 41 livres, a bunch of carrots from 2 sous to 80, a bushel of barley from 2-1/2 to 50 livres—all in a period of six months. And in the following months these prices maintained their frightening climb at a much faster pace.

Economic historians have tried to construct a price index that would reflect the full extent of inflation between April 1795 and March 1796, the period of the most violent increases. Based on figures obtained in the studies of Caron and Auland as well as prices mentioned in the records of various departments, the following table may be considered a fairly reliable approximation* of the rise in the cost of ten basic commodities from April 1795 to March 1796. All figures use the 1790 ("normal price") base: thus, the figure of 9 for the month of April 1795 indicates that the ten basic commodities then cost nine times their 1790 price, and the May 1795 prices were eleven times those prevailing in 1790, and so forth.

TABLE 1.
RISE OF TEN BASIC COMMODITIES
APRIL 1795–MARCH 1796.

1795	April	9 times
	May	11
	June	13
	July	21
	August	27
	September	31
	October	42
	November	54
	December	129
1796	January	114
	February	190
	March	388

This basic consumer index (containing such items as bread, coal, butter, eggs, etc.) reveals that living costs had undergone a breathtaking surge of 3,655 percent in a twelve-month period!

The Paris of that period reflected the miseries and chaos that a great city experiences when it is caught in the vise of hyperinflation. As soon as people got hold of a handful of assignats they would rush to buy the meager necessities they could afford before prices changed; at the end of 1795, the cost of basic items was

*See *The Assignats* by S. E. Harris. This work is perhaps the most illuminating chronicle of the French superinflation. The price index referred to above is patterned on an index formulated by Harris.

doubling daily. Arriving at a nearby bakery, a purchaser would either find it closed (having run out of goods) or—more often— he or she would encounter a long line of grim, half-starving people waiting their turn to enter. Finally, after interminable hours of waiting, the unfortunate people waiting at the end of the line would be told they could not buy their pound of bread. The shop had exhausted its small quantity of merchandise.

Shortages persisted month after month; it was the old story of too many units of money chasing too few units of production. Scarcity was aggravated by the refusal of farmers to supply prod- uce until prices mounted further. Having been forced by army requisitioning agents to sell most of their wheat at lower-than- market prices, they hoarded the remainder until the hungering population in the cities and the speculators had bid prices up to new high levels. Frequently, the long-stored grain was delivered to millers in a condition unfit for human consumption, and the bread from which it was made contained maggots and rot. But beggars could not be choosers; despite repeated wage raises, most families in Paris during 1795 and early 1796 spent more than two-thirds of their income on the four ounces of bread consumed per day per person. And four ounces were devoured, maggots or no maggots. Since wages received lost a considerable part of pur- chasing power overnight, the government promised to pay a por- tion of salaries "in kind," but the promise was rarely kept. The delegates of the Convention, however, were influential enough to have their salaries paid in wedges of cheese, which they consumed, sold, or exchanged for other commodities.

As prices shot upward (in the closing days of December 1795 bread sold at 80 livres [$16] per pound), the elderly and persons living on fixed pensions gradually sold off all their belongings and waited for death. With increasing frequency the old and the retired sought release by drowning in the Seine. This was the Paris of the common people in 1795.

But there was another side—the Paris of the newly rich bour- geoisie for whom the wild inflation had created fortunes far greater than those accumulated by former kings and nobles. These were the manufacturers of munitions, the contractors who sup- plied, at ever-escalating prices, every item that could be con- sumed, destroyed, or worn by an army; the new bankers, the foreign exchange sharpers who played the money market on margin; the successful stock riggers and the hundreds of speculators in every commodity needed so desperately by a disadvantaged population.

These new multimillionaires acquired enough paper money to buy additional lands put on sale by the government as well as the confiscated properties of the guillotined and expatriated royalists and, in addition, every jewel, coin, and object of gold or silver that came into their reach. And they had more than enough left to keep their mistresses—the *merveilleuses*—in a state of luxury Madame Pompadour could not achieve. These women could be seen in the elegant, brightly lit salons and in the cafés at night—half naked in their diaphanous pseudo-classical robes, their breasts lifted high and amply exposed, and their mock-Grecian sandals studded with jewels. They danced while the common population of Paris struggled against the enveloping inflation.

And what did the members of the Convention, the heads of committees and the various ministers (the government of France) do as prices soared upward in 1795 in response to each successive print-up of new assignats? As might be expected from purposive inflaters, they heaped more coals on the raging fire, simultaneously pretending they were attempting to bring the conflagration under control.

At the beginning of 1795 there were 8 billion livres of assignats in circulation and basic commodities sold for three times their normal (1790) price. The Convention promptly slammed 3.4 billion more into the money supply during the next four months raising the total in circulation to 11.4 billion by April 30; the index of basic commodities tripled during the four-month period to nine times the normal level.

Protests greeted the surge in living costs, but they were quickly suppressed. After having disposed of the Robespierrists, the center-of-the-road Thermidorians, in the autumn of 1794, exterminated ruthlessly the leaders of the insurrectionist Paris commune as well as the cadres of the Montagnards and the Enragés. Had these leaders been present, serious armed uprisings would have continually swept Paris and other cities during a period of skyrocketing prices and hunger. In their absence there was only a sullen desperation and intermittent abortive outbreaks.

In April 1795, the Convention decided it would no longer publically announce the creation of new assignats. Henceforth, it would authorize them in secret and make them available to the Committee on Finance,* which could then issue them without public disclosure whenever and to whatever extent seemed expedient. Government leaders could now center attention on their repeatedly announced efforts to cut down on the issuance of new assignats through a variety of revenue-raising devices. Late in April a *tontine* (a "lottery") was announced; it failed miserably. A month later another lottery—this time of certain unsold nationalized properties—was held. This, too, was a failure. Shortly afterward, and with considerable fanfare in the press, the Convention announced that "in order to stimulate trade—all restrictions against possession of and dealing in gold and silver were removed." About 200 million livres in coin surfaced as a result of this liberalization, but the assignat, which now had to compete against the newly appeared "hard money," immediately fell at a more precipitous rate.

On May 11, the government announced, with much publicity, its plan to demonetize all those assignats (amounting to over 1 billion livres) with denominations of 10 livres to 100 livres which contained the likeness of the King. After the plan was put into effect, few of the assignats were turned in; they were hoarded, and months later—when the government conveniently forgot its order to demonetize them—were once again accepted as legal tender.

On May 23, under the pretense that it had taken the action to "draw assignats out of circulation," the Convention ordered the sale of a great amount of public land at ridiculously low prices—at a time when wheat was already selling at twenty-five times its 1790 level. (Interestingly enough, the majority of the buyers turned out to be the wealthy bourgeoisie, whom the Convention represented.)

While these well-advertised "measures to reduce the circulating medium" were being propounded, the Committee on Finance was furtively throwing a prodigious amount of new assignats into the money supply. Collected evidence shows that in the four-month period between May and August, more than 5 billion livres of additional assignats were unleashed, bringing the total to 16.5 billion by August 31. The cost of living responded to the new print-up by climbing to a level twenty-seven times the 1790 level.

*Cambon, feeling that matters were getting out of hand, resigned.

But this advance proved to be moderate compared to the outburst of the next four months. Prices vaulted to 129 times the normal level by December 31, propelled upward by the manufacture of more than 12.5 billion new assignats by year-end. On December 31, there were approximately 29 billion livres in paper notes circulating through the shortage-ridden French economy. Twenty-one billion had been fabricated during the year of 1795. In the closing months of the year—while it went on proclaiming its intent "to reduce the amount of money in circulation so that prices may be stabilized" by such effete stratagems as a forced loan, a proposal to "collect taxes in kind," and the burning of several hundred million assignats—the government of France was introducing new money into the glutted monetary supply at the rate of 4 billion livres per month. Before 1790, in a period spanning more than 1,000 years, the French nation had been able to acquire a metallic money supply of only 2 billion livres.

It had become evident in the closing months of 1795 that the demise of the assignat was not far off; it had lost almost all of its purchasing power, having declined to 2 percent vis-à-vis the silver livre in November. In that month a newly elected, conservative legislature began debating the demonetization of the assignat and its replacement by another—but more restricted—paper currency. The property-oriented delegates of the newly installed legislature, many of whom had acquired great wealth during the assignat-propelled inflation, recognized that the nation urgently required a more effective medium of exchange. In December 1795, the legislature passed a decree that prohibited the creation of new assignats, once the amount in circulation reached 40 billion livres.

The Directory—a committee of five officials in whom considerable legislative power was vested—promptly manufactured a "reserve of assignats." A total of 10 billion of these were issued in January and February 1796, bringing the amount outstanding to 39 billion livres. The final 1 billion was never released, since the assignat had sunk to the point where it required 57,000 livres in paper to obtain 100 silver livres.

On the cold morning of February 18, 1796—before a mixed crowd of several thousand pauperized Parisians and a handful of men who had become enormously wealthy—the engraving machinery, plates, and the paper used in the printing of assignats were, with elaborate ceremony, smashed and burned in the Place

Vendôme on the spot where Napoleon's Column now stands.

Except for a short epilogue, the story of the assignats was concluded with the ceremony in the Place Vendôme. In the epilogue the following took place: for every thirty assignats held, the owner received one mandat, a new legal tender note. There were 2.4 billion livres of the new mandats authorized; part of the issue was to be used for the exchange of assignats and the remainder for other contingencies. So that the mandats "would be fully secured against depreciation," choice government lands having a value of 2.4 billion livres were set aside. Anyone offering an appropriate amount of mandats could at any time take possession of this property at its predetermined, fixed value. To insure a "favorable climate" for the new money a decree was passed whereby any person "who by his discourse or writing shall decry the mandats shall be condemned to a fine of not less than 1,000 livres but no more than 10,000; and in a case of a repetition of the offense shall be put into prison for a period of four years." As soon as the mandats rolled off the press they depreciated to 35 percent of their face value, a month later to 15 percent, and by August 1796 (a half year after their issue) to 3 percent.

Subsequently, for more than three years, the government of France struggled—during a period of privation for the great majority of its citizens and its armies—to revert to a metallic monetary system that would bring an end to large-scale paper money print-ups, but was forced, nevertheless, to issue small amounts of paper notes to fill the gap. Under this more restrictive monetary policy, price rises gradually lessened.

On November 10, 1799, in a coup d'état, Napoleon and his troops drove the legislature from the Assembly Hall, ending France's first attempt at parliamentary government. The future Emperor decreed, a short while later, that a completely metallic money supply should be reestablished in France. "While I live," he proclaimed, "I will never resort to irredeemable paper."

He kept his word. The printing presses were stopped and the amount of new money emitted was held to a modest level. In that way monetary order was restored and the assignat inflation was finally snuffed out.

The lesson drawn by most economic historians from the episode of the assignats can be found in Andrew Dexter White's *Fiat Money Inflation in France.* In his treatise, White graphically and correctly chronicles the destructive inflationary effects of continued input into the French economy of excessive amounts of money. But he sees the architects of the superinflation as "dreamers, theorists, schemers, declaimers, speculators (and promulgators) of that sort of 'Reform' which is the last refuge of a scoundrel." In short, he believes that the collapse of the assignat and of the economy during the French Revolution was brought about by the misguided acts of many impractical theorists and "patriots" and a few selfish speculators. In common with most economists and historians he refuses to consider the possibility that inflation need not invariably be a fortuitous by-product of fallacious policies, and that, at times, it could be a designed stratagem, and a specific tool created by the small minority at the center of power in order to maintain and expand that power and simultaneously to accumulate a mounting store of assets at a rapid rate.

The maintenance and expansion of power and the speeded-up gathering of assets by a well-placed and influential minority are readily discernible in the decade of the French Revolution. With the government of France on the verge of bankruptcy and armed mobs rioting against an ineffectual King and his uncaring "foreigner-Queen," the control of the nation had, at last, come into the hands of the bourgeoisie who had achieved a majority in the newly convened Assembly.

By 1791, therefore, the bourgeoisie—so long as it controlled the Assembly—could control France. But the same condition that had brought down the monarchy also threatened bourgeois power, namely, the highly precarious monetary situation. The creation of the first issue of nonmonetized 400 million livres of assignats and the input of 1.7 billion legal tender assignats (by the end of 1791) had temporarily staved off a declaration of insolvency by the government and had produced the usual stimulative effect on trade characteristically found in the initial phases of an inflationary cycle. But the nation's treasury remained in dangerous straits. Although the government had been able to reduce the debt by about 1 billion livres by using part of the print-up of 1.7 billion livres, the debt at the end of 1791 still stood at almost 5 billion livres and the annual interest requirement on it amounted to about 250 million livres. The funding of this massive debt posed a serious threat, and the situation was exacerbated by the serious fall-off of tax revenues. Motivated by a genuine desire to reform the high-handed and much resented tax system of the monarchy and by a thinly disguised wish to curry favor with the majority of the electorate (the rural population on whose good will the hegemony of the minority middle class ultimately depended), the Assembly in 1789 had removed many onerous taxes and had left the task of tax collection in the hands of local communities. Unfortunately, the local administrations in the farm areas regarded all taxes as undesirable. Tax revenues fell off sharply. In the summer of 1791 only one-fourth the anticipated revenues were being collected. And the trend worsened as the year progressed, despite the improved financial condition of most farmers (brought about by higher farm prices and a moderately increased yield produced from recently acquired, former Church-owned properties). In May 1792, Clavière, the incumbent Minister of Finance, announced that over 19,000 of the 40,000 local "administrations" had not yet submitted their quota of taxes due for the year 1791, and the treasury was once again empty.

The fiscal situation clearly called for a redoubled effort to collect overdue revenues. But this would have proved highly unpopular and would have threatened those at the center of power. The alternative was the constant creation of deficits and the emission of great quantities of new money to fill the budgetary gap—in short, a resort to inflation. The holders of power resoundingly opted for inflation so that they might retain their power. It is worth noting that this choice was made late in 1791 when prices were already beginning to rise, and the assignat had already depreciated to 77 percent against the silver livre.

Throughout the hyperinflation of the assignats the bourgeoisie —motivated by the desire to retain power and by the financial advantages which are ancillary to power—repeatedly chose the expediency of excessive money creation despite the inherent dangers and rejected the much-needed but considerably less popular course of diligent tax collection. In fact, as government expenses swelled (under the expansionary effect of a war effort and the galloping rise in prices), the rate of tax collection grew progressively worse. Previous to 1790 taxes (in terms of "stable" livres) normally came to just under 50 percent of government expenditures; in 1790 they declined (in "real" terms) to 30 percent, in 1791 to 16 percent, in 1792 they rose slightly to 25 percent, but in 1793 they fell to 9-1/2 percent, in 1794 mounted to 15 percent, but came to only 8 percent during the superinflation of 1795.

The problem of uncollected taxes is shockingly summarized in a statement Ramel prepared for the Committee on Finance during the final days of the assignat: "Fifteen thousand seven hundred and twenty-five million livres (15.725 billion) were assessed from September 1791 to September 1795. Thirteen billion and one hundred eighteen million remain uncollected in February 1796." This vast sum of leniently assessed taxes remained uncollected at a time when national income had risen by more than twenty times the 1789 level and about 39 billion livres of assignats were in taxpayers' hands.

But the creation of over 13 billion livres in assignats that might have been avoided by a resolutely pursued taxing program is only part of the story. The Assembly directly, or through its committees, knowingly and needlessly swelled the money supply in another way. Total government expenditures in 1794 came to 3.1 billion livres. Revenues secured by the government, including 570 million received in taxes, came to around 770 million, leaving a deficit of 2.4 billion. But the Assembly printed up 4 billion livres of new assignats, creating an unnecessary surplus of 1.6 billion for the year. A similar pattern occurred in 1795 but on a much larger scale. Total government outlays had vaulted to approximately 17.5 billion livres. Revenues received (including taxes amounting to around 1.4 billion) amounted to 1.7 billion livres, leaving a deficit of 15.8 billion livres. But 21 billion new assignats were dumped that year into the swollen money stream—a needless overcreation of 5.2 billion. For the two-year period of 1794–1795, 6.8 billion unrequired assignats were thrown into circulation. If we add to this figure the 13.1 billion created through undercollection of taxes, we get a sum of 19.9 billion, an amount which is more than one-half of the total amount in circulation when the assignat was abolished.

The overcreation of almost 20 billion livres of assignats significantly accelerated the hyperinflation and, of course, produced great suffering among millions of people. All of this callous program requires condemnation; the severest criticism, however, must be leveled at the inexcusable print-up, during 1794–1795, of almost 7 billion livres in paper notes that were not required for government use. The only purpose of that cynical maneuver was the rapid transfer of a maximum amount of the nation's wealth into the hands of the men who were part of the nexus of power. The device used by the superinflaters of that period (and one that has been employed in other hyperinflationary periods) is simple in both concept and execution. First a financial climate is created in which prices rise very rapidly and the holders of money race to acquire "things." In such an ambiance the average person is never able to secure enough money to buy anything but barest necessities because his income—though higher than in the past—has been by far outstripped by upward surging prices and whatever small savings he may have possessed have long since been dissipated. Only those who are able to command a great quantity of money can afford to acquire the items (made very expensive by a rampaging inflation) that become a reservoir of value as money depreciates. The establishment then causes the fabrication of an excessive amount of money which is made available to the relatively few influential individuals capable of securing loans through the pledging of substantial collateral assets. Using borrowed funds, the members of this privileged coterie are now able to buy up a considerable share of the nation's wealth.

The fabrication of 7 billion surplus assignats in a two-year period accomplished its purpose. Immense wealth was acquired in 1795 and 1796 by a few hundred individuals while the superinflation of the assignats and the mandats impoverished millions of ordinary people. The greatest "transfer" of wealth occurred in real property—producing farmland, urban real estate, manorial estates, chateaus, and houses. Some of these comprised the unsold nationalized properties (formerly owned by the Church, the Crown, and the emigrated royalists and nobles). These were valued, in April 1795, by Johannot—member of four committees at the time of the Convention—at 17 billion livres (in paper). Most historians of the period regard this valuation as an exercise in puffery; a consensus of reliable opinion puts the value at around 8 billion. Much of this property, by the end of 1796, passed into the hands of the upper bourgeoisie. Payment for these lands and estates came to a small extent from the accumulated wealth of the nouveau riche but the major part came from borrowed assignats that the government had so conveniently created. (The shrewd operators of that period made sure that they would not be caught with large amounts of rapidly depreciating assignats; paper money should be borrowed and invested, but not owned.)

The steady transfer of nationalized properties into the orbit of the middle class is described by Martyn Lyons in his penetrating book *France Under the Directory.* "The conditions of the sales of nationalized properties," Lyons states, "tended to favor the enrichment of the urban middle class." Possessing the resources, the bourgeoisie was always able to outbid individuals belonging to the small-peasant class. "The smaller peasant was only able to secure some of the spoils by pooling his resources with those of other peasants, to form a syndicate."

Lyons then lists the few "syndicate" operations by which small farmers were able to buy rural lands, especially in 1790, when the first block of nationalized properties (those of the Church) came on the market. Later offerings—and notably those of 1795 and 1796 —continued to favor acquisitions by the middle class. "The changing conditions of sales under the Directory did not substantially alter the balance which always had weighed in favor of the propertied bourgeoisie." Lyons explains that in the time of the Directory (after October 1795) all bids for properties were made in secret and had to be submitted in the administrative center of each department (district), far from the areas in which small farmers were situated. Moreover, conniving by administrative officials who turned down the higher bids of farmers and accepted— for an appropriate "fee"—the lower bids of favored members of the newly rich bourgeois class also disadvantaged the farming population. By the end of 1796 the great bulk of nationalized properties had fallen into the hands of individuals who never before had engaged in farming.

An enormous amount of other wealth was amassed during the superinflation of 1795–1796 by shrewd speculators who used loans for new acquisitions. Lozeau is said to have made over 100 million livres by speculating in salt (salt became an excellent store of value and, to some extent, a medium of exchange as the assignat was going through its death throes). Rovere, Le Paige, and Abolin acquired estates which surpassed that of Lozeau, by bank-financed dealings in nationalized properties. Gérard, a banker who "financed everything," is reputed to have achieved a personal worth "approaching several hundred million livres."

Various officials and legislative delegates acquired lesser fortunes (with the aid of loans) through speculation and secret profits arranged by military suppliers. Tallien, Fouche, Barras, Poulée, and Ramel—all former ardent proclaimers of Revolution—accumulated considerable wealth because their influence could be bought by shrewder and more successful men. The corruptibility of government officials and their opportunity to amass great wealth during the hyperinflation are illuminated by a statement made by Talleyrand (who was already rich) when he was raised to ministerial rank. "Now," he announced, "I must make a huge fortune! What I already own must pale into insignificance!"

But by far the greatest agglomerator of gold, jewels, chateaus, estates, and women was Gabriel Ouvrard. Son of a grocer, he made over 300,000 livres in stock speculation and came to Paris at the age of twenty with the desire to devour everything in sight. He achieved his ambition: by the time he was thirty, he was worth more than 1.5 billion livres. At one point, when the government owed him over 300 million livres (for naval supplies he had furnished at exorbitant prices and at an exorbitant profit), he said, "Well, you are right. With the way things are I may never collect. But the loss will hardly impoverish me." In 1796 his annual income came to over 40 million livres, an amount almost equal to the yearly "stipend" collected by Louis XVI for the maintenance of the entire royal court. He owned twenty-four houses in the Gers, estates at Vitry, Marly, Châteauneuf, St. Brice, and Lucinnes, as well as several houses in Paris. He bought 18,000 acres of prime farmland in Belgium. But the most celebrated of all his acquisitions was the chateau at Raincy, near Paris. It contained a vestibule lined with thirty-two Doric pillars; this led into a salon equipped with a pool twenty feet in diameter in which the light of a thousand candles was reflected, day and night. In the dining room, whose dimension approximated the size of a tennis court, fountains endlessly spouted punch, almond juice, and champagne.

Other properties—less sumptuous than Ouvrard's show place at Raincy—were systematically transferred into the grasp of entrepreneurs and sharpers as long as the government continued to supply credit through surplus print-up. When the printing process stopped because paper money was regarded as worthless, the transfer stopped. The situation that prevailed when the process drew to a close is aptly described by Von Sybel in his *History of the French Revolution:*

At the end of the year 1795, the paper money was almost exclusively in the hands of the working class (rural and urban), employees and men of small means whose wealth was not large enough to invest in stores of goods or national lands. Financiers and men of large means were shrewd enough to put as much of their property as possible into objects of permanent value. The working classes had no such foresight or skill or means. On them finally came the great crushing weight of the loss.

The American Civil War: The Greenback Era

The inflationary periods of the past stretch, like a chain of mountains, across the monetary plain of the world. In this mountain range the high, cloud-piercing peaks (the hyperinflationary eras) alternate with the lower, gently sloping elevations (the intervals of lesser price rises). The greenback period of the Civil War definitely belongs among the latter. The amount of money fabricated during that episode for the maintenance of power and the agglomeration of wealth was considerably smaller than during the Roman and French superinflations, and the results, consequently, were far less dramatic. The fiscal and monetary developments of the 1861–1865 interval are perhaps less striking than the failure of historians, historiographers, and economists to draw appropriate conclusions from them.

On the surface it appeared, even in the pre-Civil War period, that the North and the South were separated primarily by the moral dilemma of slavery. But a probing look beneath the surface would have readily revealed a more basic rationale for sectional antagonism, namely, crass economic self-interest.

The two sections had been driven apart by the thrust of economic events. While the Southern plantation owners—with their immaculate white suits and their manicured nails "unsullied by the dirt of commerce"—continued to cling to an outmoded feudal system based on a slave-produced monoculture of cotton, the more aggressive and more efficient men of the North turned increasingly and eagerly to the "dirtier" but more profitable business of manufacturing, transporting and selling of goods, and to money lending. By 1860, the mercantile society of the North—as might have been expected—by far outstripped and dominated the retrograde cavalier society of the South.

The Northern economic superiority and the South's antagonism against it were evident, day after day, in the press and in the halls of legislatures. Four years before the outbreak of hostilities, Hilton Helper declared in his book *Impending Crisis of the South:*

It is a fact well known to every intelligent Southerner that we are compelled to go to the North for almost every article of utility and adornment, from matches, shoe-pegs and paintings up to cotton mills, steamships and statuary; . . . that . . . the North becomes, in one way or another, the proprietor and dispenser of all our floating wealth, and that we are dependent on Northern capitalists for the means necessary to build our railroads, canals and other public improvements; . . . and that nearly all the profits arising from the exchange of commodities, from insurance and shipping offices, and from the thousand and one industrial pursuits of the country, accrue to the North. . . .

In one way or another we are more or less subservient to the North every day of our lives. In infancy we are swaddled in Northern muslin; in childhood we are humored with Northern gewgaws; in youth we are instructed out of Northern books; at the age of maturity we sow our "wild oats" on Northern soil; . . . in the decline of life we remedy our eyesight with Northern spectacles, and support our infirmities with Northern canes; in old age we are drugged with Northern physic; and, finally, when we die, our inanimate bodies, shrouded in Northern cambric, are stretched upon the bier, borne to the grave in a Northern carriage, entombed with a Northern spade, and memorialized with a Northern slab!

And on January 18, 1860, the Vicksburg *Daily Whig* editorialized:

By mere supineness, the people of the South have permitted the Yankees to monopolize the carrying trade, with its immense profits. We have yielded to them the manufacturing business, in all its departments, without an effort, until recently, to become manufacturers ourselves. We have acquiesced in the claims of the North to do all the importing, and most of the exporting business, for the whole union. Thus, the North has been aggrandized, in a most astonishing degree, at the expense of the South. It is no wonder that their villages have grown into magnificent cities. It is not strange that they have "merchant princes," dwelling in gorgeous palaces and reveling in luxuries transcending the luxurious appliances of the Orient! How could it be otherwise? New York City, like a mighty queen of commerce, sits proudly upon her island throne, sparkling in jewels and waving an undisputed commercial scepter over the South. By means of her railways and navigable streams, she sends out her long arms to the extreme South; and, with an avidity rarely equaled, grasps our gains and transfers them to herself—taxing us at every step—and depleting us as extensively as possible without actually destroying us.

But, though they had achieved economic hegemony, Northern capitalists had failed to win the political control that would have permitted them to wrest the nation's developing riches at a more rapid rate. Despite waning economic influence, the old Jeffersonian agrarianism (espoused by Southern slave-owners) was able to maintain a tenuous hold on the Presidency and on Congress because the entrepreneurs of the North and the "free" farmers of the West had not been able to weld a unified opposition from among their numerous "splinter" parties.

However, as the presidential election of 1860 approached, the leaders of the new Republican party were confident that they could float their way to political power on the rising wave of antislavery sentiment. Capitalizing on the mounting revulsion against slavery (whose fervor approached religiosity), Republican politicos devised an orchestrated campaign in which legislators thumped their desks against "the sin of slavery," publishers thumped their presses against it, preachers thumped their Bibles against it, and candidates thumped their breasts against it, whether they were opposed to it or not. The Republican Convention which nominated Lincoln in 1860 drafted a platform that opposed "existence [of] slavery in any territory of the United

States" and announced that: "All men are created equal . . . " and that "the new dogma [propounded by slaveholders] that the Constitution, of its own force, carries slavery into any or all of the territories of the United States, is a dangerous political heresy . . . is revolutionary in its tendency and subversive of the peace and harmony of the country . . . and we deny the authority of Congress or of a territorial legislature, or of any individual to give legal existence to slavery."

These caveats against slavery marched shoulder to shoulder with pronouncements that revealed the truer interests of the framers of the platform—their economic interests. The Republican Convention asserted:

To the Union, this nation owes its unprecedented increase in population, its surprising development of material resources, its rapid augmentation of wealth, its happiness at home and its honor abroad. . . . We hold in abhorrence all schemes for disunion [such as the proposals for secession put forward by the South]. . . . While providing revenue for the support of the general government by duties upon imports, sound policy requires such an adjustment of imports *as to encourage the development of the industrial centers of the whole country* and we commend that policy of national exchanges [monetary and fiscal policies] which secures to the working men liberal wages, to agriculture remunerating prices, and to manufacturers an adequate reward for their skill, labor, and enterprise *and* [*secures*] *the nation's commercial prosperity and independence.* [Italics supplied.]

To the agrarian South the inclusion of the single phrase "to agriculture remunerating prices" was simply an ill-disguised political ploy, but the sections against slavery sounded, for them, the same life-and-death warning that the Declaration of the Rights of Man had sounded for Louis XVI. Southerners correctly assessed that a Republican victory and the election of Lincoln would put an end to their slavocracy.

With the election of Lincoln (attained by antislavery fervor and a coalition of the "free-soil" farming interests* and the capitalists

---

*The farmers of the expanding West resented inroads made into their territories by Southern plantation owners and their slaves. Such inroads occurred as slave-owners exhausted their own Southern lands after years of regressive planting of new cotton. They became a threat to free-soil farmers who themselves sought new land for the planting of highly profitable wheat and corn crops.

of the North), the drive for secession by the South gained momentum. One after another Southern Democrats emptied their desks in the House of Representatives and in the Senate, packed their bags, and silently went home. On February 9, 1861, six states seceded from the Union to form the Confederacy; five other Southern states later followed them. For about two months a brooding truce prevailed in the dismembered nation, with the Confederacy insisting that it would abjure all acts of war unless molested. But one after another federal forts that had been built on Southern soil years before secession were occupied (without encountering resistance) by newly organized forces of the Confederacy. Then, in the predawn darkness of April 12, 1861, Confederate cannons ripped open the defenses of Fort Sumter, shattering the brief, untenable truce, and ushering in the terrible Civil War.

When hostilities erupted the two conditions habitually present at the outbreak of war immediately appeared: a spate of public assurances that the fighting would soon end in a glorious victory and—simultaneously—an empty public treasury. The inordinately difficult task of funding more than $2 billion of expenses that were to be incurred during the first three years of the war fell on the unwilling shoulders of Salmon Portland Chase, whom Lincoln officially designated as his Secretary of the Treasury, a few days after the presidential inauguration in March 1861.

The fiscal conditions cried out for another Turgot, another Colbert, or at least another Necker: a man with wide financial experience; a man with a driving, single-minded determination to deal with nothing but the concatenation of problems endlessly encountered by a government struggling against an avalanche of overdue bills. Chase had neither of these requirements. He had little knowledge about monetary matters and no financial experience. A teacher, publisher, lawyer, governor of Ohio, U.S. Senator from Ohio—he was recognized as one of the founders and pillars of the Republican party (having previously attempted to build a political base in the Democratic, Whig, Free-Soil, and Liberal parties). Handsome, of imposing stature, a forceful (though not eloquent) speaker, he had stumped the major cities and the smaller towns of the North and West—mounting every podium offered to him—during his campaigns against slavery and had finally achieved national recognition as one of the major antislavery figures. During the nomination process of 1860, he had come closest to satisfying his endless hunger for the Presidency of the United States, but lost out to "that backwoods, small-time lawyer," Lincoln. Lincoln—who, himself, had no knowledge or interest in finances—offered the Treasury post to Chase in recognition of his influence and standing in the Republican party, his antislavery zeal, and his "manifest incorruptibility." Unfortunately, a barren treasury in a time of internecine war demanded something more than "incorruptibility."

Although Chase's dedication to his new duties outran his meager qualification for finances, it, too, left much to be desired. The new Secretary of the Treasury was an earnest, conscientious, and energetic man, and an efficient administrator. In short, under him the Treasury Department—after being bolstered by some experienced and knowledgeable assistants—could have performed adequately had Chase devoted all his energies to his new assignment. Events would prove that he did not.

On the blustery March day when he walked into his office for the first time, Chase found that the ridiculously small staff of 383 employees (the Treasury now employs 122,000) was far outnumbered by the unpaid claims piled up on his desk. Suppliers to the army, many of the soldiers serving in the small peacetime force (comprised of fewer than 30,000 men), civil service employees, and members of the Congress were awaiting long overdue payment. Almost $400,000 in interest on government bonds was also in arrears. The new Secretary also learned from an assistant— John J. Cisco, an able, diligent careerist in the Treasury—that Chase's predecessor had experienced great difficulties two months before, when he had tried to raise the minuscule sum of $5 million, and had finally been forced to pay 12 percent in interest. Chase was pleasantly surprised, therefore, by the favorable reception of a 6-percent bond offering (in the amount of $8 million) he advertised on March 28, 1861. When bids were opened on April 2, it was found that the issue had been oversubscribed threefold, drawing bids running from 85 to 100, with the average bid at around 90. This welcome turn of events was ascribed to a return of confidence induced by Lincoln's election and the better feeling among moneyed people who—watching almost all of the Southern representatives leave the House and Senate—deduced that the legislative power of the country was at last in the hands of a Congress friendly to the entrepreneurial class.

But now—less than a month after he had come into office—Chase's "dream of the Presidency" took over. A man resolutely devoted to his position as the nation's chief financial officer would have filled bids not only on the $8 million he had advertised, but on an additional $9 million available for sale. But Chase's need to appear statesmanlike and to build a reputation that would some-day secure him the White House became paramount. He suddenly announced that he would accept only those bids placed at 94 and above. Since he could raise only $3,099,000 through selling bonds at these higher bids, he decided to raise the remaining $4,901,000 by inviting bids on two-year 6-percent treasury notes, to be sold at no less than par. (This alternate route was open to him through enabling legislation passed during the previous administration.) In carefully leaked statements to the press he announced his refusal to "take less than par when confidence in the government's credit seems restored." On April 8, he advertised the note issue. But by April 11, when the North announced its intention not to surrender Fort Sumter, all interest in the note issue evaporated, with only one-fifth of the offering having been subscribed to at that point. In a private letter, James Gallatin, president of the prestigious Gallatin Bank of New York, urged the Secretary to abandon the note route and advised him that, without doubt, more than $5 million in bids could be reinstated for the 6-percent long-term bonds at 87 or more. Chase rejected the suggestion, insisting that the government refused to be "knocked down" by Wall Street. Then came April 14—the beginning of the war—with financial markets plummeting. But Chase remained adamant, although subscription on the notes stayed at a standstill. Finally, the bank-ing community came to the rescue of a government beleaguered by war and the threat of imminent bankruptcy; the entire unsub-scribed portion of the note issue was immediately taken up by banks, with one New York bank subscribing to $2.5 million.

But with expenses increased by military outlays, the treasury was again bare in less than thirty days. On May 11, Chase offered the remainder of the 6-percent bonds available for sale, amounting to $8,994,000. The reception was poor from the start, since the war-induced depression of 1861 was already under way. Many Northern manufacturing plants and commercial establishments that had done a considerable business with the South either shut down as this trade disappeared or—even worse—failed when

Southern planters and importers defaulted on debts to their Northern suppliers. The defalcations gathered momentum when the Confederate government passed a regulation making the payment of debts to the Northern enemy an illegal act. (Ultimately the South would default on more than a quarter of a billion dollars, ruining numerous businesses in the North.)

The economic pall that settled on the North beginning with the spring of 1861 (it was to last for about a year) dampened interest in government securities. With bids barely trickling in, Chase announced he would also sell more two-year notes (6 percent) at par to the extent that bids were not received on bonds. Finally, after it became evident that without their aid the government would again be threatened with default, the bankers of New York and Boston again came to the rescue. After an intensive campaign by the newly formed Bankers Committee, bids ranging from 60 to 93 were obtained. Chase decided to accept all bids of 85 and above as well as all the bids at par for the notes. The sale of the bonds brought in $7,310,000 and the notes obtained $1,684,000. After a cliff-hanger, the treasury had again been saved by raising just under $9 million.

In June of 1861 Chase was again plagued by overdue bills. He tried, once again, to sell a considerable amount of the 6-percent treasury notes, but received bids for only $2.5 million. Toward the end of the month he advertised another offering, but with the existing two-year 6-percent notes selling at 97 in the open market, he did not receive any bids at par on the newly offered notes. Finally—with insurgent forces moving against Washington—the banks agreed to advance the $2.5 million as a thirty-day loan to the government, taking a corresponding amount of the two-year notes as collateral.

In this tortuous fashion Chase had tugged and pulled his way to the end of the fiscal year, June 30, 1861. Congress (which was to reconvene in emergency session on July 4), as well as the business community and banking circles, awaited the Secretary's message for the coming year with a mixture of hope and anxiety.

Unfortunately, Chase's formula for the government's financial survival proved to be—like Necker's proposal before the Estates General in 1789—essentially a blueprint for more borrowing by a treasury already held in disrepute by investors. His budget for the fiscal year ending on June 30, 1862, estimated expenditures of just under \$319 million, with "war appropriations" amounting to over \$217 million. These expenses were to be met as follows: \$240 million by borrowing and just under \$80 million from taxes. To bring tax revenues up to \$80 million (from the \$40 million collected the previous year) customs duties—on which the nation had for years depended as almost the sole tax source—would need to be raised, and \$20 million was to be collected from newly imposed direct taxes and a new income tax levied on all annual incomes of over \$800, at the ridiculously low rate of 3 percent.

Later, when critics (judiciously silent when Chase presented his "plan" to the Congress meeting in emergency session in July 1861) charged him with "blunders" for recommending unprecedentedly large borrowing instead of urging the imposition of heavy taxes, the Secretary defended himself by pleading "the impossibility of foreseeing at that time [July 1861] the magnitude and length of the war." He asserted that the imposition of a heavy, long-lasting tax burden was deemed inappropriate because it had seemed to him and to many others the war would be over in a few months.

Chase had, in fact, publicly predicted in the summer of 1861 that "the war would last only several months." But evidence clearly indicates that—despite the masquerade he acted out in public— he privately believed the war would be long and costly. In a letter dated April 20, 1861 (less than a week after the start of hostilities), he explained to a friend why he had not advocated an attack on the Confederacy during the few months of uneasy truce, as follows:*

As a positive policy, two alternatives were plainly before us: (1) that of enforcing the laws of the Union by its whole power [including making war on the Confederacy] . . . or (2) that of recognizing the organization of actual government by the seceded states as an accomplished revolution and letting the Confederacy try its experiment of separation. . . . Knowing that the former of these alternatives involved *destructive war, vast expenditure, and oppressive debt,* and thinking it possible that through the latter these great evils might be avoided . . . I preferred the latter alternative. [Italics supplied.]

*See Ellis Oberholtzer's *Jay Cooke, Financier of the Civil War* and Maunsell Bradhurst Field's *Memories of Many Men and Some Women.*

"Destructive war, vast expenditure, and oppressive debt" are not the expectations of an official who thinks that fighting will be over in a few months.

Some defense for Chase's duplicity might be attempted on the grounds that in his budget presentation he was merely carrying out—as a member of the Cabinet—the spurious charade other officials were enacting in public to heighten morale and to secure a maximum amount of enlistments into the army.

Even "Honest Abe" Lincoln, at the time of the first call-up of volunteers (April 17, 1861), asked 75,000 men to enlist for a period of only three months, but privately confided that he would have preferred a call for 300,000 men for a three-year period of service (actually 600,000 answered the appeal, cluttering the roads as they streamed—in an outburst of patriotism—toward recruitment centers). In the spring and summer of 1861, other officials, members of Congress, and editorial writers were loud in their assurances that the war would be won by autumn. However, early in April, Secretary of State Seward suggested to Lincoln that war should be declared immediately against England and France because—sooner or later—those two nations were likely to come to the assistance of the Confederacy as a result of their dependence on cotton. Had Seward (the second-ranking figure in the Lincoln administration) really believed that "victory would be won in sixty days," he would not have privately recommended the unleashing of war against Europe's two most powerful nations. His repeated public predictions of a quick victory were undoubtedly an exercise in building confidence.

It is possible, therefore, to view Chase's advocacy of a plan for massive borrowing and negligible taxes as simply the carrying out of an assigned role in a benignly intended official duplicity. His announcement of a heavy, long-term tax levy would certainly have collided with the myth of quick victory.

But he must have felt that his plan, which relied on massive borrowing, could not possibly succeed. Having just passed through a four-month period during which, with great difficulty, he had been able to raise only $24 million, he must have concluded that it would be next to impossible to borrow almost $250 million in a twelve-month interval. Why, then, did he risk almost certain failure—a failure that might produce highly dangerous consequences, especially in a time of war?

Because he wished to avoid taking a different risk that—if it failed—could prove even more damaging to his presidential ambitions. The alternate hazard he wished to avoid was that of becoming the progenitor of a highly unpopular tax program. By July 1861, no member in the government—not the President or any cabinet officer or any administrator of a governmental department or any Congressman—had recommended the passage of heavy taxes to meet the cost of war. Had Chase taken the lead in recommending them, and had they proved unpopular, his prospects of securing the White House in 1864, or later, would have been jeopardized. Thirty months later, after the press and some members of Congress had already demanded a substantial tax program, Chase publicly (though unintentionally) revealed why he had not previously proposed adequate levies. In a report to Congress in December 1863, he declared, "I can (now) see clearly that we can go no further without heavy taxation, and he has read history to little purpose who does not know that heavy taxes will excite discontent."

A discontented electorate does not vote the creator of heavy taxes into the White House. And so, in July 1861, Chase carefully refrained from advocating them. Furthermore, as might have been expected on July 9, 1861, the Congress which formally took up his message gingerly avoided imposing a war tax.

Having achieved an impressive majority through victories in the 1860 elections and through the defections of secessionist Democratic legislators who had left the House and Senate, the now-dominant Republicans did not wish to rock the boat by unleashing a squall of discontent over onerous taxes. After a single hour of "discussion"—a bitter personal tirade against Lincoln conducted by Vallandigham of Ohio—the House pummeled through a loan bill of $250 million by a vote of 155 to 5. In the Senate the measure raced through without any real opposition, passing after a few verbal amendments with which the House instantly concurred. Eight days after it was introduced, the bill was signed by Lincoln.*

Haste made waste. Two weeks later a supplemental act had to be drafted to correct some errors, plug holes, and effect minor changes. The combined acts of July 17 and August 5 (the Supplemental Act) authorized the treasury to borrow up to $250 million

---

*Designated as the Act of July 17, 1861.

in a variety of ways, as follows: through the issuance of 7-percent twenty-year bonds at par; 6-percent twenty-year bonds that could be issued at 86 and above; 7.3-percent three-year treasury notes (convertible into the 6-percent twenty-year bonds); $20 million of 6-percent treasury notes payable within one year and $50 million of treasury notes bearing interest at 3.65 percent or bearing no interest, but payable on demand. The act authorized the Secretary of the Treasury "to deposit any of the monies obtained on any of the loans. . . . in such solvent special-paying banks as he may select."

The treasury "demand notes," in the amount of $50 million (payable by the government, upon demand, in gold or silver), represent an interesting aspect of the legislation. These notes, which were to be issued in denominations as low as $5, were "receivable as payment for all public dues." In short—being immediately redeemable by the government and acceptable as payment for public debts, they were essentially "money."

On August 5, a "revenue" act was also approved in line with Chase's suggestions. Existing tariff schedules were changed by imposing duties on hitherto untaxed items such as tea, coffee, sugar, and molasses, and rates were raised on a few previously lightly taxed imports. These alterations were modifications of the Morrill Tariff Act, which had been passed in the Buchanan administration for protectionist, rather than revenue, purposes. The changes were modest in scope and were likely to produce only a moderate increase in revenues. A direct tax which was intended to yield a maximum of $20 million was likely to secure even less since $5 million was allocated to the seceded states. The 3-percent income tax levied on incomes of over $800 would also produce negligible results since only 2 million families had incomes of over $800 a year. It should have been obvious, from the start, that the new tax statute would not provide sufficient funds to cover even the $80 million of "nonwar" expenditures Chase had anticipated for the 1861–1862 fiscal year. All war expenditures were to be met by borrowing. Like Chase, the members of Congress must have felt the treasury might not be able to borrow $250 million.

In the midst of a great war requiring vast outlays, the Congress —forced to choose between a noninflationary program involving potentially unpopular taxation and an inflation-begetting (but immediately more popular) program of massive borrowing—chose the latter. In the process the legislators had opened, with almost no discussion, the way for the creation of paper money by a government which to that point had adhered strictly to a gold standard (this was done through the authorization of the $50 million of demand notes). All in all, it was a repetition of the old story: the center of power—the industrial-entrepreneurial interests of the East and the farming-entrepreneurial interests of the West—had opted for inflation to maintain their power.

The events of July and August 1861 soon proved that it was easier to shove a flawed fiscal program through a complicitous Congress than to end the fighting in the promised sixty days. By the third week of July a blockage of most Confederate ports was in force and Lincoln—having had his fill of advice on "morale raising"—had ordered a call for a half-million men for a period of three years. By that time, the Union troops, who had been ordered to "take Richmond," were driven in panic from the bloody fields at Bull Run. Then Northern newspapers raised the cry "Protect the capital! Save Washington!" The Grand Army of the Potomac took up its position to save the capital from destruction and pillage. Almost half of the Union's forces were stationed in and around Washington. The city became a mustering center and a parade ground on which inexperienced troops drilled from morning till night, but frequently carried no arms because of the shortage of guns. Thousands of women and children streamed into the confused capital for protection, cramming every hotel, boardinghouse, and private dwelling, and littering the uncleaned streets. A great, unending stench hung over the city.

By the second week of August, the cost of conducting the war had risen to $1 million per day. Chase, after testing the credit markets, came to the conclusion that it would take a long time to organize a national campaign through which $150 million of the 6-percent bonds and $140 million of 7.3-percent treasury notes could be sold to the public. He quickly made use of some of the short-term treasury notes that had been voted by Congress, including a small quantity of the demand (money) notes. Though the demand notes were immediately redeemable in gold at the subtreasuries of the government, they were at first regarded with suspicion by the public. People were not, at that time, accustomed to government-issued money and distrusted it. All paper money was issued by banks, with each bank guaranteeing to redeem, upon demand into gold, all bank notes it had issued. Consequently, when the army attempted to settle accounts with supp-, liers by paying them in demand notes or when men in the armed forces or government employees were asked to accept them in payment of their services, there was considerable resistance. In an effort to overcome opposition, Chase and other employees in the treasury issued a "notice" in which they elaborately professed their eagerness to "receive the notes in place of gold toward payment of our salaries" and Winfield Scott, then commanding general of the army, assured all fighting men that they would "find superior convenience in sending home payments of salaries made to you in notes." Ultimately the demand notes were accepted by the public as "money," but the more conservative banks refused to take them in as regular deposits and relegated them to a "special deposit" category, obviating their responsibility to convert them into gold.

But the small amount of money Chase had raised could not keep pace with soaring expenses and at last he was forced to turn reluctantly to what he regarded as a last resort: the commercial banks. Treasury officials usually enjoy a cordial relationship with the banking community, having been one of the "club" before entering government service. But the Secretary was an outsider by experience and—more important—by choice. Pompous and religious to the point of righteousness—Ben Wade, the crude Senator from Ohio, once said of him, "He pictures himself to be the fourth person in the Trinity"—Chase had a puritanical antipathy toward "money changers" and approached them in a manner which suggested that he was about to place the mark of Cain upon them. But the treasury's desperate need and the Union's precarious military position forced him to suppress his antagonism and to attempt to negotiate a sizable loan with them.

On the evening of August 9, a "quiet meeting" (the event was "withheld from the press to guard against revealing the straits of the government") was held in the home of John Cisco, the Assistant Treasurer. Present were Cisco, Chase, some of the leading bankers of New York, "and other capitalists." After considerable discussion, George S. Coe, president of the American Exchange Bank, suggested that a loan committee should be formed to study the feasibility of making large loans to the government. Six days later in a meeting (in which thirty-nine of the banks of New York as well as several banks of Philadelphia and Boston were represented)* the committee reported that the associated banks had developed a plan under which—if things went well—they would be willing to lend the government $150 million in the following way:

There would be three loans made, with the first in the amount of $50 million to be dated August 15. The banks would be under obligation to pay—if necessary—$5 million in gold to the government every six days, with the full $50 million of the first loan having been turned over to the treasury within sixty days. In return the banks were to receive from the government $50 million of 7.3-percent three-year treasury notes. The government would agree to establish a chain of agencies at its subtreasuries and other points for the purpose of selling the treasury notes the banks had taken down. As the notes were sold to the public the government, after receiving payment from the buyers, would turn the proceeds over to the banks and the banks would release the notes to the treasury, which would then deliver them to the buyer (simultaneously, in its note-selling campaign the government would attempt to sell all of its stock of 7.3-percent notes, in the hope that there would be enough funds raised so that the banks would not need to extend money beyond the $50 million of the first loan).

In case the effort to sell the notes did not secure more than $50 million, the banks would attempt to extend two further loans of $50 million each, with the second to be placed on October 15 and the third on December 15. In the case of a second and third loan, the same procedures used in the first loan would be adopted.

Chase responded favorably to the plan, saying that he did not like to pay 7.3 percent but with "the present exigency being what it is" the price was not too high. It seemed for a while that there was general agreement all around and then . . . a snag. The committee told the Secretary that the banks would—if absolutely necessary—pay $5 million in gold to the government each ten days, but preferred instead to enter a credit on their books on which the government could draw. The treasury could then issue checks to suppliers, employees, servicemen, and others to meet its expenses. The person receiving such checks could cash them and demand either gold or bank notes, or could deposit them. His

*The meeting of August 15 was reported in the press.

deposit could be drawn against, at any time, and it would be honored, on demand, in gold or in notes—whichever the depositor desired. In short, the banks wished to treat the government in the way they treated any other borrower. Their motivation was the preservation of their gold stock and the maintenance of their reserve ratio (the ratio of specie on hand to liabilities).

George S. Coe remembered the incident as follows:

Accordingly, it was at once proposed to the Secretary that—following the course of commercial business—he should draw checks (after receiving the credits of the executed loans) upon some one bank in each city representing the Association (of Banks), in small sums—as required—in disbursing the money thus advanced. . . . By this means his check would serve the purpose of a circulating medium, continually redeemed and the exchange of capital and industry would be best promoted. This was the more important in a period of public agitation, when the disbursement of large sums exclusively in coin rendered the reserves of the banks all the more liable to be wasted by hoarding. To the astonishment of the committee which represented the associated banks, Mr. Chase refused.*

At first the Secretary refused to have the treasury issue checks because the vendor or the employee or serviceman who received the check would now depend on the vagaries of banking if he wanted immediate payment in gold. While it was possible to assume—according to Chase—that some strong Eastern banks could, at all times, meet their commitments to make all payments in gold, many weaker banks, especially those in the West (because of their inadequate reserves), might not be able to honor all drafts in coin. Since the government was, by law, bound to meet its debts in gold, it did not wish to enter into an arrangement that might violate this commitment. When various bankers told him they were certain that they could work out a foolproof system among all banks, he still refused and added a new excuse for his refusal. "The independent subtreasury system of the government," he said, "required all dues to the United States to be paid into the treasury in coin." He was reminded that the Supplemental Act of August 5 specifically permitted the Secretary "to deposit any of the monies obtained on any of the loans . . . in such solvent

*Ellbridge G. Spaulding, *History of the Legal Tender Money.*

specie-paying banks as he may select," and allowed "money so deposited to be withdrawn from such deposit with regular, authorized depositories [banks] or for the payment of public dues." The Secretary stared into space and replied emotionlessly that the bill's permission to "deposit any of the monies obtained on any of the loans" implied the deposit of gold, and not "credits."

The more the bankers argued that it would be difficult in a six-month period to deposit $150 million in gold into the subtreasuries (if they were to take down the three loans), the more obdurate Chase became. He turned a deaf ear to the members of the bankers' committee when they tried repeatedly to impress him with the dangers that might arise. They admitted that although they were currently in a strong reserve condition (against liabilities of $142 million they had $43 million in specie, or a 30-percent ratio, whereas they were required to have only a 25-percent ratio); nevertheless, they were concerned because the total of the three loans ($150 million) was three and a half times the specie they had on hand. If they expended $50 million of their gold every two months by putting it into the subtreasuries, they might run out of gold unless the coin loaned to the government returned quickly and regularly back into the banks. If there was any break in the "circuit," the banks might not be in a position to honor their redemption commitments. This was particularly dangerous in a time of war when a run on the banks for redemption of notes into coin might be set off at any moment. Chase continued to sit stiffly in his chair, and the more they argued, the stiffer he became.

At last the bankers caved in: they agreed to put $5 million of their carefully husbanded gold into the government's subtreasuries every ten days. They again tried to convince the Secretary of the importance of immediately getting the gold back into the banking system and urged him to press his treasury-note selling campaign (of the 7.3-percent notes) so that the banks would receive gold proceeds for the $50 million of notes they had taken for their loan. They also warned him not to continue selling the gold-redeemable demand notes; if he pursued this course, he might wind up getting $50 million of gold with one hand from the banks and paying $50 million in gold to the government's creditors with the other hand (via the demand notes). If the receivers of the demand notes exchanged them for gold and then hoarded it, the "circuit of gold" back into the banks would be broken, forcing the banks into a situation in which they unwillingly would be violating their gold-to-debt-reserve ratio. And the more demand notes the Secretary would put out, the greater would be the public's worry over the government's precarious financial position; this, in turn, might create widespread hoarding of gold and an ultimate run by depositors to follow suit. Then the banks would be forced to suspend specie payments on demand, bringing on the danger of panic in a "time of perilous war."

Various members on the bankers' committee warned the Secretary against the continued issuance of government-generated money, stating that the precedent—once underway—would surely lead to other paper issues, bringing on the "ruin of the Nation in the midst of violent war."

Chase listened to these warnings and replied, "If you can lend me all the coin required or show me where I can borrow it elsewhere at fair rates, I will withdraw every note already issued and pledge myself never to issue another, but if you cannot, you must let me stick to United States notes."

He then implied he would issue as few as circumstances permitted, adding, however, that as the nation's chief financial officer he could not be expected to give a pledge that he would stop issuing the demand notes. Then the meeting broke up.

About a month later, in a letter written to Chase by James Gallatin, the bankers' position on the issuing of demand notes was again underlined:

When the proposed system of raising means by the banks was reported by a committee, they were unanimously in favor of affixing to it a condition that [the] government should not issue demand notes. That condition was only yielded from a reluctance to endanger or embarrass your appeal in so solemn a crisis, and because of your remonstrance against being compelled to give an official pledge against the use of a legal enactment, and still further because of your assurance that it would only be resorted to when other means of raising money should fail. The banks, therefore, feel the most implicit confidence that these issues will be confined to a very inconsiderable sum.

If Gallatin thought that he might keep Chase from issuing more demand notes by reducing the "sense" of the meeting to writing, he might have spared his efforts. Even though the treasury had already received several of the $5 million coin installments from the banks, the Secretary was forced by climbing costs to issue more of the disputed notes. But despite this, the loaned gold flowed smoothly back into the banks after the government paid it out. Contractors and other businessmen, employees, and soldiers redeposited it and the banks in turn were able to reuse the gold in meeting the next installment. In September—with specie holdings amounting to $55 million against outstanding bank notes and deposits of $173 million—the "associated" banks advised Chase they would enter into a second loan since their ratio of gold to liabilities was higher than the required 25 percent. Again, the flow of gold continued favorably.

But, again, Chase resorted to the demand notes, to the chagrin of the banking community. They protested, with no effect on the Secretary. But leaders in financial circles were really more concerned with the movement of gold in and out of the banks. They kept their fingers crossed; it was all too good to continue. Sooner or later some unfavorable event, now long overdue, was bound to "break the circuit." But the banks came back for a third loan early in November.

Then, two unconnected events suddenly swamped the "frail craft of credit." The first has come down in history as the Trent Affair. Two commissioners of the Confederacy—Mason and Slidell—had left a Southern port, evaded the blockage, reached Havana, and boarded a British packet, *The Trent,* bound for Southampton, England. On November 8, the packet was sighted by the Union man-of-war *San Jacinto* and boarded by a detail of marines. The British captain protested the search of his vessel but the two Confederate commissioners suddenly revealed themselves (their intent, no doubt, was to stir up difficulties between the Union and England). Slidell and Mason were taken as prisoners over the objections of *The Trent* captain and placed on the *San Jacinto.* When news of the incident reached the North, a wave of jubilation swept over the victory-hungry Union forces. At last there was something to cheer about. The captain of the *San Jacinto* was feted, and the Secretary of the Navy wrote a letter to him, congratulating him. Lincoln was one of the few leaders who did not participate in the rejoicing, declaring: "We must stick to American principles concerning the rights of neutrals." On November 16, the initial élan ebbed away; the stock markets plunged

over a possible war with England. Government securities fell almost three points. Wall Street was filled with rumors that the
banks were about to abandon specie payments. A run on gold
began; depositors turned bank notes into coin. Leading bankers,
in an attempt to halt the drain, issued statements that there was
"no cause for uneasiness" and "no justification or necessity for
suspension of specie payments." These reassurances did not halt
gold outflow; the "circuit" was, at last, broken. During the forty-
two days when Slidell and Mason's incarceration threatened war
with England, the exit of gold continued.

Then, on December 9, a second jolt came when Chase made his
financial report to Congress. In it he revealed that whereas he, in
his July 1861 message, had forecast expenses of around $319 million
for the fiscal year ending June 30, 1862, the swollen costs of war
were now expected to drive the figure up to $533 million—an
underestimation of $214 million. Moreover, having expected to
raise revenues from customs duties, taxes, and land sales amounting to $80 million, he now anticipated less than $50 million. His
new estimate indicated a deficit of $483 million for the year. In the
first five months (July 1 to December 1) he had been able to raise
around $230 million, mostly through the $150 million loan from
the associated banks. The treasury, therefore, would require $253
million additional funds by June 30, 1862. With characteristic
unwillingness to recommend potentially unpopular taxation, he
suggested, in his December report, only a piddling increase in
customs duties and a slight increase in certain excise taxes by
which he hoped to raise an additional $50 million. This left more
than $200 million to be met by Chase's usual resort—borrowing.
He was careful, moreover, to remove any hurdles he might possibly have created for himself along the visionary road to the White
House by apologizing for the $50 million in additional taxes he
was now forced to request. "The Secretary is aware," he declared,
"that the sum is large [but] he feels that he must not shrink from
a plain statement of the actual necessities of the situation."

The actual necessities, of course, required immediate and heavy
tax levies which would have brought in considerable income and
would have restored sufficient investor confidence to enable the
government to float whatever debt issues were required. And
Chase did shrink from these necessities by asserting, "It must be
seen at a glance that the amount to be derived from taxation forms

but a small portion of the sums required for war. For the rest, reliance must be placed on loans." And then he stood logic on its head by proclaiming, "If at any time the exacting emergencies of war constrain to temporarily depart from the principle of adequate taxation, the first moments of returning tranquility should be devoted to its reestablishment in full supremacy over the financial administration of affairs." In short, in a time of mountainous outlays, the nation need not exact required taxes, but in a time of small expenditures—when large taxes are no longer required—the government will once more be able to profess its adherence to sound financial principles (to which it had previously not adhered).

The Secretary made some obligatory obeisances to administrative economies, and then placed the capstone on his message by recommending the establishment of a national banking system. He advocated a program under which all banks would be supervised by the treasury (they were now under the control and surveillance of state banking departments). Each member bank could issue United States Treasury bank notes, but the amount of bank notes it could put out would be largely determined by the amount of government bonds and notes in its portfolio. Chase's plan—if successfully implemented—would provide a uniform currency in the place of the confusing welter of diverse bank notes the state-controlled banks were emitting, some of which were of durable value and some of which were worthless. Moreover, the Secretary, in proposing that government securities should be the chief reserve asset, hoped to promote the purchase of large amounts of treasury bonds by the banks. (Chase recommended, however, that the national bank notes put into circulation should be limited to $300 million.)

Without doubt, a reform of the highly flawed existing banking system was in order and the Secretary had some reason to believe that his proposal would be viewed as a kind of Magna Charta of American banking. It did not occur to him that the introduction of radical changes in a time of war and military defeats might be unsettling and counterproductive. He hoped that his report would be regarded as "visionary" and "statesmanlike"—the kind of plan which a future chief executive should bestow upon a waiting nation.

But from an already alienated banking community Chase's message elicited, at first, an angry silence—and then—despair. Leading bankers saw clearly that the government was now resolutely committed to an irresponsible program of deficit financing and its concomitant: inflation. Stocks and government bonds plummeted. Rumors flew that the treasury was about to suspend specie payments on its debts. The run on gold that had been set off by the Trent Affair now accelerated. The banks of New York lost almost $3 million in gold during the first five business days after Chase's report was printed. In the following week $2.5 million more was withdrawn.

Things went from bad to worse in the third week. Capitalists and entrepreneurs, after reading about the meandering and inconclusive deliberations being conducted by Congress in response to Chase's message, concluded that the nation would soon resort to the indiscriminate manufacture of paper money. They rushed to their banks, converted their bank notes into gold, and secreted the coins in strongboxes. In the six banking days of the week ending on December 28, 1861, New York banks lost $7.4 million of their gold. In the three weeks since the publication of Chase's "visionary" proposals the drain of gold of the New York banks had come to around $13 million, or 25 percent of the $42 million in specie they had held on the week ending December 7, 1861. Banks in other large cities fared similarly.

On Saturday, December 28, a committee representing the New York banks met in a stormy session lasting almost seven hours. Finally they voted (25 to 15) to take the dreaded step: specie suspension. Beginning with Monday, December 30, 1861, the holder of a bank note would no longer receive gold for his paper money. An era had come to a dangerous end. James Gallatin explained the decision: "The Government must suspend specie payments, or we must, and it is only a question of a few more days as to who suspends first and who shall hold the specie [now] in our vaults. If the government takes it, the whole will be expended and hoarded by a few people."

On December 30, most of the banks in the Union followed New York's lead and suspended gold payments. A few days later the treasury followed suit, announcing that it would no longer redeem in gold the $33 million demand notes in circulation or on "special deposit" at the banks. Chase said, at the time, that he had come to the conclusion "that the government could no longer obtain coin on loans in any adequate amounts." The treasury would go on paying interest due on its obligations in gold coin but "could not guarantee the payment in gold of any other debts or bills."

On the very day the banks suspended specie payments a bill was laid before Congress, recommending that the government resort to the issuance of irredeemable legal tender paper notes. Ellbridge G. Spaulding, a Buffalo banker and former treasurer of New York State, chaired the subcommittee of the House Ways and Means Committee that had been assigned the task of framing the legislation on Chase's national banking system. As the run on gold progressed, he quietly had set about devising a legal tender act; he was ready with it on the very day the banks suspended. The subcommittee wrestled with the bill but being equally divided between pros and cons was mired down until a member, Stratton, who could not make up his mind finally voted in favor, so that the bill might go before Congress for consideration. The measure was voted out of the committee on January 7, 1862.

Spaulding defended his legislation in the following remarks made in a letter to a certain Isaac Sherman (a businessman who had ventured "to suggest that heavy taxation was preferable to the issuing of irredeemable paper as a means of meeting expenses by the government"). "The Treasury-note bill," said Spaulding, "is a measure of necessity and not one of choice. We will be out of means to pay the daily expenses in about thirty days and the committee does not see any other way to get along till we can get the tax bills ready, except to issue, temporarily Treasury notes [the future greenbacks]. We must have at least $100 million during the next three months, or the government must stop payments." Spaulding closed his letter with a piece of gratuitous advice: unless Mr. Sherman knew of a way of supplying the needed $100 million, he would do well not to criticize the bill.

After the provisions of the legal tender bill were published, a committee of the associated banks that had made the $150 million loan descended on Washington (on January 11) in an effort to influence Chase and members of the House Ways and Means Committee as well as members of the finance committees of both chambers. Gallatin, acting as spokesman, warned of the ruinous consequences of an avalanche of government-printed paper money. In its place he recommended heavy taxation and sale of long-term securities by the government at the going market price (rather than sales at par on which Chase had previously insisted). The imposition of meaningful taxes would revive investor demand, permitting the treasury to float its bonds at a decent price (Gallatin later estimated that a sizable issue could be sold at 75 and above). He added a few minor suggestions, including a rewording of the regulations affecting the power of the subtreasuries to use banks as depositories; Chase and the bankers had previously clashed on this point. Gallatin wanted the banks to have a green light in treating the government as any other depositor. His implication was: the banks were willing—as soon as the air cleared—to resume specie payments and to furnish gold-redeemable credits to the government, but they wished to be freed from illogical demands to deposit large amounts of loaned gold into the subtreasuries in advance.

Although the bankers tried to impress the assembled government officials with the desirability of legislating heavy taxation as a precursor to the floating of reasonably priced long-term loans in the public market, Chase and various members of Congress turned their suggestions aside, insisting only that "the war had made a necessity of immediately issuing at least $100 million of legal tender notes."

Spaulding's reply to Gallatin is illuminating. He began by "objecting to any and every form of shinning through Wall Street and State Street [profiteering by stock and brokerage firms in government securities sold under par] . . ." and objected "to the knocking down of government stocks to 75 cents or 60 cents on the dollar —the inevitable result of throwing a new and large loan on the market without limitation as to price."

He next asserted that "Treasury notes [the greenbacks whose issue Congress was debating] had as much virtue as the notes of banks which have suspended specie payments, but which yet circulate in the trade of the North." And then he resolutely refused "to assent to any scheme which should permit a speculation by brokers, bankers, and others in government securities and particularly any scheme which should double the public debt of the country and double the expenses of the war to the extent of sending it to 'shin' through the shaving shops of New York, Boston, and Philadelphia."

Spaulding's response, of course, was a nonreply. He did not address himself to the suggestion of necessary tax levies, but raised the specter of large government debts (which heavy taxes would, of course, have minimized). To Gallatin's earlier warnings about the great increase in expenses the government would incur by issuing an uncontrolled, inflation-begetting currency, he spoke in emotional terms about the cost to be borne by the government if it issued bonds below par (a step which the government had taken on previous occasions). His pietistic railing against "shinning," bankers, and Wall Street was simply a demagogic maneuver designed to court favor with the electorate and with members of Congress who were opposed to his bill or were undecided. (During the 1860s, brokers, bankers, and financiers were convenient scapegoats; there was a biblical bias against them which politicians conveniently invoked.)

Unfortunately, most of the legislators whom the bankers attempted to influence were also not interested in the logic of responsible fiscal policy, and they sided with Spaulding. The bankers' committee trip to Washington ended in a resounding failure; a similar hegira a few days later also brought no tangible results in the struggle against the proposed issue of greenbacks.

Nor did the outpouring in the press and in the mails in favor of "considerable taxation" swerve legislators from their goal of "easy" money. While Spaulding was proceeding down the paper road, Justin S. Morrill of Vermont, the leading tariff authority of the period, was assigned the task of introducing a revenue bill that would enable Congress to authorize the $50 million additional taxes Chase had requested in his December 9, 1861, message. Exhortations for stiffer taxes rained in on him from all directions. Editors reiterated that, so far, no adequate tax program had been devised and that "this hesitancy, like timid surgery, can only lead to a fatal result." On January 1, 1862, the Boston *Advertiser* advised members of Congress that they must address "themselves earnestly to the great topic of government finance which oppresses every reflecting citizen. To put the truth in plain terms, however, there is a rapidly increasing feeling that Congress is afraid to deal decisively with this great subject. Taxation heavy and universal is felt to be the only solution for our present difficulties, [yet] it is whispered that members dislike to come before their constituents with a long tax bill."

With the passing of days—while Congress hesitated—the nation's support for broad tax levies proliferated, and legislators should have been able to shed their fears about "coming before their constituents with a long tax bill." They should have been strengthened by the visible evidence that, in the words of perceptive foreign observers, "Americans presented a spectacle of a people praying to be taxed."

But Congress closed its eyes to that spectacle and, in a dilatory resolution, pledged that it would raise—at some future and undetermined time—$150 million "from internal taxation." Even this effete resolve—useless as it was at the moment—rallied the markets in government securities, with some issues rising from 90 to over 100 in several days. But the more sober implications of the resolution soon took over: promises of more substantial taxes at some undefined future time were useless in dealing with present realities, and to a senator's assertion that a comprehensive tax act would "require too long a time in the present emergency," the *Journal of Commerce* retorted that "the excuse was more specious than substantial." Nevertheless, Congress refused to take the path of fiscal responsibility that might have averted inflation. (It postponed definitive action for almost six months, until July 1, 1862, when it finally voted out a new tax act. As a result of the delay, less than $52 million in taxes was collected during the entire fiscal year ending on June 30, 1862, although expenditures came to almost $475 million.)

But while legislators hesitated on taxes, they raced to bring the greenback bill to fruition. On January 28, 1862, the House took up the measure (slightly modified by Spaulding since its introduction almost a month before) which provided for the issue of $150 million United States legal tender notes ("a legal tender in payment of all debts, public and private"). Spaulding made an elaborate introductory speech in which he stressed the fact that his reluctance "to creating irredeemable paper currency" was overcome by a recognition of "necessity."

"The bill before the house is a war measure," he maintained,

a measure of necessity and not of choice, presented . . . to meet the most pressing needs of the Treasury to sustain the Army and Navy until they can make a vigorous advance upon the traitors and crush out the rebellion. . . . They [the army and navy] must have food, clothing, and the materials of war. Treasury notes issued by the government on the faith of the whole people will purchase these indispensable items and the war can be prosecuted until we can enforce obedience to the constitution and an honorable peace can be established. This being accomplished, I will be among the first to advocate a speedy return to specie payments and all measures that are calculated to preserve the honor and dignity of the government in time of peace, and which I regret are not practicable in the prosecution of this war.

During the remainder of his address and during the numerous debates that followed, he returned again and again to the theme of "necessity."

The creation of legal tender notes, he insisted, was the only way out of the dilemma—a regrettable but inescapable necessity, since the treasury could not manage to sell bonds or short-term obligations in meaningful quantities at par. He opposed sales at a steep discount—an act which would increase the debt to staggering proportions; an act that would multiply sacrifices of masses of people while it benefited a few in Wall Street.

Ringing applause broke out when he finished his speech. But Chase was not completely satisfied with it. In a private note, the Secretary—after dispensing some obligatory compliments— stated, "You do not attach, I see, so much importance as I do to the banking act as a measure of relief, nor as much as—I am confident—you will, upon reflection."

Evidently urgency and necessity were not given as high a priority, by Chase, as his desire to receive credit and acclaim for what he called his statesmanlike program of national banking, an act whose printed text required sixty sections and hundreds of pages of explanations when it was presented to the House, a measure that certainly could not be legislated with urgency.

The debate over the greenbacks ranged far and wide in both the House and Senate. Much energy was initially expended in examining the constitutional right of Congress to create legal tender notes. Finally, using some dubious precedents the House satisfied itself that it had the right to issue legal tender money. Spaulding scored a telling point when he argued, "This bill is a necessary means of carrying into execution the powers granted [to Congress] in the Constitution 'to raise and support armies.' " Thaddeus Stevens, the fustian chairman of House Ways and Means Committee (and undisputed master of invective), nailed down the legal tender dispute by summarily decreeing "whether such necessity exists is solely for the decision of Congress."

The deliberations then concentrated on the financial merits of issuing the greenbacks. A number of speakers ranged themselves against emitting paper currency. Considerable rhetoric was used to remind the House of the disastrous consequences of the assignats (one member brought along his copy of Carlyle's tome on the French Revolution and punctuated his reading of appropriate sections with dramatic gestures). Other inflationary episodes that had been brought on by the overissue of irredeemable paper were cited, namely, England during the Napoleonic Wars, the Austrian superinflation, the galloping inflation during the American Revolution, and the wild surge in prices already underway in the Confederacy (which was manufacturing paper notes by the bale).

Owen Lovejoy openly opposed the bill, proclaiming, "It is not in the power of this Congress to accomplish an impossibility in making something out of nothing. The piece of paper you stamp as $5 is not $5, and it will never be unless it is convertible into a $5 gold piece; and to profess that it is, is simply a delusion."

All the valid economic arguments that could be marshaled against fiat currency were enumerated by various representatives: prices would rise "ultimately ruining commerce," "labor will suffer," "an unscrupulous few will benefit while the public at large will be pilfered through inflation," "depositors in banks will lose through depreciation of the value of their savings," and "the road [of creating paper money], once taken, is easily sought again."

To all these arguments one stock reply was made by supporters of the bill: necessity—the necessity brought on by an empty treasury in time of war. Funds were immediately required and since there was no other available way of raising funds, they must be furnished through fabrication of paper notes.

As time went on the proponents of the bill perceived that the phrase "a war necessity" was answered less and less by the opponents. To solidify their position they induced the Secretary of the Treasury to address the following message to the House:

I have felt, nor do I wish to conceal that I now feel, a great aversion to making anything but coin a legal tender in payment of debts. It has been my anxious wish to avoid the necessity of such legislation. It is, however,

*at present impossible, in the consequences of the large expenditures en-
tailed by the war, and the suspension of the banks to procure sufficient coin
for disbursements and it has therefore become indispensably necessary*
that we should resort to the issue of United States notes. [Italics supplied.]

The opposition began to give way, finally, before the onslaught of
"necessity." On reading Chase's message, John Hickman, who
had been against issuing greenbacks from the start, said, "I have
had great doubt as to the propriety of voting for this bill, but being
assured that the Treasury and perhaps the Administration regard
this as a governmental necessity, I am disposed to waive the
question of propriety, or expediency, and to vote for it as a necessity."

W. P. Fessenden, who had considerable expertise in economic
matters and later became Secretary of the Treasury, also was
pushed aside by the steamroller of necessity after having been in
the forefront of the opposition. Reversing himself, he declared, "If
the necessity exists, I have no hesitation on the subject and shall
have none. If there is nothing left for us to do but that, and that
will effect the object I am perfectly willing to do that."

A minority protested, saying that no necessity had been proved.
"It has been asserted with the utmost sincerity," Valentine B.
Horton told the House, "that this is a measure not of choice, but
of necessity. But, Mr. Chairman, that assertion is only reiterated,
but not proved. Where is the proof that this is a matter of necessity? There may be proofs abundant, but they have not been
produced."

B. F. Thomas was more emphatic about a lack of necessity.
"Not a dollar of tax has been raised," he pointed out, "and yet we
are talking of national bankruptcy and launching upon a paper
currency. I may be very dull, but I cannot see the necessity, nor
the wisdom of such a course."

But his turned out to be a losing cause. Nine days after debate
had begun, the legal tender bill passed the House by a vote of 93
to 59. Neither party affiliation nor sectionalism was a decisive
factor in determining votes (for instance: the twenty-five Democrats who voted against the measure were joined by twenty-three
Republicans, seven Whigs, and four from splinter parties; sixteen
members from the New England states voted in favor while eleven

opposed, while delegates from the Western states voted nine to three, and those from the Central states twenty-seven to thirteen, etc.). In the Senate the vote in favor was more lopsided, with thirty for the bill and only seven against it. On February 25, 1862, the bill was signed by Lincoln.

In its final form the bill provided for the issuance of $150 million legal tender United States notes in denominations of $5 or more. Of the notes $50 million were created to "replace" the $50 million of demand notes, which were "to be withdrawn from circulation as quickly as possible." The notes were to be "lawful money . . . in payment of all debts, public and private, except duties on imports and interest on the public debt" (which were expressly made payable in coin). The notes could be exchanged at any time into a like dollar amount of the 6-percent "5-20" bonds (callable at par after five years by the government, but due within twenty years). There were $500 million of these 6-percent bonds authorized by the second section of what has become known as the First Legal Tender Act.

None of the legal tender notes were released until April 5, fully thirty-nine days since Lincoln had approved their issue. The amount put into circulation did not reach any significant proportion until the middle of May—four and a half months after the cry of "immediate necessity" had first been raised in Congress. Chase allowed overdue bills to pile up and when forced to make payment resorted to a variety of means: he issued almost $26 million additional demand notes (although Congress had ordered that previously issued demand notes should "be retired as quickly as possible"); he put out about $25 million of new certificates of deposit and certificates of indebtedness (authorized by Congress in March 1862 in emergency measures); he sold over $31 million of previously authorized 7.3-percent treasury notes and 6-percent twenty-year bonds. Altogether he raised almost $82 million in the first quarter (January 1 to March 31) of 1862 by borrowing. About $14.5 million was taken in from customs duties, and $27,019.74 from sales of public lands. In all, receipts amounted to $96 million in the quarter (while expenses were $112 million). Despite the cry of urgency the government had been able to take in $96 million in three months (or at an annualized rate of $384 million). Whatever else they were, the legal tender notes were not the offspring of necessity.

In the April 1 to June 30 quarter of 1862, the treasury's condition improved. Chase raised more than $111 million more by borrowing through a repetition of issuing more certificates of deposit, certificates of indebtedness, and 7.3-percent treasury notes. He also took in almost $14 million through the sale of the new 6-percent twenty-year notes of 1862 (they were purchased with the newly issued green-colored legal tender notes—the greenbacks). The $111 million borrowed exceeded the $98 million greenbacks used to pay government bills. About $21 million was received from various revenues, with customs duties bringing in about $19 million, direct taxes around $2 million, and public land sales, $49,558.

During the six months after the first clarion notes of necessity had been sounded in the Congress, the treasury had been able to borrow almost $200 million, and had used only $98 million of greenbacks to meet its outlays.

But in the first week of June, the expenses of war rose to a rate of $1.25 million per day and Chase felt impelled to ask for more greenbacks even though a number of legislators who favored the first issue had given their word that there would be no additional issues. He also requested permission to issue more certificates of indebtedness and certificates of deposit. The second legal tender bill was introduced into the House on June 11, 1862. This time the debate was considerably less animated with fewer objections. However, one of the opponents, Senator Chandler, of Michigan, immediately pointed out that the mere publication of the bill "without any action of the Congress on the subject, has created such a panic and has so convinced the money centers of the world that we are to be flooded with this paper, that gold has risen in price from a 2-3/4-percent to a 7-percent premium."

But the adherents of the bill again raised the contention of necessity. All opposition was met with this one argument. And when Morrill, of Vermont, declared, "The true policy is to put upon the market the small amount which will be required . . . in the bonds of the government at whatever they would bring," he was countered with the assertion that selling bonds at a deep discount would prove to be more costly than the inflation caused by the introduction of more paper money. The advocates of greenbacks, without testing the market, cavalierly assumed that only "deep discount" bids could be elicited from investors and continued to favor money fabrication over borrowing. Spaulding parried Morrill's suggestion by saying, "When money could be obtained at par on 6-percent bonds, I would prefer to have that done to the issuing of very large amounts of legal tender notes," and T. M. Edwards followed up with, "I will gladly give my consent to the sale of bonds if I were assured those bonds could be sold at par." Such responses, of course, led nowhere since the 6-percent bonds were then selling at a discount from par in the open market.

After ten days of intermittent discussion the House passed the bill 76 to 47. Again, neither party affiliation nor sectionalism was a prime determining factor in the voting. The act provided for an issue of $150 million legal tender notes; $35 million of these greenbacks were to be in denominations of under $5, with the majority to consist of bills of $1.00. In addition, a further issue of certificates of deposit was authorized. In the Senate, after a brief debate, the bill carried 22 to 13. Lincoln signed the Second Legal Tender Act on July 11, 1862, thirty days after its introduction into Congress.

Although considerable difficulties arose from the second emission of greenbacks, Chase did secure one specific benefit from them. The Secretary of the Treasury, yearning for the Presidency and convinced that he could have secured the nomination in 1860 if he had "been better known among the electorate," came to the conclusion that he had in his grasp a sure-fire method of becoming better known. He had his likeness engraved on the most frequently used greenback—the $1.00 bill. A campaign picture that would reach every prospective voter before the presidential election of 1864! Asked by a friend why he had chosen the lowly $1.00 note, he became the very model of self-effacement, replying, "I had put the President's head on the higher priced notes, and my own—as was becoming—on the smaller ones."

Some time would pass before Chase would learn whether he would obtain his desired advantage from the second issue of greenbacks, but the nation did not need to wait long before it discovered their disadvantage. As Senator Chandler, of Michigan, had pointed out, the mere discussion of a second installment of greenbacks had triggered off a depreciation of paper money vis-à-vis gold. During the first two months after their release, the greenbacks sold at near parity in relation to gold. About $275 million of gold coin had disappeared from circulation when specie payments were suspended at the end of 1861. The partial filling of this void by the emission of less than $100 million in paper between April and June 1862 had no disturbing effect because of the scarcity of money supply.

On June 11, 1862, $100 in paper could buy $96.22 in gold. On the next day, when the nation learned of the treasury's request to issue more greenbacks, paper currency immediately declined to $94.96 against $100 in gold. When the final vote was cast in the Senate on July 8, 1862, on the Second Legal Tender Act, paper slumped to $89.79. The operation of "inflationary anticipation" had immediately set in. People feared that the additional print-up of new money would lead to higher prices, and they tried to buy what gold they could in anticipation. This drove up the price of gold. In the reality of the marketplace the following occurred that day: if, as a manufacturer or an importer or a speculator playing the "gold market," you tried to buy some gold with paper, you could get only $89.79 in gold for your $100 in greenbacks, or—put another way—if you wanted to buy $100 in gold (to make payment for imports or tariff levies or your plunge into money-market speculation) you would need to present $114 in greenbacks to a gold dealer.

Through this mechanism the inflation of the Civil War was set off. Manufacturers, processors, and importers who took in only paper money from the public, since gold was no longer a circulating medium, nevertheless needed gold for goods they imported or for the payment of tariffs or for settlement, at times, with those suppliers who insisted on payment in metal money and who refused the depreciating paper notes. To compensate for the increased cost of the purchased gold, they immediately raised their own prices at least to the extent of the existing premium on gold.

Throughout the last half of 1862, gold rose in price against the greenback, until it reached $134 (against $100 in paper). Much of the rise can be attributed to the increase in money supply that came from the second installment of greenbacks, from the creation of $20 million in postage currency (on stamps to fill the need for fractional currency, since, by now, even silver and copper coins were being hoarded), and from a substantial increase in state bank notes, as well as from a massive increase in certificates of deposit and certificates of indebtedness; the latter—which circulated as money—increased by almost $200 million during the 1862–1863 fiscal year and reached a total of almost $320 million. As this greatly increased and confused volume of paper coursed through the economy, the movement out of money into "things" set in, depreciating the value of currency additionally.

Various tables have been constructed by economists and others to measure the inflation of the Civil War. Probably the most reliable is the one produced by Wesley Clair Mitchell (see his books *A History of the Greenbacks* and *Gold, Prices, and Wages*). The Mitchell index* shows that whereas prices stood at 105 at the end of 1861, they had climbed to 121 by year-end of 1862. A rise of 15 percent in living costs within a single year is hardly catastrophic, but for the lowly paid seamstresses, day laborers, clerks, and factory workers who had received only a very small advance in pay, it was a tightening of the vise.

By the beginning of 1863, despite his recourse to the printing press, Chase, too, was squeezed. With the army increased, with costly military actions flaring in various areas of the nation and with prices of supplies swelling daily, he had once again run out of money. Among the arrears at the treasury were unpaid salaries of soldiers and sailors, amounting to almost $29 million. The House of Representatives, besieged by letters from fighting men and from their dependents, voted a resolution that stated: "Whereas grievous delays happen in the payment of money due soldiers . . . [it is] resolved that the Secretary of the Treasury be requested to furnish this House the reason why requisitions of paymasters in the Army are not promptly filled."

In the duplicitous charade that followed, the stiff-necked Secretary of the Treasury—who had never learned how to wheel-and-deal with the members of Congress—was called on the carpet. One after another, various legislators—voicing a hitherto nonexistent concern about the treasury's finances—reminded the Secretary that the government would not now find itself in financial straits if he had made a diligent effort to sell the entire issue ($500 million) of 6-percent twenty-year bonds the Congress had created in February 1862, when it passed the First Legal Tender Act. Why, they asked, was the great bulk of these bonds (about $475 million) still unsold?

Chase—without admitting that he had failed to make a con-

*The Index of the Arithmetic Mean of Relative Retail Prices.

certed effort to move the bonds—replied that there was very little demand among investors for the issue, that the bonds were already selling at below par, and that it would not be possible to sell any bonds, in volume, "at the market value thereof." A large offering would immediately break the existing price level, "and so bonds could not be sold at the market value that had existed before the heavy offering."

The Secretary—without saying so outright—blamed the impasse on the language Congress had used in its First Legal Tender Act. His critics in the House and Senate responded by accusing him of legal quibbling. Representative J. A. Gurley waved Chase's explanation aside, declaring, "Everybody knows that the market value of bonds is the price they will bring when placed upon the market. No farfetched construction of this sort [Chase's] should prevent their sale."

And then Chase was lectured by members of a Congress that had, itself, been derelict in voting taxation, that had abetted war profiteering by refusing even to consider passing a war-profits levy, and that had for almost a year exerted no pressure on the Secretary to raise funds through the marketing of the 6-percent bonds they had authorized.

After three days of assorted harassment the Secretary, drawing himself up to a full, magisterial height, consented to "offer the 6-percent bonds to interested persons at a price deemed appropriate."

Finally, this exercise in high sham required—and received—a fitting conclusion. On January 14, 1863, a laconic resolution "to provide for the immediate payment of those serving in the Army and Navy" was offered in the House, together with a recommendation for the creation of $100 million additional legal tender notes. The first priority in using the new money was to be given to the overdue payment of men in the armed forces. Without any discussion, the resolution was gaveled through the House and the Senate and rushed off to Lincoln, who signed it three days later. The Congress—using the plight of unpaid servicemen as an excuse —had launched the third round of paper.

In February the joint resolution became part of the deliberations on the Third Legal Tender Act.

There was an almost total absence of meaningful debate in the

House during the February 1863 proceedings. Early in the session, Amassa Walker sounded a consensus note when he declared, "One thing is certain we are in such an emergency . . . that it is not worthwhile for us to be very particular." Spaulding, as might be expected, pumped hard for the emission of paper while he assured everyone within the sound of his voice that he found his task regrettable and almost repugnant. "I have an aversion," he insisted, "to any considerable further issue of legal tender notes and can only consent to it as an imperative necessity. I think too large an issue will tend to inflate prices, but I do not see how it can be avoided." But original adversaries of paper issues now no longer raised objections. Justin S. Morrill, an old opponent, said, "The patient has got accustomed to opiates and the dose cannot now be withheld without peril." And Horton, a consistent enemy of greenbacks, noted that "the country is launched on the current of paper money and . . . there is no turning back."

After some discussion on specific details of the loans to be raised by the treasury, the House voted to authorize $150 million additional legal tenders. The vote was unanimous. In the Senate the sentiment was almost as strong; the vote was thirty-two in favor, and only four opposed. The act was signed by Lincoln on March 3, 1863.

In addition to authorizing $150 million more greenbacks, the bill gave the Secretary the greatest latitude in borrowing that had yet been conferred on any treasury head since the founding of the nation. He could borrow up to $900 million and offer an interest rate that should not exceed 10 percent. He could issue bonds that ran anywhere from ten to forty years, with interest payable in gold coin. There could be $400 million of the $900 million in the form of treasury notes (with a maximum maturity of three years paying interest of 6 percent "in legal money"). These treasury notes were "to be made a legal tender [money] to the same extent as United States notes [greenbacks] except for the payment of duties," and were to be put out in denominations of not less than $10.

The clauses in the First and Second Legal Tender acts restricting "the negotiation of bonds to market price" were repealed (a gratuitous gesture "to avoid the confusion which has hitherto existed"). The Secretary was vested with the authority to negotiate the sale of all of the debt instruments that had been created "on terms that he might deem most advisable." The language clearly freed Chase from any real or illusory need to restrict sales of debt issues to par or to a fixed market price.

At the time, almost no public discussion was elicited by the inflationary implications of the legislation Congress had passed in the Third Legal Tender Act. Not only had $150 million more greenbacks been voted but—even more important—400 million additional dollars had been authorized through three-year legal tender treasury notes (which could be used as money), for a total of $550 million.* This amount was greater than the combined gold and bank note money stock existing in the nation prior to the Civil War.

Although he had maintained a calculated silence at the time, Spaulding admitted later on (when the damage was already done) that the creation of $550 million in additional money had "led to a dangerous expansion of credit circulation in various forms . . . and to an enormous inflation of prices, caused by the overissuing of paper money which came very near proving fatal to the finances of the government and the legitimate business of the country." Obviously, Spaulding and other members of Congress were well aware of the possibility of such consequences when they overwhelmingly adopted the legislation, yet they adopted it.

Even before Congress had completed its work on the Third Legal Tender Act, money depreciated and costs rose sharply—in anticipation of the inflation that was to follow. On January 2, 1863, $100 in paper could buy $74.70 in gold, but by January 14, when the "joint resolution" (foreshadowing the emission of more greenbacks) was passed, $100 in paper declined to $67.57, a drop of almost 10 percent in two weeks. By March 3, when Lincoln signed the Third Legal Tender bill, $100 in greenbacks bought only $58.22 in gold. Within two months the paper dollar had fallen by almost 25 percent vis-à-vis gold. During the rest of the year paper money did not depreciate further, but the cost of goods, commodities, and services continued to climb as the newly created greenbacks swelled the monetary stream.

---

*The maximum interest payable on the three-year treasury notes was 6 percent. Chase issued $166.5 million of two-year notes, bearing 5-percent interest, between July 1, 1863, and June 30, 1864. He also issued $44.5 million of one-year notes (5 percent) between January 1, 1864, and June 30, 1864.

According to Mitchell's computations retail prices in 1863 soared from an index of 121 at the start of the year to 150 at year-end, an increase of 24 percent. During the twenty-one-month period (April 1862 to December 1863) since the beginning of paper print-up by the government, living costs had soared by 43 percent. In the same interval the wages of male employees had risen by only 27 percent and those of women had moved ahead by only 14 percent. Since the rise in wages trailed the increase of prices by a considerable extent—reducing the real purchasing power of already low take-home pay—hardship and unrest developed. Strikes broke out in the major cities during the winter and spring of 1863. On March 26, 1863, the Springfield *Republican* ran an item which said:

The workmen of almost every branch of trade have had their strike within the last few months. No less than six strikes are reported by the New York papers this week, of laborers on the Erie, Hudson River and Camden, and Amboy railroads, the journeymen tailors of the city, and employees of two large manufacturing companies. In almost every instance . . . the demands of the employed have been acceded to. These strikes, which all have been conducted very quietly, have led to the formation of numerous trade leagues or unions.

Strikes "conducted very quietly" are a far cry from the looting of bakeries, warehouses, and food stores that occurred daily in Paris during the Revolution, and the laying down of shovels by railroad firemen and the dropping of scissors by journeymen tailors are very different from the parading of decapitated heads on pikes. But the job actions of early 1863 were, nevertheless, clear proof of the squeeze of inflation. Those who did not have the recourse to strike action—the aged, the several million who were "receiving alms" in the cities and small towns, and the retired living on low, fixed incomes—were the most victimized by the upward spiraling cost of food, clothing, and rent.

An objective backward look, however, would readily reveal that the ballooning of the money supply in 1863 (largely effected through the Third Legal Tender Act), the resulting inflation, and the accompanying social stresses could all have been avoided. Throughout 1863, there were continually available the financial and fiscal means to avoid the difficulties that developed. They were provided almost single-handedly by the individual who has been called "the financier of the Civil War," Jay Cooke.

Irrepressibly optimistic, he waded into adversity with an undeflectable confidence that a less superficial as well as less successful man would have lacked. Shrewd in business affairs, personable, unshakably devoted to "getting things done," he was the quintessential American salesman. After serving an apprenticeship with E. W. Clark & Co., a Philadelphia-headquartered private banking firm, he established his own banking firm in January 1861, at the age of thirty-nine. Almost from the day Chase was installed in the treasury, Cooke courted the Secretary with a series of gifts (which were accepted so long as they were made privately but were ostentatiously turned away when publicly exposed), a string of unbroken "profits" arranged in Chase's investment account at Jay Cooke and Company, and a newspaper campaign that unwaveringly enhanced the Secretary's public image.* Cooke also ingratiated himself with Chase by successfully selling a disproportionately large portion of the bonds and notes issued by the treasury in 1861 and early 1862. The purpose of this elaborate courtship was unmistakable: Cooke wanted to become the sole agent for the marketing of government debt issues. He felt confident he could interest investors in buying vast amounts of the government's bonds, he wanted genuinely to "do something patriotic in a time of war," and—last but not least—he wanted to make a tidy profit from commissions.

At last, in the closing days of October 1862, Chase—with the treasury in its usual straits and pressed by creditors—consented to have Jay Cooke and Company become the government's sole agent in the marketing of the 6-percent 5-20s (due in twenty years but redeemable, at the treasury's discretion, within five years) that had been previously offered but which the Secretary had been unable to sell. After much haggling the Secretary agreed—or so it appeared to Cooke—to pay three-eighths of 1 percent in commissions on all bonds sold beyond $10 million; one-fourth of 1 percent was to go for paying the subagents Cooke was to hire, and the expenses incurred in travel, advertising, and such "incidental charges as were experienced" in influencing the press; the remain-

---

*Jay Cooke openly controlled one newspaper at the time and successfully bought the services of writers employed by other publishers.

ing one-eighth of 1 percent was to go to Jay Cooke and Company.

Cooke now mounted the greatest selling campaign of a government issue the world had yet seen. He flooded the "Loyal States" with leaflets and posters announcing a "half-billion-dollar loan to preserve the nation, with an interest of 6 percent payable in gold." These were distributed in army camps, railroad stations, theaters, meeting halls, churches, mills, mines, factories, and even in schools. Large advertisements featuring the benefits to be derived by putting money "to work at 6 percent in gold" were inserted in newspapers. Writers were paid in cash and "with edibles and bibibiles" to push the sale of the bonds.

Then Cooke loosed the 2,500 subagents he had hired, and they swarmed into every city, town, and country crossroad of the North, with their order books in hand. And now the flood of orders rolled in from every direction. By the end of December they were being received at a rate approaching $1 million a day. They came from "capitalists" and from the well-to-do, but mostly they swarmed in from the common people. A newspaper account of a typical scene in the Philadelphia offices of Jay Cooke and Company captures the scene:

Here is a letter from a lady in Camden who orders $300 and there is one from St. Paul, Minnesota, for $12,500. Here lies one from Pottsville, Pennsylvania, for $1,000 and another from Pittsburgh for $75,000. Along comes a telegram from Norristown for $250 and close upon the messenger's heels comes another despatch from New York for $250,000. Near one of the desks is a nursery maid who wants a bond for $50 and just behind her a portly gentleman . . . he wants $25,000. And so the great current of orders constantly streams in, the letters accumulate on the desks in quires, the telegraph messengers always hurrying to and fro and our city people passing in and out from counters in never-ending procession.

By the end of February 1863, when the Senate was deliberating the creation of more greenbacks, the "never-ending procession" of orders mounted despite the unsettling effect on financial markets caused by the sharp rise in gold and the fall of the greenback. At this time the government printing office could not keep pace with the rising order rate despite the installation of additional bond-engraving facilities.

By the beginning of March when the excuse of "imperative necessity" had already steamrolled the Third Legal Tender Act through the Congress, subscriptions rose over $1 million daily. The significance of this figure can be seen in the following letter written in the third week of March 1863 to Jay Cooke by his brother, Henry:

The Governor [Chase] is delighted at the way we are rolling in subscriptions on the 5-20s. I . . . told him . . . the daily receipts could be run up to $1,250,000 and possibly more. . . . He says if he could average . . . one and a half million per day from 5-20s it would be all he wants and he would look for money from no other source.

But this admission by Chase was one made in private. Publicly—and especially in his messages to Congress—he had urged the legislation of new greenbacks because "no other avenues seem available." Nor was Congress unaware of the magnitude of the money being raised from the 5-20s, since a daily "tally" of subscriptions received was carried prominently in newspapers, and yet legislators pushed through the third issue of greenbacks as well as legal tender treasury notes.

By the last week of April subscriptions averaged $1.7 million a day and throughout May averaged more than $2 million per day, reaching $2,492,000 on May 22. But Chase—having said that he would look "for money from no other source should subscriptions reach one and a half million daily"—nevertheless issued the authorized greenbacks.

Then, suddenly, a blight set in. A few newspapers—enemies of both Chase and Cooke—demanded to know "what induced the Secretary of the Treasury to give to this house [the house being Jay Cooke and Company] a monopoly of the 5-20 funding business. That will be a useful inquiry for another time. . . . If . . . Jay Cooke and Company receive from the Government 1/2 of 1 percentum on all the notes funded we can readily see a powerful motive for that house to procure as large a sum . . . as possible."

And Congress—aping a small segment of the press—instead of coming to Cooke's defense for his service to the government and sustaining his effort, accused him of "profiteering." Cooke defended himself by citing the comparatively small sum his firm had earned by that time after paying the subagents and other expenses (the amount earned to that time was approximately $100,000). And he looked to Chase for support, but the Secretary, eyeing the primaries of 1864, remained silent.

Finally, as congressional pressure against Chase mounted, he wrote a letter to Cooke in June, telling him that henceforth the treasury could pay only one-eighth of 1 percent plus the expenses of advertising and selling. Since Cooke frequently paid his subagents more than one-eighth, he was now forced to restrict them and had no way of receiving compensation for his own efforts. Fuming, he decided to go ahead as best as he could. But for a time, the adverse publicity and the suspicions that had been aroused, as well as dissatisfaction among subagents, tended to depress sales; during June they dropped off to an average of under $1 million per day, with some days showing less than $500,000. They lagged (at around $1 million a day) through the summer and into September. Then, in October, Chase relented and advised Cooke that the treasury would return to the previous arrangement of three-eighths of 1 percent.

By the third week of October sales returned to their former level, exceeding $2 million a day. They rose beyond that in November and in December $3 million and $4 million days became commonplace. In January, when the $500 million mark (the limits of the authorized issue) was in sight, subscriptions on some days exceeded $5 million. Finally, when the books were closed on January 21, 1864, the last rush orders brought in an oversubscription of $11 million. Cooke suggested that the overage should be returned to the last subscribers but Chase, wanting every cent, asked—and received—a special act of Congress that permitted him to keep the extra $11 million.

And so ended the most successful governmental issue experienced anywhere until that time. With a somewhat hypocritical modesty Cooke wrote to Chase, "There is nothing on record in history to compare with the triumph of this appeal of yours to the people of our land, and I feel a just pride in having been, under your instructions, one of the instruments in this great work. . . . My estimate of individuals subscribing to the loan is . . . 536,000 of all classes high and low, rich and poor, white and black, and of all . . . trades, occupations and professions."

A more candid man might have added that the amount of funds secured daily by the government from the 5-20s shortly after the passage of the Third Legal Tender Act had outrun the treasury's needs; consequently, there need not have been any excuse to issue another round of inflation-begetting greenbacks or legal tender short-term treasury notes. In September of 1863—when subscriptions had fallen off because of the fracas over commissions—he had written in a private communication to his brother (published after his death): "There would have been no need whatever of . . . selling the legal tender notes . . . if Governor C [Chase] had let me alone and not disturbed the old arrangement of 3/8." But Cooke was too wedded to success to be a crusader, and so he maintained a discreet public silence. Besides, he did not want to ruffle the waters because he was considering the possibility of becoming the sole agent for the sale of the new 10-40s, which were about to be launched by the treasury.

But several developments finally prevented Cooke from performing another selling miracle. Even as the press was hailing his accomplishments with the 5-20s, Congress launched into new discussions about "excessive compensation." These forays lasted throughout the early winter months of 1864 while Chase was attempting to make up his mind regarding the method to be used in selling the new issue of 10-40s (bonds due in forty years but callable at the option of the treasury in ten years). On Friday, March 11, 1864, Thomas A. Hendricks, Democratic Senator from Indiana launched a bitter attack against "the rich banking firm which has been made rich by the drippings from the Treasury. Perhaps $1 million has been made by the firm of Jay Cooke and Company by being made the special and exclusive agent of the Treasury Department in disposing of bonds . . . which might have been disposed of by the ordinary machinery of the Department."

Cooke submitted proof that his firm had netted only $220,-059.44. But the attacks caused him to waiver about taking on the 10-40s. Two further developments soon resolved what doubts he had. Chase suddenly announced that he had decided to have the bonds carry only 5-percent interest. Cooke was appalled; he knew that at this low yield, sales would be extremely difficult since other investors had just received 6 percent (on the 5-20s). And then the Secretary just as suddenly revealed that he had decided against having Jay Cooke handle the issue as sole agent (Chase explained in a private letter to Fessenden that he did not wish to be subjected to additional criticism from Congress about "favoritism").

Undoubtedly Chase wanted to avoid such charges, particularly at the very time when Republican state party organizations were caucusing regarding their choice of a nominee for the Presidency. Private letters and memoirs reveal that this was a period of high tension for the Secretary. The chimera of the Presidency had again come into view. It beckoned to him and although, outwardly, he seemed to hesitate—pretending he did not actively seek the elusive prize, but would take it if the people conferred it upon him— inwardly he ached for it and would have given his soul to secure it. He would not discover for several months (during which he made covert efforts to secure the nomination*) that his party was not behind him and that the brooding problem-haunted "adversary" in the White House would again be chosen. But until he made that discovery, he meticulously maintained a "presidential image." Included in the presidential image-making were his decision to reduce the interest on the 10-40 bonds to 5 percent ("to husband, as much as possible, the meager resources of the government") and his decision to avoid further congressional opposition by dispensing with Cooke's services as sole agent. Both of these decisions proved disastrous, and both led to an intensification of inflation.

The 10-40s—whose sale was put into the hands of subtreasury officials and the newly established national banks—proved a fiasco as soon as they were marketed in March 1864.† This time there was no army of subagents to beat the bushes, no newspaper articles to stir the excitement of prospective buyers, no blanketing of the nation with rousing posters and circulars. Chase tried to induce Cooke to breathe some life into the flagging endeavor, but the super-salesman, who felt he did not have a salable product, gave only token support. By June 1864, only $73 million had been sold; most of these were taken by the national banks as an asset reserve for issuing bank notes. But the public, finding the yield

---

*Chase was instrumental in having a purportedly "spontaneous" newspaper campaign launched in his behalf by several anti-Lincoln publishers. But his most arrant scheming against the nomination of Lincoln was his covert instigation of the dissemination, by Senator Pomeroy, of a circular which lauded Chase and simultaneously denigrated Lincoln.

†Chase's original plan in 1861 for the formation of a national banking system was finally passed in 1863. By the time the 10-40s were offered, only approximately 100 banks had joined the system.

unattractive, shunned the issue. Deprived of any substantial funds from the sale of bonds, the treasury was strapped during the five closing months of the fiscal year (from February 1 to June 30, 1864). Some relief was secured from increased customs duties and expanded internal revenue taxes (a comprehensive tax act had been passed in 1863) but the monthly income from these sources amounted to only $22 million. An additional $20 million per month was coming in from the sale of the lagging 10-40s, for a total of $42 million. But the costs of war, alone, were running at about $75 million per month. Having previously emitted the entire issue of greenbacks that Congress had authorized in the Third Legal Tender Act, Chase no longer could use these to fill the gap. Nor could he look forward to the creation of new greenbacks since legislators had already indicated during their discussions on tax matters that no further legal tender United States notes would be voted (a formal resolution against authorizing greenbacks beyond the existing level of $450 million was adopted on June 30, 1864).

During the five closing months of the fiscal year (1864), the Secretary distributed about $170 million of small-denomination legal tender two-year and three-year compound-interest treasury notes. These—upon being paid out to suppliers and contractors— were deposited and then circulated as money, swelling the already distended monetary supply.

As might have been expected, the rate of inflation was accelerated. At the end of 1863, the Mitchell Index stood at 150, but by the middle of 1864 it had soared to 180, a surge of 20 percent within a six-month period. But the index—in common with other compilations of living costs—concealed rather than revealed the startling advance that had taken place in the price of certain commonly used items. A yard of cotton flannel that had sold for 13 cents before the start of war cost 50 cents in mid-1864, a rise of 285 percent (as against a rise of 80 percent in the general index). A pound of coffee could be bought in Boston for 14 cents before the war; by the middle of 1864 it sold for 45 cents, a rise of 220 percent. Sugar sold for 10 cents a pound in Canton, Ohio, before the war, but sold at 25 cents a pound by July 1864—an increase of 150 percent. A ton of coal that could be bought in Reading, Pennsylvania, for $2.50 in 1860 cost $5.50 in 1864, a climb of 120 percent. Wood went from $6.50 a cord in Boston to $13, a 100-percent rise. The price of beef in Camden, New Jersey, climbed by 208 percent, from 12 cents a pound to 25 cents.

Even such expansionists as Spaulding professed an alarm about the upward rush of prices. Invoking a newly discovered monetary conservatism, he declared at the close of April 1864:

It seems to me that the policy of the Treasury Department for the last three months has been that of inflation and over-issue of a paper circulating medium. It has by such a policy unintentionally stimulated and encouraged speculation in gold, stocks, and other things, rather than to encourage industry, the production of commodities and other legitimate business. . . . I know very well these evils cannot be fully guarded against during the prosecution of such a gigantic war . . . [such as] the large amount of paper necessarily issued by the government, but it is the duty of the government that these evils should be mitigated and rendered as light as possible.

Spaulding's reference to "speculation in gold" reflected the prevailing concern over the upward sweep of the price of gold, purchased—in most instances—on margin. Having sold at $151.50 at the beginning of 1864, it rose steadily to $190 by June 1, 1864 (or conversely, $100 in paper currency which was worth $65.95 in gold on January 2 declined to $52.63 vis-à-vis gold by June 1, 1864). The fall had persisted despite Chase's several attempts to prop up quotations by having the treasury buy gold on the New York Stock Exchange, in the over-the-counter market in the "Gold Room" located next door to the Stock Exchange on New Street in New York City, and in Gallagher's Evening Exchange (situated opposite the Fifth Avenue Hotel in New York) where transactions usually went on far into the night.

The Secretary tilted, with mounting anger, against the "sharpers and plungers who won fortunes in gold while the men on the battlefield lost their blood and their lives." But although he used up several million dollars of gold coin the government had taken in from tariff payments, he got nowhere. He failed to understand that it was not the power of the speculators that raised the price of gold; it was—rather—the customary depreciation of overabundant paper currency which was creating the problem. Goaded by defeat, Chase insisted, "The price of gold must and shall come down or I'll quit and let somebody else try!" Thwarted by the operations of the market, he decided to proceed along the only route left to him, namely, to abolish the market. He asked Congress to pass a bill that forbade all contracts for future delivery and all transactions of gold by a "broker outside his own office." The bill—which, in essence, would cripple all trading in gold on the exchanges—was signed by Lincoln on June 17, 1864.

On that day the price was $196.63. On June 21, when the various gold exchanges were closed by law, it streaked to $208. A period of disruption now set in. Importers paying tariff levies could not compute the amount of gold due, since no quotations were available. Business transactions payable in gold were held up until both buyer and seller could visit a broker's office to get the prevailing quotation (under the law only quotations made in person in a broker's office were permitted). Frequently the quotation submitted by two brokers varied by as much as $20. Alarmed businessmen and bankers descended on Congress demanding a nullification of the Gold Act, warning that all commerce as well as the war effort would soon grind to a halt if the act was not immediately repealed. Chase, not knowing which direction to follow, hesitated.

Then, on June 29, he wrote to Lincoln: "I cannot help feeling that my position here is not altogether agreeable to you, and it is certainly too full of embarrassment and difficulty and painful a responsibility to allow in me the least desire to retain it. I think it my duty, therefore, to enclose to you my resignation. I shall regard it as a real relief if you think proper to accept it."

The Secretary's resignation had been submitted—not as some newspapers claimed—because of embarrassment over the Gold Act, but ostensibly because Lincoln had hesitated to accept Chase's recommendation of a successor to Cisco who had submitted his own resignation for unrelated, personal reasons. In all probability, Chase's resignation grew out of his desire for "real relief" from "the difficulty and responsibility" that had weighed on him for more than three years. Moreover, he had not wanted the assignment and had taken it grudgingly as a stepping stone to the Presidency. Now that his party had pushed him aside, depriving him of his real goal, there was no point in further subjecting himself to the many irritations inherent in his job.*

On four other occasions Chase had "resigned" only to have the

*For an appreciation of Chase's disinterest and antipathy to his assignment, see *Inside Lincoln's Cabinet, The Civil War Diaries of Salmon P. Chase,* edited by David Donald.

President, with characteristic forbearance, cajole him into "withdrawing his withdrawal." It is likely that Lincoln had encouraged Chase to remain in the Cabinet so that he might better "contain" him as a rival for the 1864 nomination. By June 30, when the President read the Secretary's resignation note, such precautions were no longer necessary.

Much to Chase's surprise his resignation was immediately accepted. On that day, June 30, 1864, with rumors flying that the Secretary had quit because the government was about to declare bankruptcy, gold climbed to $250 ($100 in paper secured only $40 in gold). One day after Chase left the treasury, Congress revoked the Gold Act and Lincoln signed the repeal on July 2, 1864. But except during a few hours after transactions were reopened on the exchanges, there was no rally in the depressed price of greenbacks; paper hit a low of $37.21 on July 19 and remained under $40 until August 26, by which time the existing military threat against Washington had been removed and Sheridan had taken command in the Shenandoah. Gold declined and paper rallied in September until it reached $52.36, as Sherman captured Atlanta and Sheridan defeated Early at Opequan and Fisher's Hill. The tide of battle had swung to the North.

But news from the treasury remained bleak. There were almost $72 million in overdue bills when Chase left office and the cost of waging war had now surpassed $2.5 million per day. In addition, $162 million of certificates of indebtedness (most of which were issued during the 1864 fiscal year) had to be met. Fessenden, who succeeded Chase (and who, like his predecessor, had taken the position reluctantly), tried to sell long-term bonds, but got few takers. By September unpaid requisitions at the treasury rose to $130 million. The new Secretary then resorted to the print-up of $80 million additional short-term compound-interest treasury notes which were a legal tender and circulated as money. In addition he issued $20 million of the newly authorized 7.3-percent treasury notes (bearing interest of 7.3 percent payable semiannually). These, too, had been declared a legal tender; upon emission they increased the already teeming stream of money.

He also placed on sale through the national banks a large quantity of 7.3-percent treasury notes that had not been declared a legal tender, but they moved slowly, bringing in only an average of $700,000 a day.

Jay Cooke advised Fessenden he could easily move hundreds of millions of the 7.3-percent nonlegal tender notes if allowed to establish an exclusive agency. Again—as had occurred with Chase —haggling over commissions held up the arrangement while the efforts of the national banks proved insufficient (after several months of offerings by the banks, sales—by the middle of January 1865—had come to only $120 million). The treasury had by this time fallen behind in its payment of bills by about $175 million.

Two weeks later the desperate Secretary agreed to the terms demanded by "The Financier of the Civil War" and made Cooke the general agent for the loan. The "miracle" of the 5-20 loan was now repeated. Jay Cooke played a rerun of the circulars, the planted newspaper items, and the subagents beating the bushes— until money rolled in like a tide. On March 27 there were no notes left to sell. The words of the Philadelphia *Inquirer* tell the story: "From August 15, 1864 to February 1, 1865 (169 days) the amount . . . of the 7.3-percent loan sold under the direct supervision of the Secretary of the Treasury was $133 million, or at the daily average of about $771,000. From February 1 to March 27, 1865 (55 days), under the management of Jay Cooke . . . the sales of the loan reached $167 million, or a daily average of rate of $3,036,363."

On March 3, 1865, with Southern forces being routed everywhere and the net being tightened on Lee, Congress passed yet another issue of nonlegal tender 7.3 percents, authorizing a total of $600 million. Fessenden had by now been replaced at the treasury by Hugh McCulloch, a banker and reputed "hard-money man," who had served as Controller of the Currency under Chase. The new Secretary quickly decided to market another issue through Cooke. The selling blitz was put on again, with even more dazzling success. On April 3, 1865, the day after Lee had fled from Richmond, the fallen capital of the Confederacy, sales came to $2,108,300; on April 10, when organized fighting had stopped— and the North rejoiced amid the ringing of church bells, the ceremonial firing of cannon, and the lighting of bonfires—the sales went on, totaling $2,873,650. On Tuesday, April 11, when Trinity Church in New York was packed to overflowing by a tearful assemblage that joined the choir in singing "Gloria in Excelsis," the mails and the subagents brought in $3,312,400. On April 19, no sales were recorded. Next to that date someone had entered into Jay Cooke and Company's log: "No business. Lincoln's Funeral." McCulloch, faced by claims from contractors and eager to have on hand funds for the final discharge pay of soldiers and sailors, exhorted Cooke to keep up the campaign. With the war over, gold falling, and the value of paper rising, investors rushed to buy the high-yielding notes. On May 13, $30,451,950 poured in.

By June 30, 1865, the end of the fiscal year, $672 million of the 7.3-percent notes were either in circulation or were being held as an investment.* These represented only a part of the money supply on that date. In addition, there were $143 million of state bank notes, $146 million of national bank notes, $236 million of one-year and two-year compound-interest treasury notes, $28 million of gold and silver coin (used in business transactions and for payment of tariff dues), $161 million of certificates of indebtedness that circulated as money, as did $25 million of fractional and postal currency. And there were, of course, the greenbacks; approximately $431 million were coursing through the economy. The circulating medium, before adding the 7.3-percent treasury notes, came to $914 million.† If only the legal tender portion of the 7.3 percents is added ($20 million), the total circulating medium comes to $934 million.‡ But, to obtain a figure for the total money supply, one must add at least $700 million of bank deposits outstanding, bringing the grand total of the money stock to at least $1,634,000,000. This compares with a money supply of only $682 million on June 30, 1861. During the four years of civil war, the money stock had risen by almost 150 percent.

During the last fiscal year of the war, the increase in money amounted to just under 30 percent, exacerbating the inflation, but at a slower pace. The Mitchell Index of relative retail prices,

---

*There is no reliable estimate regarding what portion of this amount was circulating as money or to what extent the 7.3 percents were being held as an investment because of their high yield. In December 1865, McCulloch stated that the 7.3 percents were circulating freely. Even though only $20 million of the 7.3 percents had been designated legal tender, considerable amounts of the remaining "nonlegal tender" 7.3 percents passed as money among soldiers and shopkeepers. Moreover, they were discounted by contractors and therefore served as "quasi-money."

†The Statistical Abstract of the United States, using official figures, estimates a circulating medium of $983 million for the fiscal year 1865; this would indicate a circulation of about $49 million of the nonlegal tender 7.3 percents as of June 30, 1865.

‡No reliable figure for all bank deposits is available. A minimum estimate is $700 million.

having reached 180 in mid-1864, climbed to 198* by June 1865 (a gain of 10 percent) and declined to 191 by December 31, 1865, as the usual postwar deceleration set in, bringing a lessening of demand and a curtailment of the speculation in commodities that had helped to hike prices. Mitchell's findings indicate an approximate doubling of living costs during the four years of hostilities; other indexes (such as the Aldrich Report and Faulkner's tables) show a rise of almost 125 percent, as do official figures for goods purchased by the army.

But all statistical studies reveal that throughout the war (including the period of lesser inflation between June 30, 1864, and June 30, 1865) wages—though increased—continued to trail the rise in prices.

Labor agitation during 1863 and 1864 had produced some substantial gains; nevertheless, by June 30, 1865, wages had risen by 65 percent while living costs had increased by at least 100 percent. Estimates put the amount of "real" earnings lost to inflation during the 1861–1865 period at $4 billion. But this figure does not adequately reflect the extent to which female employees—who had become the major part of the work force in the paper, shoe and bootmaking, rubber, woolen goods, cotton manufacturing, and garment industries—were disadvantaged by low pay. In those industries that contained a substantial female labor force, the increase of women's pay during the 1861–1865 interval came to less than 30 percent. In cotton manufacturing, the rise was only 25 percent, in paper-making only 17 percent, in spice manufacturing there was no advance, in publishing 18 percent, in "dry goods" 4 percent. Urban primary school teachers experienced a gain of about 35 percent. In Boston a female teacher's pay rose from $400 in 1861 to $580 in 1865, in St. Louis it went from $400 to $524, in Baltimore from $292 to $520, and in Cincinnati it remained stationary at $390. But in most schools—the thousands of "country" primary schools—the rise in pay was only 15 percent, advancing from a minuscule annual salary of $175 to a slightly less minuscule total of $203.25.

The most victimized, however, were the many thousands of

---

*The Mitchell Index reflects only year-end figures, but a reworking of the sources used by Mitchell shows a level of 180 for June 1864, and 198 for June 30, 1865—the last quarter of the Civil War.

seamstresses who were employed in government armories, in contractors' sweatshops, and in their own homes. The average wage they received in direct government employ (for sewing of uniforms, shirts, blankets, etc.) was $3.10 a week. This was about twice the $1.54 received weekly for doing the same work for private contractors (most army uniforms were produced by private industry). In the Philadelphia Armory where hundreds of women were employed twelve hours a day, they received 15 cents for each army shirt they sewed; from private contractors they got only 8 cents a shirt. Those who sewed in their own homes were the worst off. A woman—supplying her own sewing machine and her own thread and working fourteen hours per day—was able to eke out only 17 cents a day. And she, in turn, was better off than the woman who sewed flannel drawers for 11 cents a day.

Manufacturers and heads of commercial establishments encouraged large-scale immigration of foreign workers willing to take pittance wages (some were actually shanghaied into the country). Some of these settled on the relatively prosperous farms in the West, but most—enduring an unexpected poverty—jammed substandard living quarters in the major cities. New York City, whose population grew from about 750,000 to 1 million during the war, contained 15,000 tenement houses, most of which had only outdoor toilet facilities. The ghettos of the foreigners—squalid, garbage-strewn, and lacking adequate hospital services—were breeding areas of disease and epidemics. In 1864, there were 12,000 cases of typhoid reported in the city, and a similar number of smallpox victims. In Washington, with its considerably smaller population, 1,000 incidents of smallpox were recorded in the last twelve months of the war. A United States senator died of the disease, and Lincoln came down with a mild case.

However, there was none of the massive starvation that swept Rome and France during their superinflations. The threefold rise of the money supply in the North during the four years of war—while substantial in scope—was not great enough to set off skyrocketing prices and the usual, attendant pandemic hunger. In the South where the creation of paper money was of gigantic proportion, the population suffered considerably, but in the North the Civil War, for most people, was a period of economic disadvantage rather than devastation.

While most of the population suffered a loss during the war,

manufacturing and other entrepreneurial interests enjoyed an accelerating prosperity. The net national wealth expanded from $16.1
billion in 1860 to $21.6 billion in 1865, a gain of 35 percent. The
immense money supply created during the war was also the basis
for an even greater peacetime prosperity during the five-year interval of 1866–1870. By the end of 1870, national net wealth had
reached $32.3 billion, twice its prewar level.

As government expenditures soared (from $60 million in 1860
to $1.2 billion in 1865) and civilian demand simultaneously
mounted, the expansion of industry and commerce grew apace.
The shipment of iron ore from the Lake Superior area more than
doubled. There was not a single iron furnace or forge in Cleveland
before the war; by 1866 there were twenty-one, producing 60,000
tons annually. Twenty new steel manufacturing plants were
erected in Pittsburgh, with six put up in one year. Before the war
the nation produced 85 million pounds of wool; at its end the
annual rate amounted to 200 million pounds. The demand for
shoes and rubbers tripled. A Lynn, Massachusetts, periodical remarked, "Operatives are pouring in as fast as room can be made
for them; buildings for shoe factories are going up in every direction; the hum of the machinery is heard on every hand." During
the four war years more harvesters and reapers were produced
than in the twenty-seven peacetime years after 1833, when Hussey
first marketed his reaping machine. The output of sewing machines rose by 150 percent; 50,000 were exported in 1864 (in the
five prewar years less than 10,000 were exported).

Lumber production increased from a prewar rate of 262 million
feet to 550 million feet in 1865 (by 1867 almost 800,000 feet of
timber were cut in the single state of Wisconsin). Furthermore, the
production of wheat and other grains soared, laying the basis for
a net surplus of exports over imports—an unusual phenomenon
during wartime.

A new industry was born in the midst of hostilities: the petroleum industry (in 1859 the first successful oil well had been drilled
in Pennsylvania). A boom developed during the next three years,
attracting over $90 million in new capital while the treasury of the
United States experienced difficulty in raising funds—ostensibly
because of "an absence of circulating medium." Thousands of
wells were drilled in a three-year period as oil rose in price to $1
per gallon ($40 per barrel). Then a glut developed which drove

prices down to $4 per barrel, but the lull proved to be short. By the end of 1864, 1,100 oil companies had been formed and the Petroleum Exchange was opened in New York. Potential oil-bearing property which had sold at $3 an acre in 1858 commanded several hundred dollars per acre in 1865.

Between 1861 and 1865 the volume of freight transported on railroads more than doubled and the earnings of carriers rose sharply. Most lines paid dividends of 8 percent or 9 percent. Railroad shares boomed; Erie skyrocketed from 17 to 126 and Hudson River Railroad streaked from 31 to 164. During the four years of hostilities the value of railroad shares rose by $200 million. Part of this rise reflected the mounting profits recorded by carriers from transporting troops and war materiel. Loaded with capital by the end of the war, the twenty leading railroads paid out dividends amounting to $114 million between 1866 and 1869.

Even the conservative banks of New York City (whose officers and directors had opposed government print-up of legal tender notes in the early part of the war) enjoyed a great prosperity. Deposits among the Associated Banks of New York City rose from $80 million in 1860 to $224 million in 1865. Profits climbed from $8 million to $21 million. Almost every bank in the city paid a minimum dividend of 7 percent throughout the war, with some distributing 10 percent to 15 percent a year. The Chemical Bank paid 24 percent in every one of the four war years.

As might be expected, powerful individuals were able to siphon off great quantities of wealth; they acquired, by legal and illegal means, hundreds of millions of the newly created dollars they had induced the government to fabricate. And they were able to retain their money and property by influencing Congress to pass tax legislation favorable to their narrow interests. The Civil War years represent the first era in American history during which there was a mass production of millionaires. The New York *Independent* observed that before 1850 there were only twenty men in the entire country who had a net worth of $1 million, but in 1863 there were already several hundred millionaires in New York City. Some "of the several hundred were worth more than twenty million [each], whereas twenty years previously there were only five persons with a worth of five million dollars" in the whole nation.

One of the wealthiest of the new multimillionaires was Alexander T. Stewart, a shrewd merchant who had built "the largest emporium" in New York City, acquired and pyramided real estate, and in 1863 paid an income tax of only $92,182 on a declared income of $1,843,637. (The exact worth of the "merchant prince" during the Civil War has never been determined, but close associates believed his estate rivaled that of Cornelius Vanderbilt, who had amassed a fortune of more than $55 million by 1866.) Stewart owned several mansions in and near New York City, one of which he donated, fully furnished, to President Grant (whose "corruptibility could always be taken for Granted"); he owned villas and resorts in the Northeast and once built an entire model community on Long Island. Most of his wealth was acquired after 1858, when his worth was reputed to have been "only $2 million."

In today's economic environment—jaded by accounts of basketball players receiving $1 million per year for throwing a ball through a hoop—an income of $1,843,637 no longer creates surprise. But in 1863 it was a startling phenomenon, worthy of lengthy press coverage. Even lesser "takes" were fit subjects for reportage, especially when the "takers" were the notorious "war contractors"—the private suppliers of guns, munitions, uniforms, horses, meat, and even women. The *London Economist* revealed late in 1861 that a leading supplier of uniforms and blankets had been able to make "$200,000 during the first few months after the outbreak of hostilities" and that "his woolen mills were being worked twenty-four hours per day, seven days a week." Another supplier reported at the same time that his profits were running at the rate of $750,000 a year and he expected much higher income the following year.

Immense fortunes were piled up by contractors who received high prices for all kinds of shoddy and defective goods. Evidence taken by congressional investigating committees indicates that the average profit on material supplied to the army through contracts came to 50 percent. One committee examining bribery involving $50 million in contracts found that bribes of senators, congressmen, army officers, and procurement personnel amounted to $17 million; despite the heavy payoffs the contractors netted themselves close to $13 million. This would indicate a profit equal to 60 percent ($30 million before bribes).

Great profits were made from the sales of guns. In the beginning of the war, rifles were turned out in various government armories as well as by private producers (the Springfield rifle was made in the armory situated in Springfield, Mass.). Those turned out by the government cost $9 each, but the "private" guns were billed to the army at prices ranging from $16 to $20 each (or at a profit of about 100 percent).

With such handsome returns available, the private gun manufacturers were eager to pile up their shipments. Consequently, by the end of 1862, the military supply centers—instead of being woefully short of firearms (as they had been in 1861)—bulged with hundreds of thousands of excess guns.

Not only did these rifles exceed requirements, but many of the privately made weapons were unusable because they were defective. There were guns that could not fire, guns that could not shoot straight, guns that fell apart, guns that exploded when fired, maiming the soldiers who used them, and there were guns in name only—being simply a piece of wood for which the army had been billed $20.

The case of *Philip S. Justice* (here was certainly a misnomer!) versus the *United States Government* tried in the Court of Claims illuminates the criminal profiteering methods of the private gun contractors. Justice, a firearms manufacturer from Philadelphia, had received, among other contracts, an order to deliver 4,000 rifles in 1861. But the government, finding the guns completely unusable, refused to pay. Justice brought suit. During the trial, William H. Harris, an ordnance officer, testified that the guns were "unserviceable and irreparable." "Many," he said, "are made up of parts of muskets to which the stamp of condemnation has been affixed by inspection officers. They are made of soft, unseasoned wood and are defective in construction. The sights are merely soldered to the barrel and come off with the gentlest handling. Imitation screw heads are cut on their bases."

A Colonel Doubleday added that "many of them burst, their hammers break off, sights fall off when discharged. You could hardly conceive of such a worthless lot of arms, totally unfit for service and dangerous to those using them." However, the Court of Claims, falling back on a pretext of "technical grounds," ruled in favor of Justice.

Clothing and blankets—which in the beginning of the war were almost as defectively made as the rifles—yielded as much profit. Uniforms in the first part of the war were made of a material that finally took on the nickname of "shoddy," a rolled-together, punched-up composition of tailings and rag ends that passed for wool. They disintegrated after a few weeks of wear and—even more important—the "blue" (the color of the Northern forces) disappeared, giving the cloth a mottled gray look. Frequently, Union soldiers mistook their comrades for the "Rebs" (who wore gray uniforms) and fired upon them, wounding and killing many. By 1863 this "oversight" on the part of contractors was corrected, but the soldiers in the Western plains and in the Cumberland Mountains continued to shiver in winter weather because the sleazy amalgam of their blankets (masquerading as wool) could not keep out the cold. While this was going on, the wool manufacturers were paying annual dividends ranging from 10 percent to 40 percent.

Considerable effort has been made to determine the total profits ripped off by the contractors during the Civil War, but no definitive amount has been established; the figures run from $150 million to $250 million. It is little wonder that the private contractors were found—in various postwar congressional investigations—to be among the frequent financial supporters of those legislators who ardently backed the creation of greenbacks and other legal tender treasury notes. Having assisted in the starting of the printing presses, the manufacturers and middlemen who held contracts with the government saw to it that the stream of notes emitted from those presses should continue to fall into their hands. Nothing better illustrates the use of inflation as a money-skimming program than the strategy of the contractors. First, they raised prices 50 percent over the cost at which such items could be produced by the government in its own facilities. Since their manufacturing plants could be kept busy around the clock in turning out high-priced goods for the army, the private producers withheld their facilities from civilian production—until they succeeded in driving up the price of civilian goods. When public pressure mounted to increase the output of government-operated facilities (so that the prices of the contractors might be driven down), the makers of "shoddy" were able to "influence" legislators to oppose such requests. As a result, throughout the Civil War government-produced material filled only one-fourth to one-third the total procurement requirements. And, as new money was created to meet the unjustifiably high cost of supplies, the contractors raised their prices additionally, heightening the tempo of their wealth accumulation. In the whole scheme the hiking of prices—inflation—became a device, and not, as is frequently supposed, a consequence of flawed policy.

The contractors made most of their money during the first thirty months of hostilities, but the fortune-building of successful speculators, stockbrokers, bankers, and railroad tycoons proceeded throughout the war and into the immediate postwar period. During the decade of the 1860s the wealth agglomerators employed the expectable stratagem: using great amounts of borrowed greenbacks the government had obligingly put into circulation, they bought up farms, gold, jewels, real estate, art works, and stocks—and then sold them at a considerable profit to people eager to acquire inflation-hedging items. As the price of objects and properties rose, a characteristically deceptive impression of prosperity was created.

In the spring of 1864 (at about the time Spaulding was manifesting a sudden concern over inflation), the New York *Independent* editorialized:

Who in the North would ever think of war if he had not a friend in the Army or did not read the newspapers. Go into Broadway and we will show you what is meant by the "extravagance." Ask Stewart [A. J. Stewart, of the several mansions] about the demand for camel's hair shawls, and he will say, "Monstrous! " Ask Tiffany what kind of diamonds and pearls are called for. He will answer "the prodigious" or "as near hen's-egg size as possible," and "price no object." What kind of carpetings are now wanted? None but "extra." And as for [race] horses, the medium-priced-$500-kind are all out of the market. A pair of "good fast ones" will go for $1,000 sooner than a basket of strawberries will sell for 4 cents."

Outlandish extravagances could best be afforded by the rail tycoons, who accomplished a massive accumulation of riches by looting and exploiting the railroads.*

*Although there is a lack of information concerning the net worth of the leading rail magnates in 1864, almost all of them added very substantially to their wealth that year through stock manipulations. The value put on their estates at the time of their death is indicative: Cornelius Vanderbilt ($105 million); John Blair ($50 million); J. W. Garrett ($10 million); Johns Hopkins ($15 million); Richard Crocker ($40 million); Collis P. Huntington ($50 million); and Russell Sage (at least $40 million). This is only a partial list of the tycoons who looked back on 1864 as a "halcyon year."

Even during the darkest hours of the war, the people of the North maintained an almost delusional hope in the economic benefits the building of railroads would ultimately bring. Congress and other governmental bodies—responding to that hope—transformed every major railroad system into a veritable treasure trove which the more resourceful acquirers of wealth depleted as quickly as circumstances permitted.

One of the more important forms of largesse bestowed upon the carriers at no cost was a vast terrain containing some of the choicest land in the nation. Chiefly as the result of enabling legislation included in the Homestead Act of 1862 (an act "brought into being to aid the landless poor"), the roads were granted outright 200 million acres. The grants included one-fourth of the states of Minnesota and Washington, one-fifth of Wisconsin, Iowa, Kansas, North Dakota, and Montana, one-seventh of Nebraska, one-eighth of California, and one-ninth of Louisiana. In all, the giveaway covered an area of 242,000 square miles—a region larger than Germany or France. The Northern Pacific received a donation of 44 million acres, the Southern Pacific 24 million, the Union Pacific 20 million, and the Santa Fe 17 million. These were grants of the federal government. In addition, the states contributed 55 million acres.

But this represents only the beginning. Based on the false premise that they were "a critical economic and military necessity," the railroads received governmental (state, federal, and local) subsidies to cover their cost of construction. For instance, the Central Pacific and the Union Pacific (created by an act of Congress in 1862) received $16,000 for each mile of construction on level terrain, $48,000 per mile through mountain ranges, and $32,000 for each mile between ranges. These costs were borne by the United States government, which took a second lien on the properties. Other lines were treated with the same munificence.

Lest they be accused of favoring one government body over another, the managers of the roads forced local and state governments to make heavy financial contributions. "We have them by the throat," explained one rail executive. "If they [the local, county, and state bodies] don't come across, we tell them we will ruin them by by-passing them. They soon get the idea. Pay up or be cut off from markets. We have them bidding against each other. The highest contributor gets the line."

Rough estimates indicate that during the 1860s and 1870s over $800 million was funneled into the railroads by various governmental bodies through outright subsidies, cash grants, and sums invested in the stocks and bonds of the various carriers. Almost $500 million was diverted in this fashion during the Civil War period,* when the United States Treasury scrounged for funds and the money supply was ballooned because of a supposed chronic "exigency."

Nor are we—yet—at an end. The Homestead Act of 1862 and the Morrill Act (also of 1862) were heralded as pieces of legislation which would open the West to the average homesteader "and secure for the American people their rightful benefits from public domain." It was, ultimately, found that only 10 percent of the half-billion acres ostensibly "opened up" became the property of average homesteaders. The great bulk of what had been the national domain either legally or by ruse came into the possession of the railroads or rich individuals. As soon as the lands became available the agents of the railroads, posing as individual farmers or small ranchers, swarmed into the land offices to stake their claims at $1.25 per acre (the price established in the Homestead Act). Individual speculators from the East also dispatched a contingent of roving agents, but in the race for the recording of land patents, the railroad agents proved to be the swiftest despite being weighed down by heavy bags of cash they carried (into which they repeatedly dipped to bribe the recording officers into giving their claims preferred treatment).

Once having secured vast stretches of terrain, the railroads either retained them for future investment or put them on sale to reap an immediate windfall. But more frequently the officers and directors in control of the carriers "diverted" them to private "land companies" they had formed and pocketed the large sums speculators were willing to pay for prime land that had ostensibly "been made available at cheap prices to the landless poor." Senator Howe of Wisconsin complained in 1864 that the land-grabbing of the railroads was turning "the whole Northwest and the whole

---

*In New York State, 294 cities, towns and villages "contributed" $30 million and 55 counties gave "subsidies" ranging from $5,000 to $3 million. Massachusetts, hardly a great railroad-building state, joined the parade as 171 of its towns and cities raised funds for the railroads.

West into but little more than a province of New York." And the Senator was well aware of the methods used by the rail magnates to secure large grants of land which they could later divert for their private benefit. Although he was never caught with his hands in a railroad agent's bag, some of his associates in Congress were less scrupulous and made themselves available to discreet bribery. In 1864, the Union Pacific was successful in having its charter revised so that it could obtain a doubling of its land grant. Success came after its directors spent a half-million dollars in the private offices and homes of various legislators in Washington. J. B. Stewart, a railroad lawyer (and no relation to the "dry goods King"), "also lubricated the rails by dispensing $200,000 to key officials and legislators."

The amount of money made by the railroad tycoons from diverted land sales was augmented by large sums ripped off through other devices. One of the most profitable was the so-called construction company. Directors of a newly chartered railroad would secretly band together to form a separate company of which they were usually the sole stockholders. The private company would then carry out the building of the railroad at prices greatly in excess of costs. The stockholders of the construction company (directors of the railroad) then pocketed the difference between the actual cost and the amount charged to the railway. Collis P. Huntington, head of the Central Pacific Railroad (who obtained a charter in 1861 by judiciously distributing $200,000 among various congressmen), was one of the originators of the construction company scheme. He and several of his fellow brigands established the Credit and Finance Corporation, which was formed "to purchase all material for and carrying out all the building work" of the Central Pacific. The officers of Credit and Finance charged the railroad $79 million, which was about $36 million more than the cost of construction. The $36 million, of course, lined the pockets of Huntington and his associates. The extra expense was actually wrenched from the United States government, which subsidized the cost incurred in the construction of railways.

The directors of the Union Pacific were even more enterprising. Forming a corporation loftily named Credit Mobilier,* they

---

*Most of the Credit Mobilier windfall came during the years between 1866 and 1869 when the major portion of the UP system was constructed. Even though only a minor part of

charged the UP $94 million "for construction and other services," but during subsequent congressional investigations the highest estimate placed by experts on the cost of building the line came to only $44 million. Not all of the profit of $50 million went into the coffers of Credit Mobilier, since there were a number of other shareholders who knew something about the windfall and expected to share in it. These well-informed stockholders consisted of a number of senators, congressmen, and some Cabinet members, including James A. Garfield, future President of the United States. In 1873 when the full impact of the Credit Mobilier scandal broke, one of the founders of the UP, Oakes Ames, a former manufacturer of shovels, revealed that he "had won favor" in Washington "by emoluments to legislators and men in high office." He confessed also to a distribution of Credit Mobilier stock "in Congress, where it would do the most good." When asked why stock was distributed, he replied, "There is no difficulty in getting men to look after their own property."

There were also a number of public stockholders in Credit Mobilier who, of course, knew nothing (until the scandal occurred) about the bribery of officials; they had bought their stock as "a good thing" when Credit Mobilier had "gone public" to lend legitimacy to its operations. They shared, in a small way, in the $50 million profit when, several years after its formation, Credit Mobilier declared its first dividend amounting to $2.5 million, and its stock boomed to $260 a share. But the major rewards, of course, went to the officers and directors of Credit Mobilier who owned the great bulk of the stock outstanding. They were able to grab off for themselves approximately $33 million of the $50 million "take."

Members of Congress who were treated so generously by railroad executives returned the generosity. They enacted legislation that exempted the carriers from all taxes. In July 1862, the roads were required to pay a 3-percent levy on all passenger receipts but none on freight. In 1864, the schedules imposed a 2-1/2-percent levy on both freight and passenger receipts. But the railroads merely raised their charges to customers to the extent of the levies,

the rip-off occurred during the Civil War, the episode illustrates the scope of "profits" that must have been taken in during the war by companies whose operations were never exposed.

leaving their profit unimpaired. Solicitous legislators also favored the tycoons with a law that restricted the tax on dividends received from railroads to 3 percent. Officers and directors who had voted themselves millions of shares (through unwarranted mergers and by exchanging personal properties of dubious merit which they threw into the railroad companies) were then able to pay themselves large dividends and retain 97 percent of the distribution.

The government's personal income tax and corporate tax policies also helped the railroad owners—as well as others who were in a position to make a good deal of money—to retain and pile up their wealth.

Despite heavy federal budget deficits, no personal income taxes were leveled during the first fifteen months of the war. Congress finally managed to impose a personal tax on July 1, 1862, at the ridiculously low rate of 3 percent on incomes up to $10,000 and 5 percent on incomes above that figure. (No taxes were paid on incomes under $600.) In the fiscal year ending June 30, 1863— when the budget deficit came to $606 million, only $456,000 was raised from income taxes. In the late spring of 1864, when stocks were booming and the price of gold was skyrocketing (and while a new batch of legal tender notes was being printed to fill a freshly denuded treasury), Congress finally got around to debating an increase in income tax rates and the possibility of installing graduated rates on higher incomes. After considerable debate, a tax of 10 percent was set on incomes of over $10,000, but all attempts to impose graduated, higher rates on incomes of more than $10,000 were beaten down. The advocates of increased rates were told flatly in a resolution adopted by the Ways and Means Committee that in "its opinion the principle [of higher, graduated rates] was a vicious one." Morrill, who had found no principles violated in raising tariffs that ultimately led to an increase in prices the consumer paid, countered proposals that would have significantly increased the tax payments of agglomerators by stating, "This inequality is in fact no less than a confiscation of property." Stevens, chairman of the Committee on Ways and Means, echoed him with, "I see no reason why a man should be punished in this way because he is rich."

As a result of this approach, less than $15 million in personal income taxes was collected during the 1864 fiscal year, when the deficit came to more than $620 million. Only $20.5 million in income tax came in during fiscal 1865, when the deficit rose to $970 million. During the whole Civil War (which was waged at a cost of over $3 billion), the total amount of income tax collected came to only $35 million. Of this amount, about $18 million was received from persons earning less than $10,000 per year.

The accumulators of wealth paid less than $17 million in income taxes. To this must be added less than $13 million they paid on dividends and interest received from railroads, canals, insurance companies, and banks—for a total of less than $30 million. This represents only 6 percent of the estimated wealth amassed by the superrich during the Civil War. Had Congress leveled a 50-percent tax on all incomes over $25,000 (not an unreasonable rate in time of war), an additional $250 million in taxes would have been received, obviating the creation of the last two greenback issues and the inflation those emissions produced.

But, of course, no adequate tax policy was implemented; the legislative representatives of entrepreneurial interests were more concerned with the needs of their benefactors than with fiscal responsibility to the nation.

The same bias was reflected in the failure to enact taxes on the profits of corporations and other businesses. The only exceptions were insurance companies and banks.* All other corporate enterprises escaped a tax that might have reduced profits. Considerable amounts of revenue were extracted from enterprises (especially after 1863) that masqueraded as taxes but were actually charges passed on to consumers. These were the "taxes" on gross receipts, liquors, tobacco, manufactures, and sales. A total of about $237 million was raised from these sources. Evidence indicates that these levies did not impinge on profits. As soon as a producer incurred a charge (such as on gross receipts), he immediately defrayed that charge by raising prices.

The same inflation-begetting pass-through occurred in the col-

---

*In 1864, a special charge against capital used and notes in circulation was leveled on banks, not so much as a revenue-raising device but as an attempt to force the still hesitant state banks to enter the national banking system. The conversion was finally effected in 1866 after a punitive and prohibitive 10-percent tax on the circulation of state banks was enacted in December 1865. About $7.2 million was raised during 1864 and 1865 from charges leveled against the banks.

lection of $305 million from customs duties. Manufacturers, processors, and merchants routinely hiked prices to offset duties paid, and again profits were maintained.

The revenue-raising system designed during the Civil War took in $542 million from various pass-through charges on business ($237 million) and customs duties ($305 million). The average consumer—already beset by an inflation induced through rapid money fabrication—bore the increased costs. A treasury department and a Congress less responsive to special interests would have designed a fiscal program that contained extensive taxes on business profits and would have instituted wage-price controls.

Instead, deficit-financing and money print-up were used to fill the deep budgetary gap (during the war total revenues from all sources amounted to only $753 million but expenditures exceeded $3.3 billion). The implementation of these fiscal and monetary policies brought on the inflation of the Civil War. They might have been avoided and the inflation they induced might have been averted. But that would not have suited influential wealth-accumulators. In essence, they got what they wanted: (1) the furnishing by the government of substantial assets (land) and large amounts of new money that might be gathered in by those who were most skilled in the art of appropriation; (2) a tax program that facilitated wealth accumulation and wealth retention; and (3) the establishment of an ambiance of inflation in which it was possible to pyramid wealth to higher levels.

A few epilogic remarks are required.

In the spring of 1865, with hostilities ended, demand for commodities and goods fell sharply. Thousands of employees who had worked for the war contractors were dismissed and hundreds of businesses were forced to close. Prices fell; the wholesale price index declined from its high of 216 in January 1865 to 173 in April 1866, a drop of 20 percent in fifteen months. Retail prices pursued a similar course. Even though a vigorous economic recovery got underway in 1866 (one which was to last until 1873), wholesale and retail prices continued their downward path; by year-end of 1873 the wholesale index had fallen to 130, accompanied by a somewhat lesser drop in retail prices. By the second quarter of 1879, wholesale prices had declined to a point where they were 12 percent under their prewar level.

The fall in living costs was matched by a decline in gold vis-à-vis the greenback. At the end of the war gold stood at $150 against $100 in greenbacks; by the end of 1866 it declined to 126, and by 1873 to 106. By the end of 1878, when convertibility of paper into coin was reestablished, it was selling at parity with the greenback.

The greenback, again, came into Chase's purview although he was no longer associated with the treasury. Soon after his reelection in 1864, Lincoln—with characteristic forbearance and humaneness—appointed the man who had schemed against him to the office of Chief Justice of the Supreme Court. It was in that position that Chase once again was required to deal with the greenback. In the case of *Hepburn* versus *Griswold,* the Court was asked to rule on the legality of the "legal tender" quality which was imputed to the first issue of greenbacks. Surprisingly, on February 7, 1870, Chase issued an opinion that Congress had had no constitutional right to declare the greenbacks to be "legal tender." He observed that although the notes had been declared "legal tender in the settlement of all debts" in a time of war and great stress, there had been no basis in law for that action. The Chase of 1870, secure in the position of Chief Justice, had reversed the Chase of 1862. A "packed" Supreme Court reversed his opinion several months later.

In 1872, when he was sixty-four, Chase considered making another try at the Presidency. But the partial paralysis which had stricken him grew worse as the year wore on, and he decided he was too ill to make the attempt. He died in May of the following year.

His friend Jay Cooke survived him for thirty-three years, but events proved that he had reached his zenith during his prodigious fund-raising for the treasury during the Civil War. In 1873, having overextended himself in his attempt to finance the building of the Northern Pacific Railroad (the government, by that time, was no longer handing out millions for the construction of carrier systems), he was forced into bankruptcy. He lost all his property, including his mansion (dubbed "Cooke's Castle" by Chase) situated on the 200-acre Ogontz estate near Philadelphia. The castle contained fifty-two rooms most of whose walls were ornamented with frescoes "and reornamented" with many paintings. It contained also a theater, conservatories, a miniature "armory," fountains, and Italian gardens. It had been built—as had several of

Cooke's other properties—from proceeds made in banking, gold speculation, and stock market operations during the Civil War.

The failure of Cooke's financial empire swept away other banks, brokerage houses, and railroads, unleashed a financial panic, and brought on the depression of 1873. But the astute agglomerator rose from his "premature demolition," resurrected the Northern Pacific, and became a multimillionaire once again during the boom that followed. An optimist to the very end, he died in 1905, at the age of eighty-four.

With the long Civil War drama ended and with the leading financial figures having left the scene, the customary process of reassessment took place. Biographers, historiographers, economic historians, and economists who dealt with the inflation of 1861–1865 were finally confronted with the usual questions: What went wrong? Who was responsible?

The writers who believed that history is a bare Baedeker of places, persons, and events, of course, did not address themselves to these questions. Others, seeking the easiest way out, never arrived at definite conclusions or, if they did, found safety in withholding them. Among those who were willing to venture an opinion, the most frequently assigned cause for the onset of the inflation was the emission of greenbacks, with a general agreement expressed that—given the pressing needs of the treasury for immense amounts of money with which to prosecute the war—the creation of greenbacks was inevitable. Once having made this assumption, the great majority of historians and biographers attributed the continuation of the inflation to a series of miscalculations, to "human" errors.

Although some observers* came close to the edge of the precipice, very few took the final leap to assert that the Civil War inflation—regardless of its origin—was calculatedly maintained in its last stage to facilitate the transfer of wealth.

Andrew Johnson, however, had no difficulty in making a blunt assessment. Stripped of his powers during the concluding part of his term, and with nothing to lose by telling the truth, he described

---

*See *The Greenbacks and Resumption of Specie Payments* by Don C. Barrett; also *The Age of Enterprise* by Thomas C. Cochran and William Miller and *The Rise of the American Civilization* by Charles and Mary Beard.

the men in office and in Congress as members "of a government for the benefit of industry" and he characterized the rich who had become "beneficiaries" during the Civil War as "an aristocracy based on nearly two billions and a half of national securities that has arisen to assume political power."

The German Hyperinflation, 1922-1923

In the autumn of 1923, Lotte Hendlich, a German widow in her fifties, returned to her native Frankfurt after an absence of more than four years in Switzerland. In 1919 she had gone to spend a few pleasant weeks in a Swiss village where her relatives lived. But almost immediately, Frau Hendlich broke her hip in a fall. During her long convalescence her chronic cough became worse, and the doctor attending her advised her that she was suffering from advanced tuberculosis. The months and years of her illness dragged on interminably even though her relatives were genuinely solicitous (they insisted on defraying all her expenses, including the fees of the doctor). At last, in September 1923, she was "cured" and considered well enough to return home. Her much longed-for homecoming soon became a nightmare.

In the stack of accumulated mail she found three letters from her bank; they delineated her ruin. The first—written in mid-1920 by a minor bank officer who had befriended her—advised her "to invest most of the funds in your rather substantial bank account" (amounting to over 600,000 marks, or the equivalent of more than $70,000 at the exchange rate prevailing in 1919). "It is my judgment," the writer continued, "that the purchasing power of the mark will decline, and I suggest you try to guard against this through some suitable investment which we can discuss when you come into the bank."

The next letter, dated in September 1922, and signed by another officer said, "It is no longer profitable for us to service such a small account as yours. Will you kindly withdraw your funds at the earliest opportunity?"

The third letter, dated several weeks before her return from Switzerland, announced, "Not having heard from you since our last communication, we have closed out your account. Since we no longer have on hand any small-denomination bank notes, we herein enclose a note for one million marks."

With gathering panic Frau Hendlich looked at the envelope that had contained the letter and the million-mark note. She noticed that affixed to it there was a canceled postage stamp of one million marks. Her bank account—which four years before seemed large enough to provide her with a serene existence to the end of her days—had been utterly consumed by inflation and could no longer pay for an ordinary postage stamp.

The German hyperinflation of the early 1920s that victimized Frau Hendlich and millions of her compatriots must be viewed as the pinnacle of the world's monetary disturbances. In no other era was so prodigious an amount of new money fabricated, were prices driven to such inordinate heights, were so many lives disaffected by economic chaos; in no other interval did inflationary pressures so violently rend the fabric of society. There was an exceptional aspect even in the rationale put forward by the perpetrators of inflation to justify their policies; in previous periods of surging prices the so-called exigency of war had been employed as a cover-up to explain away an inflationary monetary policy, but during the German experience several new covers were devised, notably the exigency supposedly created by onerous reparations and the exigency of constantly threatening Bolshevism.

But the program pursued by the successful agglomerators of the period was manifestly unexceptional. Repeating the devices employed by their counterparts in the past, the appropriators of the early Weimar Republic were able to sweep up immense assets by purchasing them with the torrent of money their government had loosed at their behest. But whereas previous inflationary periods had produced millionaires, the German hyperinflation created billionaires and trillionaires—sometimes overnight. In 1923, when the nation was suffering its worst financial difficulties, the world's first quadrillionaire emerged.

The catastrophe of 1923 had its beginnings in the inflationary fiscal and monetary policies pursued by the German monarchy during World War I. On July 23, 1914, Germany's ally, the Austro-Hungarian Empire, served a forty-eight-hour ultimatum on Serbia, ushering in "the war that was to make the world safe for democracy." During the next week the Reichsbank (the nation's central bank) lost more than 100 million marks of gold coin, its gold reserves decreasing from 1,357 million to 1,253 million, as war jitters set in. On July 31 the Reichsbank—in a breach of its legal obligation—suspended its function to redeem paper marks into gold on demand, even though its gold "cover" still amounted to 43 percent of outstanding paper marks (the statutory requirement set the cover at 33-1/3 percent). On August 4, 1914, three days after Germany had entered the war through a declaration of hostilities against Russia, the Reichstag (the legislative chamber) met in a somber session but summoned the usual, optimistic prediction that the war would be short. Notwithstanding this assurance, it took certain steps which proved that the legislators believed the war would be costly and long. The Reichstag immediately suspended all specie payments and armed the Reichsbank with a new power: the right to issue new bank notes through discounting of short-term treasury bills. Until August 4, 1914, the central bank had been prohibited from including treasury bills in its asset cover for the emission of new money. It had been able, under an old regulation, to include discounted commercial bills in its "cover" for additional print-up, but had refrained from widespread use of this because of its announced "conservative approach in the creation of banking credit and in other monetary matters."

By August 7, three days after the new monetary policies were put into place, the treasury flung out 2 billion marks of new three-month bills. The Reichsbank promptly "bought" most of them and paid them off (after deducting 4 percent in annual interest) with almost 2 billion marks of newly printed bank notes that were dutifully dispatched to the waiting treasury. And the treasury then loosed the new bank notes into the nation's money* stream by paying its debts with them. By year-end of 1914 the amount of outstanding bank notes was pushed to almost 6 billion through the same mechanism, and by the end of the last war year —1918—the total rose to just under 33 billion. In four and a half years the amount of paper circulating medium expanded nine times (from about 3-1/2 billion marks to almost 33 billion).

Short-term indebtedness (mostly in the form of three-month bills) represented but a small portion of the treasury's wartime borrowing. A continuous war-bond selling program was mounted until the accumulated long-term loans escalated to 97 billion marks (during the preceding half-century outstanding indebtedness had amounted, year after year, to less than 5 billion). Almost 80 percent of Germany's total wartime expenditures of 164 billion marks were defrayed by borrowing. Only 31 billion marks were obtained from nondebt revenues, including customs duties, transfer-payments received from the various state (*land*) administrations, and—belatedly—from taxes. Less than 20 billion marks were furnished by taxes—an amount equal to only 12 percent of expenditures. (During the same war Great Britain raised 33 percent through taxes, and, in World War II, tax receipts in the United States amounted to approximately 40 percent of expenditures.)

Germany's meager wartime tax revenue was no accident; predominantly it was the result of a program whose aim was the preservation of wealth of the privileged class, rather than the raising of adequate revenues for the nation.

Many economic historians have attempted to dispose of the subject of inadequate revenues by pointing out that the Reich had entered World War I with severely limited fiscal powers, and with almost no apparatus for collection of taxes. Funds received from

---

*Not all of the three-month bills emitted by the treasury were immediately monetized; some were taken up by the banks, others by financial institutions, and, in a small way, by individuals. Such "taking down" outside the Reichsbank did not immediately result in the printing of money, and in the beginning of the 1914–1923 decade kept the Reichsbank's issue of new bank notes lower than it might have been. But in the worst period of the hyperinflation the percentage of unmonetized bills shrank and finally dried up.

customs duties and from monies contributed by the *land** (state) governments were used by the Reich to defray outlays for national defense, the upkeep of the monarchy, and the bicameral parliament and certain courts. But prior to the war, most of the taxes were gathered—and were used—by the various *land* administrations, which were responsible for carrying out most civilian governmental functions in Germany, but were, of course, subservient to the Crown. With this background it is not surprising—according to usual explanations—to find the Reich hamstrung during the 1914–1918 war years in the area of tax raising and collection. Hence, the lean revenue crop.

This defense of a retrograde tax policy overlooks certain facts. The imperial government under Wilhelm the Second was a semioligarchy, empowered to impose programs virtually by fiat. Although the Reichstag was an elected body, its powers had been rendered largely illusory. All legislation had to be submitted by officials of the various secretariats and departments (Interior, Foreign Affairs, Navy, State, Treasury, Justice, etc.). Each of these departments was headed by a Secretary who had been appointed by the Chancellor who was, himself, the designee of the King. In short, the King, through his administrative surrogates, originated legislation. The Reichstag then deliberated on the legislation and voted on it. Later its enactments were sent to the Federal Council, the upper house, which determined whether the legislation was in keeping with legal precedent and was "administrable." The Federal Council—composed of delegates hand-picked by the King and chaired by his chief representative, the Chancellor—was really an administrative instrumentality of the royal family and of the Junkers (the feudal landed aristocracy and officer corps) who obtained most of the seats. In all important legislative matters the King "proposed," the Reichstag went through the shadow show of deliberation, and the King finally "disposed."

Moreover, during the early part of the war the King's power became even more absolute, since the only truly "opposition" party—the badly splintered Social Democrats—was almost totally ineffectual because its 110 delegates in the Reichstag had

---

*The German Reich consisted of a confederation of laender or states, each of which contained its own administrative structure, although it recognized the undisputed hegemony of the monarchy.

adopted a resolution to suppress its opposition during the duration of hostilities "out of loyalty to the Fatherland."

Endowed with near omnipotence, the government—if it had wished to do so—could have established an effective tax system that could have achieved the high degree of success attained by other emergency "programs" mounted by the monarchy during wartime, such as food rationing, manpower controls in war-oriented industries, mobilization of strategic materials, and the management of industrial and agricultural production. A substantial amount of taxes could have been gathered had there been a will to do so. Actually, there was a will to avoid doing so.

Karl Helfferich, Secretary of Finance—and a steward of the King despite his bourgeois origin—shied away from vigorous taxation that might have inconvenienced persons of wealth. From the beginning he announced that taxation would be unnecessary because the war would be short and because Germany would soon recoup its expenditures through reparations obtained from its defeated enemies. This assurance was repeated in various newspaper interviews and proclaimed before the Reichstag in March of 1915. In addition, Helfferich devised a ploy to show that taxes were unnecessary because the budget was already in balance. His device —a threadbare fabrication—was the essence of simplicity. He excluded all war expenditures from the ordinary budget and placed them in an extraordinary budget with an appended footnote: "to be repaid from reparations at the conclusion of the war." He then applied the small annual income from customs duties, transfer payments received from the *land* administrations and some miscellaneous revenues against the regular expenses, and announced that these funds covered the ordinary budget. The rapidly proliferating war expenditures remained out of sight because eyes were closed to them even though the Reichsbank was issuing rising amounts of bank notes (through the purchase of the treasury's bills) to meet these "obliterated" expenses.

As the war dragged on through 1915—bringing rationing and deprivation to the home front and a stream of wounded men and death notices from the war fronts—pressure rose to impose taxes, especially on the war profiteers. The insistence to "spread the sacrifices equally" mounted to such an extent that the Kaiser suggested privately to Helfferich "that some action might be in order."

But neither the Secretary of the Treasury nor his conservative associates who held seats in the Reichstag were imbued with a sense of urgency. Finally, in June 1916, the first rudimentary tax regulation was put into effect. It levied a "turnover" (value-added) tax at the incredibly low rate of one-tenth of 1 percent. According to Helfferich, most articles manufactured in Germany turned over five times in the process which moved them from raw material to finished goods. The full tax on most items, therefore, came to only one-half of 1 percent. The second tax adopted—the "war profits" tax—was heralded as a formidable levy against war-goods manufacturers, many of whom were important supporters of the King and influential members of the centrist and right-wing political parties. But various "investigations" conducted by postwar commissions revealed that sufficient ambiguity had been created during the drafting of the tax measures to enable the profiteers to pay considerably less than the "intended" share. And so the total tax yield in 1916 remained under 15 percent of expenditures. (After the Weimar Republic was established several committees appeared to labor arduously to determine and recover the debt owed by the profiteers, but except for some token "restitution" by small fry, the attempt ended in a predictable failure.)

Although the 1916 tax legislation contained Helfferich's imprimatur (he had worked on the bill in the early part of the year), he was no longer head of the treasury when it was put into force. On May 22, 1916, he had been promoted to one of the highest offices in the Reich—that of Vice-Chancellor—and simultaneously was made Secretary of State. Among his many duties as Vice-Chancellor was the "overseeing" of the Reichsbank. He was required also to "work in close association with the Treasury Department." He was now, de facto, the controller of the government's fiscal and monetary policies. He was only forty-three, and —barring some stroke of bad luck—could some day become Chancellor of the Reich although, to his regret, he had not a single drop of royal blood in him (he was the son of a well-to-do textile manufacturer).

Judging by the past, he had good cause to be optimistic about the future. In 1903, at the age of thirty-one, he had achieved international fame through the publication of his major economic work, *Das Geld.* Massive in scope, and reflecting the workings of a highly organized mind, it raised Helfferich to a position of preeminence among German economists. Although it offered no new insights, it remained, for years, a standard text in Germany and was translated into many foreign languages and employed as a reference source throughout the world by economists, bankers, governments, and universities.

It is worth noting—despite the inflationary monetary policies Helfferich continued to advocate from 1914 to 1924—that in *Das Geld* his position was that of a "hard money" man. In his publication he maintained that money "not backed by gold" was soon likely to lose its monetary function. In his book he advocated a strict adherence to a gold standard and asserted (and the dictum is particularly illuminating in the light of antithetical statements made by him in the decade between 1914 to 1924) that "the unlimited possibility to create money"* (the power to issue inconvertible paper money) would soon become far too seductive for the State to resist. A large section of the book dealt with the need and the mechanics of establishing an international monetary system backed by a gold standard. But here again he issued a caveat against the seduction of issuing large amounts of money fashioned out of nothing but the desires of the issuing institutions.

Riding a rising wave of plaudits, he became a director and monetary adviser at one of Germany's leading banking institutions, the Deutsche Bank. There he made valuable contacts with various industrialists and the then president of the Reichsbank, Koch, who believed that "Helfferich had one of the most probing minds and the most prodigious memories I have ever encountered." In 1910, and now regarded as one of the Reich's most eminent authorities on monetary affairs, he was selected, with the Kaiser's approval, to serve on the Central Committee of the Reichsbank. During his four years at the central bank he created a favorable impression with the Kaiser and was finally elevated to the post of Secretary of the Treasury. In that position his value to the monarchy—especially his raising of almost 100 billion marks in the various war-bond campaigns—won him new commenda-

---

*In *Das Geld* Helfferich's exact words were: "Even to the State, itself, the unrestricted possibility of making money out of nothing is too tempting for us to feel that there would be no misuse of the power for fiscal purposes . . . an economic system based on an irredeemable paper currency appears like an acute malady which ends in the complete depreciation of the paper currency or in its redemption at a small fraction of its original value."

tions. His appointment to the vice-chancellorship surprised no one; it was a reward for valuable services rendered.

And so, in mid-1916, the next rung on the ladder seemed easily within reach; it was only a matter of time. But things went awry for Helfferich, for the monarchy, and for the German Reich.

In 1917 the financial situation became more onerous as military outlays climbed and the cost of conducting the ordinary affairs of government ballooned. Massive expenditures were required for the purchase of grains and bread to feed a population systematically starved by the Allied blockade. With the need for additional revenues mounting and dissatisfaction spreading on the war-weary home front despite the temporary successes on the battlefield, the pressure for further increases in taxes proliferated. For a while Helfferich tried to mute these demands by insisting that "the ordinary budget continues in balance." Finally the turnover tax was raised, as was the rarely collected tax on the so-called war profiteering. But by far the greatest boost in revenues came from the imposition of certain heavy excise taxes, the most important being a levy on coal used in homes and in public transportation —neither of which fell heavily on the rich.

The new regulations did raise revenues (from a low of 2.4 billion marks in 1914 to 7.8 billion in 1917). But the failure to impose and collect comprehensive inheritance, income, capital-gains, and corporate taxes kept receipts considerably below the swollen expenditures. As a result, annual deficits mounted. New efforts to push the war-bond sales were exerted. But these—like the insufficient taxes—did not close the budget gap. Then the government resorted to the speeding up of its engraving presses (the usual procedure was followed: the treasury issued debt in the form of three-month bills, most of which the Reichsbank purchased with freshly printed marks). In the single year of 1918 the volume of paper marks rose by almost 15 billion, an amount nearly five times the total that had been accumulated during Germany's long history before World War I. In addition, commercial bank deposits—stimulated by the multiplier effect of the newly created paper marks—rose from a prewar level of just under 5 billion marks to over 19 billion at the end of 1918. The high-powered money supply (currency* and demand deposits) rose from 8.5 billion to 52 billion

*No reliable figures exist for coins in circulation.

marks or more than six times within a period of four and a half years. The swelling of the money stock had its inevitable consequence: inflation.

By the end of 1918, the wholesale price index stood at two and a half times its 1913 level. No official cost-of-living price index was published in Germany during the war; it is therefore not possible to determine with reasonable accuracy the size of the inflation at the consumer level. But there is no question that the two-and-a-half-fold rise reported in wholesale prices deeply understated the true increase. It reflected "official" prices, rather than those that prevailed on the black market for basic commodities "controlled" by the government. According to published reports, many so-called controlled items actually sold far above their "regulated" levels. Whether the rise in prices amounted to 150 percent, as official sources claimed, or 300 percent, as many contemporary observers insisted, is uncertain. It is certain, however, that the later hyperinflation had its beginnings during the war years.

The emission of the first 2 billion marks by the Reichsbank during August 1914 may have been required to meet the initial costs of mobilization, but the steady stream of subsequent wartime print-ups—and the accompanying inflation—could have been avoided through appropriate taxation.

But, increasingly during 1917 and 1918 taxation, monetary difficulties and even the proliferating inflation became secondary to the more vexing problems of impending military defeat and political instability. The Russian Revolution of March 1917 had a destabilizing effect on Germany. It emboldened the more radical factions among the Social Democrats—the left-leaning Independent Socialists and the revolutionary Spartacists—to demand a negotiated end to the war, a greater role in government for the proletariat, and universal suffrage. The leaders of the Majority Social Democratic wing—gradualist in viewpoint and supported by most of the 2.5 million members of the "Free Trade Union" —were pushed, almost against their will, into proclaiming slogans for "bread and universal suffrage."

After news of the events in Russia reached Germany, a few red flags (clandestinely hung) appeared in Berlin. In April, at the instigation of the Independent Socialists and Spartacists, the first massive wartime strike by 200,000 workers (who demanded cancellation of a recent order that would have further reduced their starvation-level rations) was held. Threatened by the successful demonstration put on by their rivals, the Majority Social Democrats arose in the Reichstag and cautiously called for an end to annexationist demands and "enough bread for all," and they pushed their program for political reform, especially in Prussia, the most reactionary of the laender. Members of the Conservative and National Liberal parties—the spearhead of reaction, and closely tied to the German Supreme Command—charged all Social Democrats with being "wartime traitors and agents of murderous Marxism."

In the midst of the turmoil—and just weeks after the overthrow of the Russian monarchy—the United States reluctantly renounced its neutrality and entered the war. With this development and with the Allies beginning to score some notable military successes, the moderate elements in the Reichstag were encouraged to launch the "peace resolution of 1917." Actually this modest proposal (introduced by Matthias Erzberger, a representative of the moderate Center [Catholic] party), was not a call for cessation of hostilities; rather it was a plea for the renunciation of revanchist aims by all the belligerents at "such a time when the war would be brought to a close."

Ludendorff*—who had conferred the title of First Quartermaster General upon himself—raced furiously to Berlin and insisted that the Kaiser put an end to the treachery, demanding that the courtly and gentle Chancellor—Bethmann–Hollweg—should crush the "plot" or be forced to quit. For a while the Chancellor held out, but finally caved in when Ludendorff threatened to "quit the field and leave the Army in the lurch"; finally, Bethmann–Hollweg resigned. Michaelis, a hack hand-picked by Ludendorff, took over and tried to stem the growing tide in favor of the "hateful peace resolution." But he proved too weak; a coalition of the Social Democrats, the Center Party, and the Progressives pushed it through the Reichstag, by a vote of 212 to 126. The first real exercise in democracy had taken place in Germany; time would prove it heralded the end of the monarchy.

---

*Ludendorff was a man constantly consumed by an insatiable ambition. Crafty, ruthless, and imperious in manner, he never attained the popularity enjoyed by his rival, Hindenburg. But, by sheer force and the charisma born of battle successes, he was able to elbow his way, during the war, to the forefront of the political arena.

Michaelis did not last long. In September 1917, two ringleaders of a mutiny conducted at Kiel by a group of disgruntled sailors were sentenced to death. The Independent Social Democratic delegates to the Reichstag accused the government of silencing loyal citizens who dared express unpopular views. The coalition of Social Democrats, Center members, and Progressives once again acted in concert and pressed the King to replace Michaelis who —in their view—was only playing into the hands of the radicals in the Kiel matter. Their line of reasoning moved the usually vacillating monarch into taking a rarely invoked position against Ludendorff; he dismissed Michaelis. On October 26, 1917, the entire staff of the Chancellor was turned out of office, including Helfferich. Although Helfferich's name was included for consideration by Wilhelm as a Vice-Chancellor, under the new Chancellor (Hertling), it was rejected by the "coalition" because of his increasingly reactionary views, his growing imperious manner toward other members of the government, and because he had alienated large segments of the Social Democrats. (He frequently turned his back on the Socialist section while he excoriated them in his appearances at the Reichstag as Secretary of State and Vice-Chancellor, on one occasion announcing that "I will not address representatives of traitorous Marxism.")

Helfferich's career in the chancellory had lasted only seventeen months; it had begun on such high hopes and ended in failure and a seething and bitter anger. The fallen Vice-Chancellor blamed everything on the "Marxist traitors and their willing associates, the Socialist Democrats."

He found additional cause to rail at his "enemies" in January 1918, when 1 million munitions workers in various cities went into the streets and clamored for an end to the war and its accompanying deprivations. The mobilization had been directed by the Independent Socialists who had organized the workers and shop stewards into councils. Dragged in against their will, the middle-of-the-road Majority Social Democrats—following the counsel of their leader, Ebert—sabotaged the strike by bringing it to a premature end, lest their adversaries, the leftists, should accrue power from a successful demonstration.

As time went on the program and political acts of the Majority Social Democratic leaders were increasingly motivated by the effect they would have in their rivalry with their leftist and Communist counterparts, and they came to regard their adversaries as a much greater threat than the enemy they had for a long time invoked in their propaganda, namely, the capitalists, the Junkers, and the ruling members of the monarchy. And, as they moved increasingly against the Marxists and Bolsheviks, the more willing were the capitalists in and out of Germany to regard them as a suspect but effective bulwark against the supreme threat: the establishment of a Communist Germany.

By the summer of 1918 the specter of defeat hovered over the broken German lines. Both Hindenburg and Ludendorff recognized the end was near but refused to surrender their spent and suffering armies (a half-million Germans were killed in battle during 1918), in the hope that they could work out a suitable deal for themselves. But no deals were in the offing for them or the royal family.

Woodrow Wilson on several previous occasions let it be known that no peace treaty could be entered into if the monarchy were to survive. On October 23, he issued a note that sealed the doom of the High Command and the Kaiser. It read, "If it [the government of the United States] must deal with the military masters and the monarchical autocrats of Germany now or if it is likely to have to deal with them later on in regard to the international obligations of the German Empire, it must demand, not peace negotiations, but surrender."

Wilson's note hastened the disintegration of the monarchy. During the autumn of 1918 and the first two weeks of November events tumbled over one another with a speed that defied perception. Cabinets fell; private notes about the impending armistice conference flew back and forth between German and Allied officials; Ludendorff and Hindenburg resigned (the latter's retirement was not accepted because it was thought he could exert a "symbolic stabilizing effect" on the seething nation); the Majority Social Democrats were invited into a coalition government (and thereupon the Independent Socialists and Spartacists left the party, denouncing "revolution from above" and advocating setting up a workers' republic); a number of democratic enactments were pounded through the Reichstag, over the rabid opposition of rightist delegates (and much to the chagrin of Helfferich, whose expression of opposition appeared in the reactionary press). And the Reichstag, having "achieved the foundations of democracy," quixotically suspended itself at the time when it was needed most. To escape the mounting turmoil of Berlin, the Kaiser—refusing to abdicate—sequestered himself, on October 29, at Spa with his coterie and waited for a miracle.

None came, but on the following day there was a mutiny at Wilhelmshaven when sailors refused to participate in a last-minute suicidal attack against a vastly superior British fleet. The revolt spread to other ports, and, by November 4, newly formed navy "councils" and "soviets" had hoisted a red flag on every vessel. Neither the use of the word "soviet" nor the red flags were indications of a desire for revolution, as later events showed; they were merely symbols of dissatisfaction, but at the moment their use was ominous. Workers joined the mutinous sailors. The Majority Social Democrats, fearing the situation was getting out of control, threatened to leave the government coalition unless the Kaiser immediately resigned. At this juncture the Spartacists urged a massive uprising on November 9. Ebert, fearing an immediate Communist putsch, organized a counter-demonstration "which would last until the Kaiser left."

At the height of the Ebert-led mobilization Prince Max of Baden, who had been acting for Wilhelm while the latter remained at Spa, announced the Kaiser had abdicated. He also proclaimed a provisional government headed by Ebert (as Chancellor) which would remain in power until general elections were held and a constituent assembly was convened. The milling crowds that overflowed Berlin's main squares roared approval.

But the threat of revolution by a newly risen Communist movement still hung over Germany. In response to a growing pressure from the centrist Social Democrats and in effort to thwart the fomentations of the radicals, the German representatives signed a long-delayed and draconian surrender on November 11, 1918.

A new but equally troubled era for the nation had begun, in which military matters would be secondary and in which monetary affairs would become paramount.

In the immediate postwar period, with Germany's fiscal policy even more inflation-inducing than during the war, expenses (notably for relief, war pensions, and reconstruction) soared far ahead of the limited revenues. During the 1919 fiscal year (April 30, 1919, to March 31, 1920) revenues were equal to only 30 percent of expenses, whereas during the war—with heavy sales of war bonds raising the government's income—they had equaled 80 percent of expenditures.

But the sale of long-term debt was not undertaken by the treasury after the Armistice (virtually no bond-offerings were made throughout the whole postwar hyperinflationary period until some time in 1924) despite the Reichsbank's very comfortable gold position in 1919. As a result of an intensive "patriotic" campaign to gather up the Reich's gold supply in wartime, the central bank, at the beginning of 1919, held 2.25 billion marks in gold. This should have encouraged investors to purchase long-term government issues, especially if the interest had been made payable in gold. Moreover, though most of the population was worse off at the end of hostilities, the middle class had expanded and the rich —protected by a tax policy that favored them—had become wealthier. A considerable store of money had been accumulated in banks; the total of deposits in commercial and savings banks had almost quadrupled from the end of 1913 to the end of 1919, rising from about 29 billion to just under 120 billion marks, an amount equal to almost 1,850 marks per capita, or more than four times the per capita money supply (in dollars) in the United States in the same year (1919). The per capita money stock of Germany at the time was far higher than that of the North during the American Civil War and represented a pool from which the government could have attempted to draw funds via attractive bond offerings. But no Teutonic counterpart to a Jay Cooke—nor even an S. P. Chase—mounted a campaign to sell the nation's debt issue. Even Erzberger—who was appointed Finance Minister in June 1919 and was regarded as "fiscally tough"—made little effort to sell long-term obligations.

Having failed to provide for adequate revenues from taxes and long-term debt, the government financed the deficit—as it had during the "war emergency"—by having the Reichsbank print new marks for the flood of fresh treasury bills it discounted. Almost 18 billion new marks were created in fiscal 1919 to help bridge the gap between meager revenues and swollen outlays, bringing the total number of marks outstanding to almost 51 billion. Again the predictable occurred: by the end of 1919 the wholesale price index climbed to over eight times its prewar base. It more than tripled during 1919 (from a 2.5 level at the end of 1918), as prices were driven up by the surging supply of money and as controls were lifted from many items. The 1919 experience represents one of those infrequent anomalies in which high prices and low industrial activity go hand in hand.

The accelerating inflation of 1919 (which touched off numerous demonstrations and essentially futile attempts at revolution) was discussed at the time by the then vice-president of the Reichsbank as follows: "The real causes for the increasing amount of notes [marks] issued are the hoarding of money and to speculation abroad." In other words, the printing of a large amount of new money (and the resulting inflation) was required because there was an actual shortage of marks brought about through hoarding and exporting funds abroad for speculation. This canard—the supposed shortage of money while the nation was choked with money —was to be repeated intermittently throughout the hyperinflation by the Reichsbank.

New revenue acts were passed in 1919; as a result, marks received in tax payments rose considerably, but that benefit was negated by the soaring expenses incurred by government (the substantial rise in government outlays in 1920 was predominantly attributable to inflation). Nevertheless the new tax laws did raise revenues to 33 percent of expenditures (against 30 percent in the previous year).

But the government's deficit—a whopping 67 percent of expenses—required more financing. Again no long-term debt was raised, and again the mechanism of having the Reichsbank issue fresh money after discounting new treasury bills occurred. As a result the amount of marks circulating at the end of the 1920 fiscal year increased to 81 billion, a jump of about 30 billion in the year (the increase was about equal to the total increase experienced in all the war years). Prices, naturally, followed the path of money up the mountain, rising to 14.4 (in the wholesale price index). In the two years since the end of the war prices had almost sextupled. In the international money market the mark had depreciated even more precipitously. Whereas 4.2 marks could purchase $1.00 before the war, 70 marks were needed at the end of 1920.

In the fiscal year between April 1, 1921, and March 31, 1922, the collapse of the mark in foreign exchange markets and its disintegration as an effective store of value in domestic dealings were greatly accelerated by a new phenomenon: the payment of cash reparations.

The peace treaty signed at Versailles in June 1919 charged Germany with sole responsibility for the war and stripped the Reich of an enormous amount of wealth and productive means. In part payment for damages sustained, it extracted vast, rich territories from Germany, notably Alsace-Lorraine, Posen, Upper Silesia, much of western Prussia, and most overseas colonies. The loss (exclusive of overseas colonies) amounted to almost 15 percent of Germany's arable land, 75 percent of its iron ore, 68 percent of its zinc, and 28 percent of its coal deposits. The loss of Alsatian potash deposits to France had a disruptive influence on the Reich's chemical industry; the loss of important coal and other mineral deposits in Upper Silesia had an initially disturbing effect on German steel production and the loss of Alsatian textile plants to its chief competitor severely affected one of the nation's chief exports: textiles.

The treaty also stripped Germany of much of its commercial and fishing fleets, a considerable portion of the rolling stock of its railways, the entire railroad system in Alsace-Lorraine, and all material and properties left behind in the ceded areas (the German government was ordered to recompense the German owners of properties that had been expropriated). In addition to these deprivations, the treaty laid down certain terms which seriously affected German exports but forced the Reich to extend "most favored nations" treatment to the exports (imports into Germany) from its former enemies.

All of these stipulations had a profound economic effect on Germany, disrupting its output and exports and initially causing severe unemployment.

But there were other punitive stipulations. The full extent of the reparations (both in cash and in kind) that Germany would eventually be forced to pay to its victors would not be announced until May 1, 1921. In the meantime the Reich was to post a bond of 100 billion "gold" marks, the first 20 billion of which was to be redeemed through payments in kind at a date not later than May 1, 1921. Details on the method of liquidating the remaining 80 billion portion of the posted bond would be outlined at some future date.

Members of the German government reacted with shock and anger when the enormous "bill of reparations" was handed to them. The press and the government maintained that the contem-

plated extraction of over 100 billion gold marks would bankrupt
the nation. It would create chaos; it would create the worst of all
fates: revolution by the left. The most onerous aspect of the demands—apart from their size—was the insistence that cash reparations be made in "gold" marks. The Allies stipulated—quite
understandably—that Germany could not deliver depreciating
paper marks to meet cash reparations, but could pay them in gold
or in the currency of the country to which the payment was due.

This meant that Germany would need to enter the international
exchange market and with its constantly depreciating marks buy
the appropriate foreign currency needed for delivery. The lower
the mark sank in international markets, the greater would be the
amount of marks required. This mechanism would touch off an
additional need for the printing of new marks which, in turn,
would lower the international market price of marks, and so forth.

The cash reparation payments would prove to be highly inflation-provoking in the fiscal year 1921 (April 31, 1921, to March 30,
1922) and the first part of the succeeding fiscal year. On April 27,
1921, the Reparations Commission (before which Germany intermittently appeared in the role of testifying prisoner) finally handed
down its verdict. The full bill would amount to 132 billion gold
marks, most of which was payable in kind. Two billion gold marks
per year would be required in cash payments in each subsequent
year, with 1 billion in cash payment due by the end of December
31, 1921.

Germans fulminated at the reparation terms. Riots broke out
in major cities. Angry street-corner orators pointed out that 132
billion gold marks (at the ongoing foreign exchange rate) was
equal to one-half the total prewar estimated wealth of Germany,
and Maynard Keynes in his blistering book *Economic Consequences of the Peace* castigated the Allies for their greed and
stupidity, forecasting that the Weimar Republic would soon be
forced into suspending reparation payments. But despite all protests the Allies stood their ground and part of their armies still
stood on German soil to "police the peace" and to insure reparations. The Germans had no choice but to meet the draconian
demands.

The first cash installment was made before the end of May 1921
and the final 1921 payment was made before the close of the year.
These payments came at a time when the full benefits of Erz-

berger's tax reforms were being felt. Had there been no reparations expenses during the 1921 year, later government statistics revealed, the tax revenues would have covered almost all other expenditures. But the demands created by cash reparation payments pressed against the beleaguered government.

Again the printing presses were turned on by the Reichsbank. The total of outstanding paper marks which had amounted to 81 billion on January 1, 1921, and had remained virtually unchanged until May 1921 (the first month of cash reparation payments), finally ended the calendar year at 122.5 billion. The rise of more than 41 billion in the year was largely brought on through the issuance of paper marks that were then converted into foreign exchange for reparations. The wholesale price index immediately reflected the surge in money supply: having actually declined to 13.7 by June 30, 1921 (from 14.5 in December 31, 1920), it shot up by more than 21 points in the next six months of heavy reparations payments, to 34.9 by December 31, 1921. The average German citizen keenly felt the inflationary hurt brought on by reparations. Having been squeezed by rising prices that had reached, in mid-1921, a level fourteen times their prewar base, he was forced to pay prices thirty-five times their prewar level by the end of the year.

Reparations exercised the expectable, devastating effect on the exchange value of the mark. In May 1921, before cash reparations began, the mark stood at about 70 to the dollar, but by year's end it sank to a level of 174 to the dollar (it was then worth 1/43 its prewar price in relation to the dollar).

In 1922 the destabilizing effect—both monetary and political—of reparations became more evident. In January of that year a conference was held at Cannes in which the German government presented its case for the postponement of reparations. But the middle of the meeting witnessed the fall of the more liberal Briand government and the elevation of the vindictive Poincaré to the French premiership. The Reparations Commission, now stiffened against any break in the German payments, required installments of 31 million marks in cash every ten days (under further German pressure and the behind-the-scenes maneuvering of the United States the amount was reduced later in the year to 60 million gold marks monthly in cash and payments each month in kind having a value of 120 million gold marks).

Until July 1922 the government continued its installments and then—seeing prices skyrocket and the exchange value of its monetary unit evaporate—stopped all cash payments, protesting that it could not go on without incurring a complete financial and social collapse.

During the first seven months of the calendar year of 1922, revenues from taxes remained high and again almost covered nonreparation expenditures, but the stiff reparation cash disbursements once more induced a deficit which the treasury met in its usual fashion, and the volume of paper marks issued by the obliging Reichsbank soared to a new high. From a level of 122.5 billion on January 1, 1922, the total number of marks outstanding streaked to 202.6 billion, by the end of July, an increase of over 80 billion in just seven months. The glut of paper marks reflected itself on the foreign exchange market: from a price of 174 to the dollar on January 1, 1922, the mark sank to a quoted price of 770 to the dollar (having been worth 20-odd cents before the war, it had an exchange value of only 1/35 of 1 cent in July 1922).

Although foreign exchange fluctuations were of vital concern to speculators, businessmen, and the government, they had no recognizable significance for the average German. But the sweep of inflation had an unmistakable impact. During the seven-month period (January through July 1922), the wholesale price index leaped from 34.9 to 100.6.

In the hot, sullen summer of 1922, Berliners were paying prices that were 100 times as high as those prevailing before the outbreak of war in the comparatively carefree summer of 1914.

A pair of shoes that could have been bought for 10 marks in 1914 was now priced at 1,000 marks. A pumpernickel loaf, priced at 40 pfennigs (four-tenths of 1 mark) in prewar days now sold at 30 marks. A coarse shirt that would have found few buyers in 1914 at 3 marks would—in the summer of 1922—disappear the moment a weary salesgirl displayed it in a store window, despite its price tag of 500 marks. It would be snapped up because the buyer wanted to get rid of his ever-cheapening money and because he knew that next week he could find someone willing to pay 600 marks. The second buyer, like the first, would not need the shirt; he—like everyone else in the population—was merely getting rid of his depreciating money and was putting it into anything that retained its value. The race to dispose of money and to put it into *Sachwerte* ("things that retained their value") became a way of life; in fact, it became a major portion of life by mid-1922.

The powerful industrialists, of course, had understood the necessity of putting cheap money into *Sachwerte* before 1922. From 1920 on, with money they borrowed from banks and other financial institutions (money that had been ostensibly fabricated to finance the deficits of the government), they systematically built up their plants. And as the process of inflation swelled their profits, they repaid their debts with the great quantity of cheap marks they took in. "It was absolutely necessary to have a large debt," Minoux (one of the major agglomerators of the period) once said. "You borrowed 100 million marks in a year when your profit was only 40 million. You then spent your borrowings on building up your plants. Two years later—with the mark down to 1/50 of its worth from the time you borrowed, and your profits up to 2 billion marks—you could repay your whole debt of 100 million with only 1/20 of your bigger profits. By that time the worth of your plants that had cost you 100 million (but which really did not cost you anything since you used other people's money to build) were now worth over 5 billion marks. Really, you did not have to be clever in those [1920–1923] days to make a fortune; all you had to do is borrow and put the money into solid things."

What Minoux did not add, however, was that in order to borrow one had to be considered "creditworthy," and that the banks extended their swollen deposits and bank notes almost entirely to a small group of entrepreneurs—for the most part the officers and directors of the cartels who frequently owned or controlled the banks themselves.

The piling up of *Sachwerte*—plant and equipment—by German industry during the hyperinflation of 1922–1923 through the use of depreciating money is illuminatingly revealed in Pearl S. Buck's *How It Happens,* a collection of conversations with Germans who lived through the 1922–1923 hyperinflation. The following is excerpted from one of the statements made to the author by a person who was interviewed:

We were deceived. . . . We used to say all Germany is suffering from inflation. It was not true. There is no game in the whole world in which everyone loses. Someone has to be the winner. The winners in our

inflation were the big-businessmen in the cities . . . and in the Green Belt
. . . the Junkers. The great losers were the working class and above all
the middle class, who had the most to lose. . . . You see the great winner
in inflation—big business. When inflation ended big business had not
only recovered its industry but had modernized it tremendously. The
bourgeois press called it "the miracle of German industry" which had,
despite war and inflation, recovered and reorganized completely, thus
enabling Germany to face competition on the world markets. Sounds
beautiful, doesn't it? The opposite however was true, for German industry did not recover despite inflation, but by means of inflation.

And while industry was piling up assets, the losers—the rentiers
and other members of the middle class—were being pauperized as
they had been during previous hyperinflationary episodes. The
hundreds of Lotte Hendlichs who had squirreled away a modest
fortune from which they had hoped to secure an income of 2,000
or 3,000 marks a year, and a genteel existence, were already
ruined. Like their French counterparts during the early 1790s, the
pensioners, the aged, and anyone living on a fixed income gradually sold the few *Sachwerte* they still owned and applied for the
woefully inadequate public assistance (which could not keep up
with leaping prices) or slipped into the final, death-producing
malnutrition.

But the winners were not greatly disturbed by the hard fate of
the losers. In mid-1922, Hugo Stinnes, arch agglomerator of the
period (who, by using borrowed funds, had amassed more industrial, banking, and mining companies than any other individual in
recorded history), printed a public appeal in one of his newspapers
for the issuance of additional marks by the Reichsbank—at a time
when the German economy was already awash in a high tide of
money and the exigency of cash reparations no longer existed (the
cash payments having been suspended). Stinnes's newspaper exhorted, "There is a shortage of money. We must have additional
money to maintain industry and order."

At the same time (in June 1922), the government was informing
the "losers" that inflation had been forced on Germany after the
war largely by the Allies through the odious reparations. According to this theory reparations had caused a deficit in the balance
of payments and, hence, a fall in the value of the mark on exchange markets. This set off a decline in the purchasing power of

the mark within Germany, leading to higher prices and the need to print more money by a government beset by higher expenses.

The government's Office of Central Statistics stated, "The fundamental cause of the dislocation of the German monetary system is the disequilibrium of the balance of payments. The disturbance of the national finances and the inflation are in their turn the consequences of the depreciation of the currency. The depreciation of the currency upset the budget balance, and determined with an inevitable necessity a divergence between income and expenditure." And Helfferich (whose counsel greatly influenced the conduct of the Reichsbank although he no longer held any administrative office in the government after 1918) echoed the same theory.

Not inflation, but the depreciation of the mark [on the foreign exchange market] was the beginning of this chain of cause and effect; inflation is not the cause of the increases of prices . . . but the depreciation of the mark [on the exchange market] is the cause of the increases in prices and of the paper mark issues. The problem of restoring the circulation [the problem of restoring the purchasing power of the mark in domestic markets] is not a technical or banking problem; it is in the last analysis the problem of the equilibrium between the burden and the capacity of the German economy to support this burden [the burden of reparations and the negative balance of payments].

Of course, Helfferich knew better; he was merely acting out the usual duplicitous role assigned to or adopted by men of influence during an inflationary era. One need only to remember his caveats (in the first edition of his *Das Geld*) against vesting any government with the power to create limitless amounts of paper money and recall his predictions that such power will inevitably lead to overissuing of money to the point where the purchasing power of the money will become dangerously eroded. He knew the disastrous effects of swollen money supplies, but obviously he had chosen to "forget" what he knew.

But his views—which at all times (1919–1923) minimized the effect of the immense money fabrication—were heralded by the industrialists and those who spoke for them, namely, most economists, government officials, and much of the press. Klockner, head of a major manufacturing conglomerate, insisted that it was necessary "to have much greater amounts of money available so that the mark would remain cheap and so that Germany could continue to export cheaper-priced goods . . . but if there were a shortage of marks, the consequence would be a disaster of considerable magnitude." One of his associates added, "An appreciable and unforeseen improvement in the mark would paralyze the export trades and provoke vast unemployment." He then referred darkly to the "threatening Marxist Armageddon."

In August—fearful that the chorus of voices advocating the profuse emission of marks might die down—Stinnes published the contents of a hitherto little-noticed remark he had made in June about "the lack of necessity for a foreign loan which would raise the exchange rate of the mark to a level the German economy could not endure."

And so more money was manufactured by the Reichsbank. From 202.6 billion at the end of July 1922, the amount of outstanding marks more than doubled within the next three months, shooting up to 484.7 billion by the end of October. The cost of living followed dizzily upward, reaching 566 times the prewar level (as measured by the wholesale index).

But still the cry for more money continued. Julius Wolff, eminent professor of economics, assured everyone: "In proportion to the need, less money circulates now in Germany than before the war. This statement may cause surprise, but it is correct." Elster —during this period and later in his book *From the Mark to the Reichsmark*—asserted, "However enormous may be the apparent rise in circulation in 1922, actually the figures show a decline [the decline in the exchange value of the total paper marks outstanding]."

Most establishment economists in Germany continued to insist during 1922 and 1923 that—in terms of their aggregate value in "gold" marks—the vast volume of paper money was not "excessive" and that "there was no true inflation." Occasionally, an "opposition" economist, in a burst of excoriating revelation, would dissent. One of these was Georg Bernhard. Referring to Stinnes as "that archetypal beast of prey," he stated:

He [Stinnes] has created intrigues against every Government which he feared would put in order the internal conditions of Germany. Every time any problem . . . was considered—whether it was the question of reparations or that of German finances—he has always raised his voice and declared that the premises necessary for solution of that problem did not exist. . . . The classes on which he exercised a great influence opposed in a most violent manner all attempts to reconstruct the [national] finances and restore the currency. . . . By means of credits [loans] amounting to billions, whose [repayment] value was constantly reduced by inflation, he bought one firm after another . . . he appropriated banks, financed shipping firms, acquired participations abroad and controlled numerous commercial enterprises. And all this he coordinated with the system of his politics, which aimed at the maintenance of inflation and disorder.

But such transitory opposition was easily overwhelmed by pronouncements of the government and the majority of the press, which in November backed the industrialists' latest exhortations for a still more accommodative stance by the Reichsbank (at that time Stinnes released a statement that "there is neither money nor goods"). As he was making the allegation the supply of marks in Germany exceeded, by far, the combined money supplies of all the capitalist nations that had fought against Germany in World War I.

Nevertheless, the Reichsbank again responded to the demands of men at the center of power. In the last two months of 1922 about three-quarters of a trillion additional marks roared into the swollen money stream, raising the total to 1,295 billion by year-end. In mad pursuit the wholesale index galloped to 1,475 times the prewar level. The sullen women and men who lined up before the food and department stores were now obliged to carry their money in knapsacks, cartons, and valises; their wallets and purses were too small to contain the hundreds of thousands of marks required as payment for everyday items.

The gaunt Germans queuing up for the astronomically priced merchandise would ask one another, "When will it all end?" Little did they know that it was only the beginning, for the Reichsbank —despite all its obfuscating assurances—had embarked on a new and disastrous program: the creation of money through the discounting of commercial bills.

Having refrained, for years, from using commercial bills as an asset "cover" for the fabrication of new marks because of a professed "conservative approach in the creation of bank-

ing credit and in other monetary matters," the central bank—
in midsummer of 1922—reversed itself and opened the flood-
gates.

In July 1922, the Reichsbank suddenly announced that "in
order to meet the growing needs of commerce and industry which
find the existing store of marks inadequate," it would "resume the
discounting of commercial instruments of credit presented by
banks and "creditworthy businessmen."

This meant that the following chain of events could take place:
any major business firm considered creditworthy could borrow a
large sum of money from a commercial bank by issuing a debt
instrument; the bank would then turn over to the Reichsbank the
commercial bill that had been executed and would, in return,
receive from the central bank the full amount of the commercial
bill (less a small discount) in the form of newly engraved marks.
The creditworthy firm could also borrow directly from the Reichsbank by issuing a commercial bill which the central bank would
discount and for which it emitted new marks. As in the case of
treasury bills, the creation of new money against commercial bills
was limited only by the judgment of the directors of the Reichsbank and the speed of the printing presses.

Over 417 billion new marks were slung into the already bulging
money stock during the last five months in 1922 (after cash reparations had been terminated) via the discounting of commercial
bills. These hordes of new marks were created for the sole use of
the large German industrialists and other capitalists in the concluding months of 1922 even though the commercial banks bulged
with close to 500 billion marks on deposit in August of 1922 and
ended the year with over 2 trillion 200 billion. The accommodation of the central bank was openly proclaimed in July of 1922,
when its directors promised "to make credit available for production and trade at low-interest rates."

The accommodation of the Reichsbank is clearly visible in the
ridiculously low discount rate it maintained on discounted commercial bills. In July 1922, when commercial banks were already
charging 50 percent in interest to small private and commercial
borrowers, the "creditworthy" large borrowers were charged only
5 percent by the central bank on the commercial bills they issued.
In August the central bank discount rate was apologetically raised
to 7 percent, in September to 8 percent (while the commercial

banks were already charging 75 percent), in November to 10 percent, in January 1923, to 12 percent, and in April 1923, to 18
percent. But by that time small borrowers were already paying 300
percent. In all aspects the Reichsbank pursued a thinly disguised
program to deliver—at low cost—the means (billions of marks) by
which Germany's chief agglomerators could buy up or erect additional productive assets. In *The Economics of Inflation* (the semi-
nal work on the German hyperinflation) Constantino Bresciani-
Turroni, the eminent Italian economist, described the
"accommodative" attitude of the Reichsbank during the summer
of 1922 in the following terms:

In Reichsbank circles it was denied that a rise in the discount rate would
exercise a depressing influence on the inflation, and on prices. . . . Rather
than raise the discount rate (on commercial bills) it was thought more
appropriate to apply a certain rationing of credits, only the more deserv-
ing being allowed to benefit therefrom. But such a method favored a
privileged class, to whom the Reichsbank presented enormous sums of
money, to the detriment of classes to whom the depreciation of the mark
was disadvantageous. People who enjoyed the favor of the Reichsbank
could make sure of purchasing goods and foreign exchange. Speculation
against the mark was in such ways financed by bank credits. The credit
policy adopted by the Reichsbank reinforced the effects of the governmental inflation and helped accelerate the fall of the mark, which indeed
had never been so rapid as it became after the Summer of 1922.

During the five-month period in 1922 after cash reparations were
suspended (August through December 1922), more than a trillion
new marks were fabricated. More than 400 billion came into being
through discounted commercial bills, and the remainder of about
600 billion were emitted through the discounting of treasury bills.
A substantial part of the latter—probably somewhere between 400
billion and 500 billion—erupted to meet government deficits, and
close to 200 billion were manufactured for the benefit of capitalists
through additional discounting of treasury bills. (The increasingly
confused record-keeping by the government involving paper-mark
expenditure and receipts makes it impossible to arrive at completely accurate budgetary statistics.) While the creation of 400 to
500 billion for government deficits can be at least partially con-
doned, not even an iota of excuse can be found for the emission
of over a half-trillion new marks for the benefit of capitalists.

The half-trillion exceeds by more than three times the 135 billion new marks created during the cash reparations period. Nevertheless, long after cash payments stopped, establishment economists in Germany and elsewhere continued to blame cash reparations as the chief cause for the country's hyperinflation. They were not dissuaded by the statistics of the ballooning money supply after July 1922, or the fact that the wholesale cost of living had advanced only from 13 to 100 during the cash reparation period (an 87-point gain), whereas the index had shot up by 1,375 points during the final five months of 1922 (surging from 100 to 1,475 times the prewar figure).

The continued invoking of cash reparations for the enveloping superinflation was a smokescreen used to obscure the highly successful, wealth-gathering activities of the already superrich industrialists. In the second half of 1922 and the first part of 1923, the wealth-strippers were able to grab hundreds of small firms through private purchase or by obtaining control through transactions on the stock exchange where the rise in share prices failed to keep pace with inflation. Legislation abetting the formation of conglomerates was enacted. The Reichstag also put through tax regulations that exempted the vertical trusts from paying most "turnover" taxes, enabling them to force smaller competitors (who could not escape the value-added taxes) out of the market and make them easy prey for takeover. As in all inflations, the largesse of the central bank was synchronized with a discriminatory fiscal policy that enabled the tycoons to multiply their assets. The greatest headway in the formation of "vertical" trusts was made in the mineral, coal, steel, and chemical industries. The cartelization in coal is a good example: by the end of 1922, the Stinnes group controlled 19 percent of all coal output. Krupp and Haniel each controlled 9 percent; Phoenix, Hoesch, and Thyssen, combined, had 15 percent. Thus the six top firms controlled more than 52 percent of all coal produced in Germany. In the prewar years the twenty-eight leading firms controlled less than 50 percent.

Taking advantage of their "creditworthiness," the major wealth accumulators of the period—Stinnes, Ganz, Minoux, Karstadt, Michael, Bosel, Kahn, Krupp, Thyssen, Herzfeld, Klockner, Haniel, and several "minor princes of inflation"—all heaped company upon company and asset on top of asset, until the value of each "pile" rose into the hundreds of billions of marks—and in several cases—into trillions.

It is Stinnes, however, who emerges as the personification and the archetype of wealth-gouging in that era. By adding to his considerable inherited wealth the vast amount of credits that were made available to him, he was able to erect a "colossus that bestrode the continents"—the first true, international conglomerate, whose extensiveness has yet to be equaled.

The "Midas of Mülheim" frequently boasted of being a self-made man, but he did get his start with some ancestral aid. His grandfather, Mathias, who established a coal business at Mülheim in the early part of the nineteenth century, left various mining properties and a tidy amount of cash upon his death. These eventually passed on to Hugo and his brother. Itching to devote his time to the piling up of property and power, Hugo Stinnes discarded his father's advice that he educate himself extensively; he quit the Berlin School of Mines after six months and, in 1892, established his own firm, Stinnes Gesellschaft, with a capital of 50,000 marks. He was then twenty-two. During the next twenty-two prewar years he expanded rapidly into other fields. He bought into one of Germany's leading industrial combines (the Deutsche Bergwerke) with coal-mining interests in the Ruhr and iron mines in the Rhineland as well as steel-products manufacturing plants and a shipping enterprise. In 1907 he obtained control and became the firm's president. Together with Thyssen he also established one of the largest electric power companies in Germany (Rhenish Westphalian). Next, he went into overseas shipping and developed a fleet on the Elbe.

He was now well set for all the opportunities that could be seized by a scoundrel during a great war, and he devoted himself relentlessly to those opportunities during World War I and its aftermath.

His companies sold coal and steel to both sides (the clandestine wartime sales to France were frequently at lower prices than the "open" sales to Germany). While he was busy putting up new plants within Germany during the conflict, he arranged a "concession agreement" with the owners of Belgian mines and mills that were seized when the German forces overran Belgium. Paying nothing for the privilege, he extracted an agreement that provided him the profit of these enterprises (less a small participation to the

former owners) with the proviso that he would buy out the operations for a specific sum plus the amount of profit that he had
"extracted." The purchase would be made within a brief period
after the vanquished Belgian nation would sign a surrender agreement at the end of the war. (Of course, Stinnes never had to carry
out his bargain; he carried out only the profits.)

Stinnes now became a slavedriver incarnate. He drove the Belgian workers—sometimes at the point of bayonets—until they
dropped from exhaustion. (He said during this period, "I do not
believe in charity. The sooner an inefficient worker dies, the better.") His siphoning activities in Belgium also included discreet
but frequently repeated looting. Much productive equipment and
considerable coal and ore were "stripped" and shipped, without
any compensation, to Stinnes's various enterprises in the Fatherland.

The lost war, of course, stopped such income, and some of the
plants that Stinnes had established were taken from him when
certain territories were ceded to the Allies under the Versailles
Treaty. But the "King of the Ruhr"—as he was now known—was
able to influence the German government to compensate him for
these losses to the extent of 300 million marks (characteristically
he had borrowed most of the funds to buy or build these properties
—debts he did not meet until the mark's depreciation made the
repayments insignificant).

By the time he received his "compensation" he was worth about
a half-billion marks. Some of this he converted into foreign currencies that were kept in Dutch vaults. Some was invested in
newly established foreign corporations. In either case the money
left the purview of the German government's tax collector. The
remainder of his money was put into new plants or into new
investments in corporations he would eventually take into the
omnivorous holding company which has come down in history as
the Stinnes Concern. Except for funds required to buy everyday
necessities (he was always unostentatiously dressed and lived what
he considered to be a spartan life), Stinnes kept almost none of his
personal funds in marks.

Throughout the post-Versailles period when Germany continued to make reparation payments in kind, Stinnes railed against
the "shameful penalties placed upon the Fatherland," and made
prodigious profits from the payments. As a leading supplier of

important so-called compensation items—steel, coal, lumber, minerals—he contrived to put prices up artificially, gouging millions of additional marks from the government when it purchased the necessary supplies from him.

During the gathering hyperinflation, in a driven, compulsive fury, he acquired company after company until he had a full or partial interest in 1,555 prime firms that possessed 2,888 plants. Although he extolled the efficiency inherent in vertical organizations (combines that began with raw materials and ended in the manufacture of the finished product), his octopus reach took in almost everything. He became "monarch of a kingdom" that included banks, newspapers (it was estimated he controlled at least 40 percent of the German press), inland waterway and transocean shipping fleets, firms dealing in foreign exchange, chemical and explosives producers, paper and printing, film producers, brass and copper works, automobile manufacturers, oil producers, exporting enterprises, mortgage companies, hotels, and—of course, his original interests in coal, iron, steel, and mining.

Through the Stinnes Concern he became the leading multinational industrialist of the world, with iron, shipping, and marketing organizations in South America, China, and the West Indies. He acquired steel producers in Austria, Czechoslovakia, Switzerland, Poland, and Rumania. He obtained major participations in oil in Rumania, Russia, South America, and Mexico. By 1924 the Stinnes Concern had a part or full interest in the following foreign operations: 20 coal mines and fields, 21 iron mines, 4 oil fields and numerous exploratory companies and refineries, 16 stone and ceramic works, 29 smelters, 20 metal processing and machine works, 7 locomotive works, 3 telegraph companies, 4 shipyards, 80 electrical goods plants, 8 paper and chemical plants, 47 electrical and gas utilities, 9 shipping companies, 14 newspaper and printing companies, 3 cotton and coconut plantations, 10 banks and bankholding companies, and 254 selling agencies. All of these—and almost all his many domestic companies except those acquired before the war—were bought up or were created with borrowed money.

Using the "weapon of inflation" Stinnes was able to increase his personal estate from the equivalent of $10 million (over 40 million marks) immediately prior to the war to a reputed level of over $1 billion at the end of 1923, or an amount exceeding 4,200,000,-000,000,000,000,000,000 marks (four octillion 200 septillion marks). (A reliable estimate of his personal wealth has never been established. Much of his personal fortune was secreted in foreign countries, to escape detection by the German tax office and by the Allies.) The value of his share of the assets in the Stinnes Concern at the end of 1923 is beyond calculation. In the last nine months of 1923 that firm piled up a galaxial profit amounting to 428,-946,709,598,344,462 paper marks (almost 429 quadrillion marks).

Figures on the wealth of Stinnes's major contemporaries, as well as the amounts they acquired during the hyperinflation, are not available. Attempts to estimate their estates—impeded by devices to thwart inquiry—have been too inconclusive. Scattered evidence indicates that the worth of each of his nearest rivals—Thyssen, Krupp, and Rathenau—ranged somewhere between 1.7 billion and 2.2 billion prewar marks. In each case the major portion of accrued assets was attained during the inflationary decade between 1914 and 1923.

The year 1923 was the zenith of Stinnes's fortunes, but it was also the year in which Germany was overwhelmed by anarchy in both the monetary and political areas. The fabrication of new money was driven to lunatic heights and the upward rush of prices assumed a cyclonic fury.

During the first three months of the year almost 4.25 trillion new marks roared out of the Reichsbank's printing presses, raising the total to 5,542,900,000,000 (almost 5 trillion 543 billion). But in the next three months almost 11 trillion 800 billion additional marks spewed out, with the amount outstanding surging to 17 trillion 340 billion.

It was after July 1, however, that the torrent smashed through the dikes. In July, alone, almost 26.5 trillion new marks erupted; in August an almost incredible 625 trillion, and in September a sanity-defying 27,575,705,000,000,000 (27 quadrillion 575 trillion 705 billion). By the end of September the grand total of marks outstanding had reached 28,244,405,800,000,000 (almost 28.25 quadrillion). During the nine months since the beginning of the year over 28 quadrillion new marks had been manufactured; about 4.5 quadrillion of this amount had been created directly for the benefit of major industrial interests (through the mechanism of discounting commercial bills) at a time when the nation was already drowning in marks.

The problems produced by the emission of these myriads of Reichsbank notes were cataclysmic, but not the least of them were the difficulties encountered in the printing of the money. Despite all its heroic efforts the Reichsbank could not turn out the depreciating marks with sufficient speed. Various devices were tried to draw even in the constantly failing print-up race. Since almost nothing could any longer be bought with marks in denominations of 10, 20, 50, and 100 (the most frequent denominations issued until 1921), the Reichsbank cut down on the engraving of these and in 1922 began issuing large amounts of notes denominated in 500 marks, 1,000 marks, 5,000 marks, and 10,000 marks. Between May and December, 426 billion of the 10,000-mark notes were printed despite the Reichsbank's public announcement in its 1922 report that it "had encountered difficulties in the procurement of paper suitable for the printing of such notes." The manufacturing of sufficient amounts of money presented even greater dilemmas in 1923. The central bank's report for 1923 announced, "Keeping pace with the progressive depreciation of the means of payment in circulation, the devalued notes streamed back into the coffers of the bank.* Again and again the currency circulation had to be replenished with new money with large denominations." Therefore, in 1923 the 10,000-mark notes were followed by notes of 50,000, 100,000, and 200,000 marks. But by mid-1923 a 200,000-mark note could not buy a pound of potatoes. So there followed, in quick succession, notes ranging from 1 million to 500 million, and then those ranging from 1 to 500 billion. Finally, in the anarchic days of October and November 1923 notes ranging in denominations from 1 trillion to 100 trillion were rammed out of the presses.

But the Reichsbank continued to lose the race. It doubled, quadrupled, then octupled its existing plants, bought new printing plants, and then, in the spring of 1923, it began engaging outside firms to assist it. By November, 132 private firms were also print-

---

*Havenstein, president of the Reichsbank (who issued the report), meant to convey the following: as the increasingly useless small denomination notes were returned to the banks with a request that they be replaced by an equivalent amount of marks in large denominations, the Reichsbank fell progressively behind in its attempts to print up a sufficient amount of notes of large denominations.

ing up notes on 1,783 machines working around the clock, and 32 private pulp and paper firms were used to satisfy the devouring engraving machines.

Despite all these draconian measures, the Reichsbank was not satisfied with its efforts to cure the "shortage of the circulating medium." In their 1923 report the directors of the central bank declared, "The wholly extraordinary depreciation of the mark has naturally created a rapidly increasing demand for additional currency, which the Reichsbank has not always been able to fully satisfy.... The dispatching of cash sums must for reasons of speed be made by private transport. Numerous shipments leave Berlin every day for the provinces. The deliveries to several banks must be made . . . only by airplanes."

Havenstein then announced—as further proof of the assiduousness with which he had labored to produce "sufficient" marks— that the Reichsbank had spent the following sum in a single year for the manufacturing and printing of bank notes: 32,776,899,-763,734,490,417 marks and 5 pfennig. Almost 33 quintillion marks spent on the production of money—and, of course, one must not forget the 5 pfennig!

The difficulties experienced by the Reichsbank in fabricating "enough marks" were dwarfed by the problems created from its gargantuan emissions. By March 1923 the wholesale index had raced up to 4,827 and by June to 24,618 times its 1913 base. But from July 1—in keeping with the lunatic quantum leaps in the money supply—prices exploded into the ionosphere. By the end of July the wholesale index streaked to 183,510; by August to 1,695,109 and by September 30 to 36,223,777. At that time the mark was quoted at over 154 million to the dollar. A half-dozen eggs—if they were available in an economy increasingly overtaken by shortages—cost almost 3 million marks; before the war they were priced at less than half a mark. A pound of beef (priced at eighty pfennig, or eight-tenths of a mark in prewar days) now sold at 3.5 million marks. A suit—which sold at 75 marks in 1913—was advertised by Wertheim's department store in Berlin at 225 million marks.

In his autobiographical book *The World of Yesterday,* Stefan Zweig, the famous Austrian author, gives an eye-witness account of Berlin in the autumn of 1923:

I sent a manuscript to my publisher on which I had worked for a year. To be on the safe side I asked for an advance payment of royalties on 10,000 copies. By the time the check was deposited it hardly paid the postage I had put on the parcel a week before. On street cars, one paid in millions. Trucks carried the paper money from the Reichsbank to the other banks, and a fortnight later one found 400,000 mark notes in the gutter—a beggar had thrown them away contemptuously. A pair of shoe laces cost more than a shoe had once cost, no—more than a fashionable shoe store with 2,000 pairs of shoes had cost before; to repair a broken window, more than the whole house had formerly cost—a book more than the printer's shop with a hundred presses. For $100 one could buy rows of six-story houses on Kurfürstendamm. . . . Some adolescent boys who had found a case of soap forgotten in the harbor disported themselves for months in cars and lived like kings, selling a cake every day, while their parents—formerly well-to-do—slunk about like beggars. Messenger boys established foreign exchange businesses and speculated in currencies of all lands. . . . I have a pretty good knowledge of history, but never, in my recollection, has it produced such madness in such gigantic proportions. All values were changed . . . the laws of the State were flouted. . . . Berlin was transformed into the Babylon of the world. Bars, amusement parks, honky-tonks sprang up like mushrooms. . . . Along the entire Kurfürstendamm powdered and rouged young men sauntered, and they were not all professionals; every high school boy wanted to earn some money, and in the dimly lit bars one might see government officials and men of the world of finance tenderly courting drunken sailors without any shame. Even the Rome of Suetonius had never known such orgies as the pervert balls of Berlin, where hundreds of men costumed as women, and hundreds of women, as men, danced under the benevolent eyes of the police. . . . Young girls bragged proudly of their perversion: to be sixteen and still under the suspicion of virginity would have been considered a disgrace in any school of Berlin at that time.

All this went on, said Zweig, while most people "were being stretched daily on the rack of inflation."

The stretching continued in October and November. In October, 2,476,711,294,000,000,000 (almost 2.5 quintillion) additional marks were disgorged. And in November an astronomical 397 quintillion 833 quadrillion erupted, bringing the total outstanding to over 400,338,326,000,000,000,000 (more than 400 quintillion 338 quadrillion). Of the 400,337,031,172,000,000,000 (more than

400 quintillion 337 quadrillion) spewed out during the eleven months of 1923, 347.3 quintillion were created in the process of "furnishing credit" to the major cartels by discounting commercial bills. Over 346 quintillion were printed for the same purpose in the single month of November, when the discounting of treasury bills was finally prohibited as the government—beset by seething unrest and what was thought to be the first stages of a Bolshevik takeover—at last put through a monetary reform program calculated to end the inflation.

By the end of November—with the mark having been rendered virtually worthless—the cost of living was driven to sickening heights. The wholesale price index as of November 30 had skyrocketed to an extraterrestrial height of 1,422,900,000,000 (almost one trillion four hundred twenty-three billion times its 1913 level).

By that time most farmers and tradespeople refused to sell anything for marks. To fill the need for an acceptable monetary medium the government permitted the creation of "emergency money" by so-called reputable industrial and commercial concerns, utilities, railroads, *land* administrations, and city governments. By November 1923, approximately 118 quintillion marks of such legal emergency money was in circulation; it had been emitted for the payment of salaries and for settlement with vendors. In addition an even greater amount of bogus emergency notes had been loosed by small firms not on the government's approved list, by individual debtors who issued their own medium of exchange, and by counterfeiters. So great was the need for "circulating medium" to meet the fantastically high prices, and so intense was the insistence of sellers of goods and services to avoid the useless Reichsbank marks, that even the spurious emergency issues were —for a period of months—accepted. Side by side with these makeshift devices an active barter exchange had developed. In the closing months of 1923, Germany had reverted to a medieval economy. At that time the few sellers who were willing to assume the risk of receiving payment in marks demanded 224 billion for a one-pound rye bread (slightly more than one-fourth of a mark in 1913), 80 billion for an egg (less than one-twelfth of a mark in prewar days), 3 trillion marks for a pound of butter, and 2 trillion, 500 billion marks for a pound of beef. A newspaper was priced at 200 billion marks and a pair of shoes at 32 trillion. In international money markets, the dollar was worth over 4 trillion marks.

Clearly the end had finally come. The mad race the German people had been forced to run against the vaulting mark had gone beyond the limits of endurance. The population was exhausted from chronic malnutrition; throughout 1922 and 1923 almost the entire work force—despite the receipt of a weekly pay that ran into seven or eight figures (compared to two digits in the prewar period)—lived below the German Statistical Office's definition of the poverty level. Despite endless work stoppages and strikes, workers had not been able to extract sufficient raises to meet more than 60 percent of their minimal daily needs. In the early part of 1922—as prices shot upward—they had insisted on a pay scale that was based on the spiraling cost-of-living index. After much agitation the demand was met. But by mid-1922 this no longer sufficed since costs rose so drastically within a week. Labor leaders then demanded and obtained payment of salaries twice per week. But the galloping inflation outran this compromise, and the government finally decreed that salaries "shall reflect the anticipated rise of the following week's cost-of-living index." Of course, not even the most diligent employer could foresee the lunatic leaps that would occur in prices, and so wages—to the very end of the inflation—continued to trail onrushing living costs.

No one becomes inured to slow starvation, and the German population deeply resented their gnawing hunger. But even more disturbing was the continuing destabilization of daily life. Oriented toward orderliness and balance in their lives, the average German reacted with despair and anger toward the anarchy which had overtaken all aspects of daily existence. The constant change in prices became an anathema. Berliners cursed a fate that put the price of a kilo of bread at 15 billion marks at two o'clock and 25 billion at three o'clock. They could not endure a situation in which a restaurant meal was priced at 100 billion marks when the diner began eating, was already priced at 115 billion when he began his main course, and cost 125 billion when he was handed his check. Toward the close of 1923 most small restaurants shut their doors, partly because people could not afford the cost but predominantly because patrons could not abide the constant change in prices.

Nor could people tolerate waiting a long time on food lines only to see a sign suddenly appear in a window: "Store closed. No more merchandise." Or "Store will reopen 3 P.M. Inventory being repriced." And they could not abide an existence which forced them to run for a streetcar from their place of employment, burdened by a half-bale of marks they had received from the paymaster, to run again (after leaving the streetcar) to the nearest bakery—only to be told after an interminable wait on the *Schlange* (the snakelike line on which the German population waited day after day) that the establishment could not accept the "small-denomination" currency the buyer was presenting.

As destabilization grew, the German people yearned for a return of the old prewar life—for a return of quiet, of a decent order, and for rest from daily uncertainties. Instead, as 1923 progressed, the chaos increased.

On January 11, 1923, French and Belgian troops, at the instigation of the revanchist (and Germanophobe) Poincaré, had invaded the Ruhr on a long-sought-for pretext. Germany, although it had been forced to suspend cash reparations, had assiduously maintained its payment responsibilities involving materials and kind. But in December 1922, through an oversight, it had neglected to send 140,000 telephone poles to France. The French steel industrialists, who coveted the rich coal supplies of the Ruhr, saw their opportunity. The foreign troops were ordered in, ostensibly to guarantee the fulfillment of reparation payments (their real purpose was to put into place the first segment of France's plan to detach the Ruhr from Germany).

For months French troops occupied the Ruhr, depriving Germany of income from one of its most productive regions. In retaliation, the Ruhr workers laid down their tools. Rioting flared intermittently as French soldiers and German miners fought one another. In the first week of September the government was forced to expend 18 billion marks to support the idled workers and their families; in the following week the bill came to over 30 billion marks. Unable to stand the drain, the Weimar Republic capitulated, ending the nine-month struggle by ordering its miners back to work and agreeing to resume reparations in kind.

The right-wing parties denounced "the surrender." The right-of-center wing of the Volkspartei (which Helfferich belonged to and represented in the Reichstag) and the Nationalists (a mixture of

industrialists, Junkers, farmers, and army officers) who had gradually begun making headway to reduce the bargaining power of the
unions now foresaw the failure of their efforts, with the end of the
emergency and the abatement of sacrifice-inducing patriotic fervor.
The National Socialists—robbed of the so-called misery that they
hoped would gain them adherents and ultimate hegemony—ranted
about a "new" stab in the back by "international Marxists and
Jews" (the "old" stab-in-the-back charge had been leveled against
Social Democrats and leftists during World War I when they had
advocated an end to hostilities that would bring a just peace). And
the Communists accused the government of a sell-out of the German proletariat to French industrial interests.

The rivalry between the far right and the far left now became
supercharged. The Communists organized what was described as
a state of siege in Berlin and staged revolutionary demonstrations
in Thuringia, Saxony, and parts of Bavaria. Separatist riots broke
out again in the Rhineland, and in the major cities of the nation
the Hitlerite S.A. men, carrying hidden pistols, patrolled the roads
in their military trucks, loudspeakers blaring their inflammatory
slogans.

And as the mark was going through its death throes, farmers
hid their produce from plundering bands that stole cattle, sheep,
goats, horses, and even dogs—anything that could be eaten. In the
cities provision-stocked warehouses were ransacked and the
empty ones were set afire by the embittered unemployed (now
increased to 28 percent of the work force) who had been thrown
out of work because small plants and lesser business establishments could no longer function in the monetary chaos.

On October 13, a bill was laid before the Reichstag, giving the
government wide latitude to deal with the crisis. The Nationalists
and Communists ceremonially left the legislative hall before the
bill was enacted. The law authorized the government to take any
steps deemed necessary "in financial, economic, and social" matters. If required, the government could suspend the democratic
rights of citizens embodied in the Weimar Constitution. The legislation was the forerunner of the financial reforms of November 15,
but it also was a weapon to suppress extremist political activity of
both the right and left. But its passage was really aimed at smashing the left. The Social Democrats—as might be expected—insti-
gated it and they voted for it after their centrist colleagues in the

Reichstag agreed to give them a token victory: the retention of the eight-hour workday.

After the enactment of the Emergency Law the Reichswehr (the small but well-trained army of the Weimar Republic permitted for defensive purposes by the Versailles Treaty) quickly suppressed some of the Communist-leaning *land* administrations although they had been legally elected. This did not put an end to Marxist agitation. Strikes erupted in Leipzig, Dresden, and Berlin. But these mobilizations led nowhere; the German people wanted only surcease from difficulties, not revolution. Furthermore, Moscow got the cue and—unknown to all but the inner councils of the German Communist party—suggested that "proletarian unrest" be abandoned for the moment.

But Hitler and his cohorts believed the time was ripe for them. On the evening of November 8, Gustav von Kahr, rightist Premier of the Bavarian *land* government—a royalist who became virtual dictator of Bavaria—addressed an anti-Bolshevik meeting in the Bürgerbraukeller, a beer hall that had increasingly become the haunt of rightist louts. While Kahr was disposing himself of his rather boring address, Hitler and his machine-gun-toting storm troopers moved quickly into the hall; Hitler raced to the platform and—screaming at the top of his voice—proclaimed "a National Revolution." While der Führer's men blocked the exits, Kahr, Ludendorff, and several others were forced to join the revolutionary government Hitler was to head. (Ludendorff was to be commander-in-chief of the Reichswehr and Kahr was alloted the rather lowly position of "head of Bavaria.")

The meeting broke up and Kahr returned home. He promptly repudiated his "enforced participation." On the following day the power-hungry Ludendorff and Hitler decided to lead a march on Munich. At the center of the city they were confronted by police and armed troops loyal to Kahr. The police opened fire. Hitler's men, for a brief moment, returned fire, and then Hitler jumped into a car and—temporarily—escaped. Ludendorff haughtily marched a few steps toward the armed force that stood in his way, hoping that the lowly soldiers would defer to the former First Quartermaster General. The soldiers stood their ground guns ready; Ludendorff halted and was arrested.

The others involved in the beer-hall putsch were apprehended. Kahr's involvement was completely overlooked, but Hitler and

Ludendorff were brought to trial on February 26, 1924. Ludendorff was acquitted by the groveling judge despite the copious evidence of his involvement of high crime against the government. Hitler was given the minimum sentence for high treason—five years—of which he served less than nine months. The concluding part of his imprisonment was spent in the fortress at Landsberg, in which he had the run of the place and lived in comfort. A steady stream of visitors came to pay homage. Among them was the future inmate of Spandau, Rudolf Hess, whose conversations with his martyred leader centered on one subject: the establishment of a "world order" dominated by Fascism.

On the books of the Weimar Republic there was a statute stipulating that a foreigner convicted of treason must be deported after serving his sentence. Hitler, an Austrian national, was not deported. He was a good man to have around in a nation perennially obsessed by the possibility of a Communist takeover.

The beer-hall putsch—though a point of considerable interest to historians—seemed of little consequence to the German people, and was quickly forgotten. But it had a galvanizing effect on the government, which by now realized that the chaotic conditions created by the superinflation had to be terminated immediately. And so, on November 15, the "stabilization plan" involving the rentenmark which the government had devised in October—but which it hesitated to impose largely because of the pressure against it by the more expansionary cartelists (notably Stinnes)—was finally put into effect.

On November 16, the newly formed Rentenbank began issuing rentenmarks to both the government and major commercial borrowers. The rentenmark was not legal tender for settlement of private debts but was a unit of account for the settlement of transactions with government agencies. A holder of 500 rentenmarks, upon demand, could convert them into a bond having a nominal value of 500 gold marks (therefore, 1 rentenmark equalled 1 gold mark). These bonds were to be supported by funds received into the Rentenbank from taxes levied against agriculture and business. The gold clause had absolutely no validity, since the bonds had no gold cover and would be redeemed in paper; it was used simply for its cosmetic value, which turned out to be rather considerable.

At the same time the value of the paper mark (of which almost

400 quintillion were outstanding) was set at 1 trillion marks to 1 gold mark (or at the rate of 4.2 trillion paper marks to the dollar). Actually this stabilization of the paper mark vis-à-vis the dollar was another cosmetic exercise. In international monetary markets the dollar continued for a time to sell at a higher level than the stabilization base. Moreover, there was no attempt to revalue the existing paper mark into a new so-called gold mark at the ratio of 1 trillion of the old into 1 new gold mark. The gold mark was —pure and simple—a mirage. Its purpose—like the gold clause attached to the convertibility feature of the rentenmark—was a fiction used to impart a sense of stability to the rentenmark. And to a considerable extent the fiction worked.

It worked for two reasons. The population desperately yearned for a new stable money system. Even though the new rentenmarks could not be used for buying bread or paying rent, and other necessities, they were eagerly accepted, were progressively discounted at banks, and gradually took on a character of quasi-money. The second reason for the rentenmark's success was the government's promise that it would issue only a limited amount of rentenmarks.* This assurance—contrasting so glaringly with the Reichsbank's monumental issues in the past—also worked its benefits.

Prices stabilized for a brief period. But then early in 1924 the Reichsbank—claiming the usual urgency of a "lack of circulating medium" and under pressure from industrialists with large indebtedness who ardently opposed "stabilization" and the contraction of the money supply—again began issuing prodigious amounts of fresh marks. Prices of goods and services bought by the public soared again and a rekindling of inflation seemed imminent. This time, however, the government did not succumb to the threats and pressures of Stinnes and the new super-rich; it stopped the mass fabrication of new marks. As a matter of fact—seeing the handwriting on the wall—the "old" industrialists (Krupp, Thyssen, et al.) used their influence at this stage to contract the money supply to bring down their inflation-begotten rivals.

With the printing press stopped, prices stabilized again by the late spring of 1924. With order reestablished in Germany, foreign exchange rolled into the country as exports boomed. Tax rates

*A promise that was kept.

were raised and, in contrast to the past, there was a serious effort made to collect revenues from industry, banking, and commerce. After incurring a budget deficit in 1923 that exceeded the combined deficits experienced in its entire history, Germany produced a slight surplus in 1924.

The monetary transformation achieved in 1924 was frequently described as "the miracle of the rentenmark." Like so much else in those tenuous times, the phrase was used for its thaumaturgic effects. If the "stability" produced could be considered a miraculous achievement by enough people, then perhaps the miracle would become self-validating.

There was nothing miraculous in the rather transparent scheme. The world's history is replete with episodes in which a repudiated monetary supply was replaced by a new, readily accepted money system. In early periods the tribal chief or local ruler (already having decided upon the new monetary unit) would stage a ceremony (usually held at night) in which the "holy advisers" would chant, dance, and commune with the gods. They would go through a ritual of successively throwing into the air one money form after another (beads, bones, bits of tusks, shells, etc.) and inspecting the designs formed as these objects struck the ground. Then, suddenly, the head wise man would proclaim, "The gods have chosen! Their message is shown on the earth before us. They have chosen shells for our money!" Then the chief (who had previously chosen shells) would give thanks to the gods for their favorable intervention, and the assembled population would celebrate the advent of their new money. And that ancient system worked until, for one reason or another, too many shells were put into circulation; then a new money was introduced.

The Weimar government, resorting to the more sophisticated methods of mythification employed by modern societies in monetary affairs, did not invoke the gods.* Nor did it entirely replace an old repudiated currency. It introduced a new monetary unit that circulated side by side with the old discredited money and—in the process—created a climate in which fiscal and monetary order could be reestablished.

Finally, on October 11, 1924, the old paper mark was replaced

---

*Of course, U.S. Federal Reserve Notes ask for divine intercession; they contain the words: IN GOD WE TRUST.

by a new monetary unit, the reichsmark—into which it could be converted at a ratio of 1 trillion old paper marks into 1 reichsmark. The rentenmark was convertible into the new currency on a one-to-one basis. By June 25, 1925—with most of the paper marks having been converted—they were withdrawn from circulation and ceased to be legal tender. The reichsmark became—and remains until today—the nation's sole monetary unit. Its advent formally brought to an end the most violent inflation yet experienced, an episode that saw the making of instant billionaires and overnight paupers. The process that had been characterized by Bresciani-Turroni as "the governmental inflation" was—at last —abandoned.

In the six years between the appearance of the reichsmark and the beginning of the worldwide depression of 1930, Germany experienced a surging prosperity. Under the Dawes Plan and the Young Plan it met the reactivated (but more realistic) reparation demands put upon it. In those half-dozen years the nation's living standard was outdistanced only by that of the United States.

With the coming of the Great Depression of the 1930s, markets shriveled and the flood of investment capital into Germany dried up. Unemployment rose and a frustrated and embittered nation— fearful of a return of the harrowing days of 1922–1923—turned to a demagogue who had constantly raised the apocalyptic specter of the hyperinflation. The daemonic, wild-eyed man who had jumped to the platform in the Bürgerbraukeller just one week before the stabilization plan of the rentenmark was put into effect —the man who had repeatedly prophesied that he would be carried into power on a wave of misery—was ready.

And now, to tie up a few loose ends:

Within four months after the introduction of the stabilization plan, death claimed three individuals who so adversely affected the financial condition of Germany during the stormy decade between 1914 and 1923.

On November 20, 1923—just four days after the first issue of rentenmarks was released—Rudolf Havenstein died at the age of sixty-six. Trained for the law, he became a district judge, but his interests gradually veered toward finance. In 1890, he served as Finance Minister of the state of Prussia, and a decade later as president of the Prussian State Bank. Recognized as a faithful steward of Junker interests he was elevated to the presidency of the Reichsbank in 1908, and occupied that position until his death.

A dull, gray man who constantly clung to the uses of yesterday, Rudolf Havenstein was awed by the court life of the monarchy and by the display of naked power by the industrialists during the early years of the Weimar Republic. Pliant and assiduous, he became the willing tool of the wealth-engrossers who insisted on a continued print-up of marks during the 1914–1923 decade. Perhaps this most prodigious of all money printers will be remembered above everything else for having submitted the highest printing bill in the history of mankind: almost 33 quintillion marks and 5 pfennig.

One of the chief beneficiaries of Havenstein's policies expired suddenly on April 10, 1924. About two weeks later, the American publication, *The Independent,* stated, "It is almost like reading that a natural force has been removed from the earth to read of the death of Hugo Stinnes. It is doubtful whether any man ever enjoyed greater economic and industrial power during his lifetime than he."

" 'Industry,' he had said," the article went on, " 'is the only force remaining in Germany. Its development alone can save her. Now, it is I, Stinnes, who have contributed most to her [Germany's] prosperity, who am best placed to make it fruitful in the future for I shall soon have established my control over everything that is worthwhile and so it is my ideas the government ought to follow and my decisions which ought to be its guide.' "

The article concluded with a final illuminating paragraph. "When Isaac Morrison [in the only interview ever granted by Stinnes to an American newspaper man] had asked, 'What are you working for? What do you hope to accomplish with this tremendous structure you have built up?' Stinnes looked at him with a frozen anger, then at long last replied, 'That question I will not answer!' "

Deprived of the cohesive force that had held it together, the overbuilt, hastily assembled structure that Stinnes had created quickly collapsed. Many of his corporations—burdened by mountainous debt—had to be sold off by his two sons to meet the demands of creditors. Some historians have suggested that his survivors might have continued his enterprises if they had had the will and the talent to do so, and if they had not worked at cross-purposes. Others have said that had he been alive, Stinnes would have managed to extricate himself from the difficulties that lesser individuals could not overcome. Perhaps they are right. But three years after his death the colossal empire he had built on the ruin of a monetary system was, itself, a ruin.

Less than two weeks after Stinnes was buried, Helfferich died in a train wreck, on April 24, 1924. Throughout the mounting monetary and political chaos of 1923, Helfferich had continued to seethe with resentment over his failure to achieve a paramount role in the German government, and he continued to nurse the hope that the elusive prize would yet be grasped.* His villa on the Hitzigestrasse became a focal point for monarchist and militarist counter-democratic activities. Believing that the "right" would soon come to power he increasingly became the purveyor of ultraconservative policy in the Reichstag and the dispenser of ultraright invective.

But Helfferich's greatest influence—and a most destructive influence it proved to be—was exerted in his monetary writings and his frequent testimonies before committees and official bodies. Regarded, until his death, as the nation's leading financial expert, he was able to legitimize the hyperinflation in his writings and speeches.

Alternating unblinking lies with obfuscating rhetoric, Helfferich maintained the fiction that the disgorging of quadrillions of marks had not created the superinflation. As late as June 1923 (when the wholesale index had already leaped to 24,618 times its 1913 base and when it required more than 145,000 marks to purchase \$1.00), Helfferich testified before the Committee of Inquiry into the Fall of the Mark that "since the total value in international exchange of all the [paper] marks circulating now in Germany is more adequately covered by the store of gold in the Reichsbank than had been the outstanding circulation before the war, there cannot, in truth, be said that there was a decline in the soundness of money."

In two articles that appeared in a now-defunct London financial

---

*Although he continued to serve, until his death, as a delegate to the Reichstag, the last administrative post he held in the government was the unprestigious assignment as Foreign Minister to Russia in 1918. He lasted about a month in that post and was recalled by an embarrassed Foreign Office when his counter-revolutionary activities were exposed by Soviet authorities.

journal shortly after the stabilization plan had been put into effect (but which had been written by him several months before that date), he continued to absolve the Reichsbank from the responsibility of the havoc it had created through its gigantic emissions (a policy he himself had constantly egged on). "Any observer," he wrote, "who looks deeper into the matter discovers that this monetary catastrophe was provoked by general, economic and by political conditions—as well as by the collapse of the mark. The former were the primary and decisive cause of the unprecedented demoralization of German finances . . . although it must be added that the financial collapse *in turn* helped to precipitate the catastrophe of our currency."

And then—shortly before his death—and when it was already obvious that the great industrialists, even against their will, had come to the end of excessive money fabrication and had begun to realize that, for the time being at least, the wild expansionary era was over—he at last permitted himself the luxury of truth. "The attempt," he said, "to stop the depreciation [the monetary depreciation] by creating a new money with a backing of real values was surprisingly successful considering that the new money was not based on gold itself."

He then went on to list all the factors that were leading to the reestablishment of a sound currency: increased taxes, cutting down of expenditures, attempts to balance the budget, refusal of the Reichsbank to discount bills, and other measures—in short, all the efforts that should have been made, and could have been made, before the winds of the hyperinflation had begun to roar.

Several weeks after his last article appeared, he died in the wrecked train near the small town of Bellinzona.

Hundreds of economic historians have produced books on the hyperinflation of the Weimar Republic, most of them in German. The great majority of these works give unqualified recognition to the inordinate wealth stripped off by the major industrialists in a period when the bulk of the population was being pauperized. Some go beyond that point and—with recognizable trepidation—summon enough courage to state that the superinflation hastened the transfer of assets.

But most historians of the period insist that the aggrandizers became the beneficiaries of chance, of erroneous government policies, and the fortuitous opportunities the inflation thrust upon them. Conversely, the millions of common people—lacking the propensity and the ability to turn financial chaos to their advantage—became the victims of monetary "mistakes."

A few come down on the side of chance. Frank D. Graham is a notable proponent of the chance theory. In his book *Exchange, Prices and Production in Hyperinflation: Germany 1920-1923* (published in 1930) he asserts, "Inflation came to be regarded—not as a blind god playing capriciously though not destructively with human fortunes—but rather as a malevolent deity bent on smashing."* To Graham the German experience was a game dominated by blind fate; by undiscriminating gods. For him the motives and ambitions of highly placed men had little or nothing to do with the course of events.

But the bulk of historians and economists subscribed to the theory of "mistakes" and of failed governmental policy. In his book *The German Reichsbank and the Economy of Germany,* Salomon Flink—while commenting on the relentless print-up of marks by the Reichsbank while prices were rocketing—observed, "The Bank *mistook* cause and effect." In another section he stated, "In July 1922 the Reichsbank advocated an increased utilization of the commercial bills of exchange as a means of payment without any change in the discount rate which was then 5 percent. The new policy offered the businessman the opportunity of procuring purchasing power which he could pay back at maturity with a fraction of its cost."

And then he adds the following telltale sentence: "The great *fallacy* of the Reichsbank becomes apparent if one considers the fact that the discount rate was left unchanged at 5 percent when the banks . . . charged 50 percent." In yet another section he declared, "Many outside factors contributed to the self-deception of the German credit institutions and enabled them to provide the necessary funds to the business world." In short, the Reichsbank and the banks did not know what they were doing ("self-deception").

Ignorance . . . errors . . . faulty decisions . . . but not a hint of planned "accommodation" to the aggrandizers.

---

*Despite its questionable conclusions regarding the benefits and causes of the German inflation, his work is a veritable gold mine of tables, charts, and economic data.

Rufus C. Dawes, chief of eight economic advisers attached to the International Committee of Experts (a multinational group sent to Berlin in 1924 to investigate economic conditions and the country's ability to pay reparations), struck a similar note in his semiofficial book *The Dawes Plan in the Making,* published in 1925. "The whole system of direct taxation," he wrote "went to pieces in 1923, and for that reason and on account of the confusion occasioned by the inflation, there was a very low scale of taxes upon the incomes of the very rich men. . . . The profits made by repaying in depreciated currency, the credits granted by the banks and the payment of taxes in money of depreciated value have resulted in great accumulations of unearned wealth in the hands of a relatively small number of German businessmen."

He follows these remarks with a statement so incredible that it requires rereading. The rich, he says, should be taxed more heavily because they "are demonstrably able to meet it [the heavier tax] and because whatever is taken from them by this sort of a tax is, in fact, the recovery of a part of what has—*through no intent of their own*—been taken by them, without compensation, from others." (Italics supplied.)

The agglomerators grew rich—Dawes implies—because the tax department was faultily administered (it "went to pieces") and the major industrialists simply became the innocent beneficiaries of a malfunctioning tax system. What Dawes carefully omits are the following facts: in 1923 over 95 percent of all revenues were secured from taxes levied and withheld on workers' salaries, with corporations and the wealthy paying less than 5 percent. Evidently the tax authorities were quite efficient in collecting from semi-starving employees, but they "broke down" when they needed to enforce levies on the rich.

Dawes's Committee of Experts knew that the great majority of tax returns submitted by the wealthy and by major corporations were "late filings," tardily submitted so that the so-called taxpayer could defer payment until the wild depreciation of money rendered his payment meaningless. The rich "broke down" the system, and the tax authorities helped them break it down by imposing a minuscule penalty on late filers.

Dawes knew also that until the Emergency Act of October 1923 was passed (by which time it was far too late), the major cartels were able to evade a substantial portion of their taxes by hiding profits in foreign subsidiaries. Nor was he unaware of the fact that the schedule of inheritance taxes of the Weimar Republic was the lowest among all industrialized nations. A 2-1/2-percent rate was in force on most inherited wealth.

All the evidence encountered by him and the Committee of Experts* should have indicated, beyond the shadow of a doubt, that the men of power had sabotaged the gathering of taxes so that they might retain the massive assets they had accumulated and that the government—despite ritualistic demurrals—cooperated with them. Dawes and the men who worked with him evidently preferred not to ascribe blame where the blame lay, and they resorted to the stale shibboleth of "mistakes" and "breakdown of administration."

Quite the opposite approach was taken by a small minority of economic historians who, daring to grasp the sharp nettle of pejorative conclusion, put forward the proposition that the scooping up of wealth by a small powerful group was achieved through a deliberate inflation policy that was maintained at the behest of the wealth-accumulators. Those few "revisionists" who advanced this theory concluded that the inflation would not have become as destructive nor as lengthy were it not for "a calculated abetment by the government and the Reichsbank, an abetment carried out for the benefit of the industrialists and others capable of borrowing great amounts of depreciating marks for the purpose of obtaining appreciating assets."

Bresciani-Turroni—without doubt the quintessential economic historian of the German hyperinflation—cogently advanced this theory. For several years he had studied monetary records and political documents of the momentous 1914–1923 decade, first as a member of the Reparations Commission, then as head of the Export Control, and finally as an economic adviser to the Agent-

*Most members of the Committee of Experts probably felt that it would be impolitic to engage in ex post facto accusations. This feeling was undoubtedly heightened by the resounding defeat suffered by the Social Democrats and "centrist" parties (the tenuous coalition that had formed previous administrations). The Nationalists (on the right) and the Communists (on the left) had scored impressive gains in recent election campaigns. The Americans on the committee and on the Reparations Commission were apprehensive about the rising tide of Communist support and did not wish to antagonize the important industrialists and other men of wealth on whom they would need to depend. The massive loans subsequently offered to Germany under the Dawes Plan—although explained in lofty language—had as its chief goal the "checking" of Communist influence.

General for Reparations. In his wonderfully lucid work *The Economics of Inflation**—after presenting a mass of evidence—he asserted:

The example of all countries with a depreciated currency shows us that the depreciation of money *creates a vast net of interests vested in the maintenance and continuation of the depreciation itself, interests* which are disturbed by the possibility of a stabilization itself of the exchange, and which therefore are assiduously opposed to the return of normal monetary conditions.

This is just what happened in Germany. There is no doubt that the inflation would not have assumed such vast proportions if it had not been favored in many ways by people who drew a large profit from it. It is clear from the discussion held in 1922 and 1923 in the *Economic Council of the Reich "that representatives of those classes used their influence on the government to impede the reform of the public finances and to sabotage all proposals for the stabilization of the German exchange,* which they only accepted when, at last, an economic catastrophe threatened Germany, and it was evident that the consequences of the inflation would rebound against their *authors. . . ."*

It is most astonishing that huge private fortunes and imposing concentrations were amassed in the years 1919–1923—years which were not on the whole a time of general economic prosperity. The fact is certainly surprising, although the surprise is lessened if we consider that even past times of economic regression, of social dissolution and of profound political disturbances have often been characterized by a concentration of property. In those periods the stronger recovered their primitive habits as beasts of prey. [Italics supplied.]

Another reputable observer who drew his conclusions from official German records and from personal on-the-scene observations also gave an insight into the manner in which the Weimar inflation was maintained for the benefit of "the industrialists" so that they might annex "one domain after another." On November 20, 1923 —the day on which Havenstein was at last removed, by death, from the presidency of the Reichsbank—J. K. Morgan, brigadier general in the British army and former deputy adjutant general on the Inter-Allied Military Commission (headquartered in Germany), gave a lecture at the University of London on conditions he had encountered during his several years' service in the Weimar

*Published in 1933.

Republic. His remarks are given particular weight not only because they are based on official contacts, but also because they come from a highly conservative man who cannot be accused of anticapitalist bias, and whose power of observation must have been considerable since his counsel was frequently sought by Austen Chamberlain.

"The inflation of the currency," Morgan said,

by destroying the middle classes and enslaving the workers has undermined the political basis of the Republic and concentrated all real power in the hands of a few, namely, the great industrialists. No one in this country can have any conception of how great their power is, and they are daily annexing one domain after another. They control the banks; they have bought up the two great news agencies; they have obtained command of a very large portion of the German press, and they have cornered the supply of paper.

Until now* they had been largely responsible for the discount policy of the Reichsbank, which is itself governed by the representatives of the great banking corporations—which are only the industrialists under another name. Obtaining money for a long time at 18 to 30 percent they have rediscounted the bills of smaller people at 500 percent. With the Ruhr credits they have made untold profits.

It is they, not the government, who tax the people. The assessment of their own earnings by the revenue authorities has been farcical and their balance sheets have represented the most impudent evasion of taxation in fiscal history. The whole system of taxation—especially the income tax —instead of operating as in other countries to redress the inequalities in the distribution of wealth, has actually operated to promote them. The worker pays taxes on his weekly wages which are known—the capitalist on his yearly profits which are never ascertained. The assessment of the former was in current values, the assessment of the latter in values so obsolete as to be nominal by the time payment was due.

In no other country in the world is capital so strong or politically so despotic. The economic form of society fails to correspond to the political theory; a republic in name, it is a capitalist despotism in fact.

Proof of Morgan's allegations existed in government documents, and this evidence was known to all sorts of government officials, to members of the Reichsbank, and to economists employed within the government. Such individuals, nevertheless, purblindly

*The stabilization plan had been put into effect five days before Morgan spoke.

accepted official explanations that the inflation was being maintained solely "to create more money so that the government might
continue to function, and to furnish the necessary funds for commerce and industry, and afford the means that would produce
conditions of stability and order." And those few individuals who
perceived the government's intercessory role in maintaining the
inflation for the benefit of the "rich industrialists" decided it was
judicious to observe a discreet silence.

Nor were establishmentarian economists and historians dissuaded from taking the "official" view when, in 1958, there suddenly surfaced an authoritative—though unintended—admission
of the purposive role of the government in the maintenance of the
German hyperinflation. Almost thirty-five years after the superinflation had finally been extinguished, Gert von Klass published his
authoritative biography on Hugo Stinnes. The biography revealed
a hitherto unknown entry Stinnes had recorded in his secret diary
on June 23, 1922.* On that day he had suddenly been called by
Walter Rathenau (Foreign Secretary of the Weimar Republic) to
the American embassy so that he might give the American Ambassador and a visiting banker (representing the Morgan interests)
an official overview of the growing financial chaos. Stinnes's view
was elicited because he was not only the nation's leading industrialist but also one of the most influential members in the Reichstag
and he represented the Weimar Republic in international confer-
ences. When he snapped his fingers, ministers of the government
jumped.

"At the request of Dr. Rathenau and of the two other gentlemen," Stinnes had recorded,

I analyzed the situation in all its details. . . . First the reasons why
Germany *carried out the inflation policy,* which it did after the war, were
established. I pointed out that after the lost war it had been absolutely
necessary for Germany to bring 4 million men then in the field [men who
had served in the army and navy] . . . back into the regular routines of
regular activity, and for that, raw materials and employment were neces-

*See p. 287 of Appendix for the text of that part of Stinnes's secret diary entry that dealt
with the use of inflation as a "policy" and a "weapon." The translation of the entry was
made by Professor Fritz K. Ringer and appears in *The German Inflation of 1923* (edited
by Professor Ringer and published in 1969 by Oxford University Press).

sary. It was necessary to sacrifice some capital for the purpose of sustaining the life of the nation . . . for if the masses had remained unemployed Bolshevism would have seized Germany. . . . I also informed the gentlemen that the *weapon of inflation* would have to be used in the future too without regard to the resulting capital losses [the capital losses brought about through the depreciation of money and savings]. . . . The Americans did agree that lives were worth more than money and from this standpoint they understood why Germany followed a policy of inflation. [Italics supplied.]

So there it was out in the open: the world's first recorded, official admission that governments, on occasion, knowingly used inflation as a "program." Here was proof that inflation was not invariably—as conventional economic theory had always claimed—the by-product of "fortuitous" malfunctions within the economy, or the result of "errors." It could, at times, be the creature of purposeful "policy." The dictionary definition of "policy" is: "A settled course adopted and followed by governments, institutions, or individuals." A reading of Stinnes's entire diary entry will reveal an a priori acceptance on the part of the participants in the clandestine conference of the concept that a rapid depreciation in the purchasing power of money could be the outgrowth of a *"settled* course adopted and followed by governments."

Of course, Stinnes attributed the use of inflation to benevolent motives (the saving of his nation from the clutches of Communism), and the Americans concurred on the advisability of pursuing the "program" for the same beneficent purposes, although a close reading of the text of the memoir indicates a strong suspicion on the part of the Americans that the "policy" may actually have been pursued for the benefit of "rich [German] profiteers," such as Stinnes himself. Their skepticism is borne out by his need to underscore, once more, that the "inflation program" was being implemented solely for the benefit of the nation and that any thought that the monetary depreciation was pursued for his (and others') benefit was ridiculous.

"It was further established in the discussion," he went on, "that the American gentlemen had been told not only by Germans—but especially by the French—that I deliberately aimed at growing inflation as something economically desirable. . . . I called the gentlemen who had expressed views like that to the American gentlemen—fools."

But Stinnes's attempt to exculpate himself from the charge that he and others were abetting the inflation to "acquire one domain after another" was followed within weeks after his meeting at the American embassy by the sudden revelation of a secret, heated exchange between himself and the Minister of Finance, Hermes, who had announced certain measures to stop the fall of the mark against other currencies. (Hermes properly contended that the domestic inflation was being fueled all the more by the immense creation of marks used to buy up foreign exchange for reparations payments and that the lower the German money went, the more marks had to be printed.) Immediately upon hearing about the Finance Minister's plan, Stinnes fired off a private memorandum to him. "I have such strong doubts," the master stripper of assets had written, "as to the efficiency of this type of *foreign exchange politics* that you may expect extreme measures from me, if I do not directly oppose them!" (Italics supplied.)

But such glaring revelations left majority opinion unshaken. The establishmentarians went on insisting that the hyperinflation had been entirely an "economic disaster brought on by accidental, uncontrollable events." There had been no planned abetment— they insisted—no perpetuation of the inflation by "vested interests" who obtained an economic advantage from its continuation.

The Modern U.S. Dollar: The Coming of Fiat Money

During the past quarter-century, the physiognomy of inflation has been utterly transformed. Prior to 1952 the typical inflationary interval proved to be a paroxysm that suddenly gripped the economic corpus and soon passed away. Usually each brief seizure had its origin in some "emergency" (frequently in the outbreak of war) and ended soon after the real or purported exigency was over. There then followed a considerable period of cooling off.

Before the middle of the twentieth century inflation had been an exceptional phenomenon, an aberration that interrupted a protracted period of relatively stable prices. When the exception had run its brief course, the rule of stability was reestablished and prices fell. Frequently, living costs declined to a point equal to or lower than the level that had existed prior to the onset of inflation. This cooling off precluded any long-term, cumulative inflationary build-up. As a result, prices remained fairly stable over long periods of time. For instance: living costs actually declined from the end of the Civil War until the outbreak of World War I (the New York Federal Reserve Index of Consumer Prices declined from a level of 102 at the end of 1865 to 100 in 1914). It was not unusual during the nineteenth century for a man of sixty to buy a loaf of bread for the same price his mother had paid when he was a boy of six. All this has changed. Inflation has become a malady that endures year after year—decade after decade—persisting without interruption and offering no real hope of cessation.

Proof of the chronic nature of modern inflation abounds in the cost-of-living tables released by the leading nations of the world.* The consumer price index of the United States registered its 160th consecutive monthly advance in April 1980. Unbroken since January 1967, this string of month-to-month cost-of-living increases is by far the longest in the sixty-five-year history of the index. Since 1913 (when the index was established) there have been only eleven cycles in which consecutive rises in living costs went beyond six months. The longest previous interval—created by the vast economic pressures of World War II—lasted only twenty-two months and was brought to an end by wage-price controls. But the average span of consecutive rises came to only four months, or one-fortieth of the duration of the current cycle.

Almost thirteen and a half years of constantly climbing prices without a single monthly break is a record not easily equaled. In the past, those nations that experienced a long, unabating depreciation in the purchasing power of money were finally overwhelmed when the velocity of inflation became unbearable.

For us, too, the wind has begun to pick up ominously. In the 1953–1962 decade the rise in the cost of living proceeded at an idyllic annual compounded rate of 1.1 percent. In the next ten years (1963–1972) the pace tripled to 3.3 percent on average, but reached a 6-percent level in some of the later years of the decade. Then, during the next five years (1973–1977) prices sprinted ahead at an

---

*See table on page 290 in Appendix. The facts contained in that table reveal the persistence of inflation in Canada, France, Italy, Japan, Germany, and the United Kingdom (our six leading trading partners), as well as in the United States. The data is obtained from *International Financial Statistics,* published May 1978 by the International Monetary Fund.

annual compounded rate of 8 percent. In 1978 they accelerated by 9 percent, and in 1979 swept upward dismayingly by 13.3 percent. Assuming the continuation of a 13-percent annual rate during the next three years (a distinct possibility since costs rushed upward at an already greater rate in the opening months of 1980), the consumer price index will soar to almost 300 by 1982—a surge of almost 175 points from the 125 level at which it had stood at year-end of 1972. If these projections are proved correct, the purchasing power of the 1972 dollar will have shrunk to 40 cents in a ten-year period.

The landscape beyond 1982 appears even more bleak. The likelihood is that the 13-percent inflation pace of 1979 will give way to a rate of between 25 percent to 30 percent unless stringent, long-term wage-price controls are installed. The persistence of such a trend would ultimately produce the social destabilization that invariably accompanies a gathering hyperinflation.

In the initial stages of past inflationary episodes, there existed a deceptive prosperity and "growth" accompanied by a gradual rise in prices that seemed, for a time, entirely containable and "manageable." Later events, of course, proved that the perpetrators of inflation did not know when to stop; the forces they unleashed—seemingly innocent and even beneficent in the beginning —brought disaster in the end.

Have we already begun—unawaredly—to reenact the opening segments of the old scenario? The existence of certain similarities suggests that possibility. In addition to the most ubiquitous symptom—a rapid acceleration of all living costs—there now prevails a simultaneous presence of the four phenomena that have coexisted during all major modern inflations, namely: (1) a massive expansion of money and banking credit; (2) continuing and burgeoning governmental budget deficits; (3) the race to buy inflation-hedging possessions (ranging from rare postage stamps to entire corporations); and (4) the rapid transfer of wealth to persons of power and influence (although these four phenomena now prevail in many nations, the scope of this book limits our discussion to their existence in the United States*).

---

*See table in Appendix (page 289) for data on the increase in money experienced by the seven leading capitalist nations during the quarter-century between 1953 and 1977.

(1) Massive expansion in money and banking credit.

The great surge of money that has occurred since 1933 (when the government renounced its obligation to convert banknotes into gold) can be seen in the following:

TABLE 2.
RISE IN MONEY SUPPLY (M²)*

Year	Money Supply (billions)	Per Capita Money Supply
1933	$ 34.0	$ 272
1942	78.9	585
1952	168.5	1,074
1962	242.9	1,302
1972	525.3	2,516
1973	571.4	2,715
1974	612.4	2,890
1975	664.3	3,111
1976	740.3	3,441
1977	806.5	3,720
1978	879.0	4,032
1979	952.6	4,702

*M² consists of money in circulation plus demand and time deposits in commercial banks, but does not include deposits in mutual savings banks, savings and loan institutions, credit unions, and the postal savings system. Nor are certificates of deposit of $100,000 or more included. Their inclusion (an imperative inclusion, in our opinion, but one which is conveniently overlooked by most economists and analysts) would have raised the M² money supply by $74.7 billion at the end of 1977 to a figure of $881.2 billion. Note also that we have used the M² supply as a measure of money, rather than the narrower, less-revealing and by now outmoded M¹ supply commonly reported in the press.

From a low base of $34 billion at the end of the bleak depression year of 1933, currency and deposits rose by $45 billion during the next ten years. Then, in the decade between 1942 to 1952 (during which we printed up vast sums to finance two wars and an interbellum boom) there was a bulge of almost $90 billion. In the moderate decade (1952–1962) before we became mired down in the Vietnam War the rise was smaller, amounting to $77 billion. But in the following ten-year period (1962–1972) the stock of money soared by an unprecedented $282.4 billion as we flung out dollars to finance our military venture in Southeast Asia and to fund a domestic expansion and the acquisition of overseas assets by our leading multinational corporations. In that single expansionary decade we created more money than we had accumulated in the 186-year history of our nation prior to 1962.

But during the next five years (1973–1977)—with fabrication of money even more hectic—we piled up another $281 billion. In the single year of 1977 we put out an additional $66.2 billion. If the rate of print-up during the next five years proceeds at the pace set in the 1973–1977 period, the money supply will surge to more than $1.24 billion by the end of 1982. If that projection proves to be correct, a credulity-defying $1 trillion will have been added to our money stock in just twenty years. Such an exponential growth would deeply exacerbate the already undesirable rate of inflation. (Note: In March of 1980 the Federal Reserve Board—ostensibly to "achieve an improvement and refinement of monetary data"— discontinued the use of the various money supply measures it had been issuing for years [including the M^1 and M^2 measures referred to in this book] and replaced them with a new set of money indexes. The narrowest of these new money supply figures is the "M1A" measure and the most comprehensive is the "L" supply.)

(2) Continuing and burgeoning governmental budget deficits.
Before the Great Depression of the 1930s (that is, before the leading nations of the world forsook the gold standard), governments usually stayed within their means. Heads of nations or empires who ran chronic deficits were regarded either as irresponsible weaklings or charlatans or madmen. Heavy debt spending was excused only in time of war, and since wars were always started with the promise that they would be "short," budget shortfalls were countenanced only during brief periods of "dire exigency."

Subscribing to these theories, the government of the United States had accumulated a debt of less than $1.25 billion by the beginning of 1930, after 154 years of operation, during which annual budget surpluses were commonplace and the occasional deficits were small. But the Depression brought on the fatal metamorphosis, as nations abandoned gold so that they might fabricate enough paper money to revive their stagnant economies. The national debt of the United States quickly mounted to just under $43 billion by 1940 (the end of the Depression decade) as the Federal Reserve System accommodated to a pump-priming President and Congress.

By 1946—after heavy shortfalls incurred to finance the most costly war in history (World War II) and the vast outlays associated with demobilization—the national debt soared to over $269 billion. By 1952—despite the heavy drain of the Korean War —it had been reduced to around $259 billion.

But from that point on (except in 1956, 1957, and 1969) budget surpluses became obsolete. The constant progression of budgetary shortfalls sustained during the twenty-five years after 1952 drove the total of gross federal debt up by an additional $450 billion, until—at the end of 1977*—it reached $709 billion. In just five years (1973–1977) immense budget deficiencies had propelled the total up by an additional $272 billion, a figure greater than the total debt outstanding until 1952.

The trend continued into 1978 when the year's deficit came to $49 billion. During the three peacetime years of 1976, 1977, and 1978, a combined shortfall of $173 billion was recorded. Clearly, we have entered a new phase. Budgetary deficits are no longer the short-run response to a sudden exigency—such as war or society-destabilizing depression. They have become an almost perennial feature of fiscal policy, occurring in peacetime as well as in time of war and during lush periods as well as in years that are lean.

Actually, substantial government deficits have become commonplace not because the Treasury has been unable to raise additional revenues to meet expenses, but because the makers of fiscal policy have purposively employed deficit financing as an economic stimulus (more about this later on).

During the past quarter-century the government has relied on the largesse of the Federal Reserve System for the means to fill the budgetary gap. The central bank has also provided gargantuan amounts of new funds to other borrowers whose proclivity to incur debt has exceeded that of the government, namely, consumers and corporations.

(3) The race to buy up inflation-hedging possessions—usually with borrowed money.
"The orthodontists are driving up the cost of [musical] instruments to the point where young musicians simply cannot afford them." This appraisal was made recently by Joseph Lufkin to describe the ongoing worldwide scramble for "value-retaining" objects.† Mr. Lufkin's remarks contained no animus against dentists. As a consultant to the nation's leading auctioneers and appraisers of antiques and artworks (Sotheby Parke Bernet), he welcomes their presence—and the growing presence of newly rich business executives, physicians, and motion picture and television celebrities who—in addition to the

---

*Fiscal year ended on September 30.
†See article of January 14, 1979, in *The New York Times* written by Deborah Dankin, titled "Early Violins, the Latest in Collectibles."

coterie of traditional collectors—are buying everything in sight.

In a single auction held in December 1978, at Sotheby's New York branch, the hectic bidding for rare musical instruments brought in a record-breaking $1.8 million. Among the old Italian instruments auctioned off was an Antonio Stradivari cello; it went for $287,000. A Guiseppe Guarneri del Gesú violin owned by Yehudi Menuhin, the world-famous violinist, sold for $221,000. "Stradivari violins," according to W. H. Wells, another expert at Sotheby's, "are absolute gold dust." A rare Stradivari that fetched $35,000 in 1950 now commands a price of close to $300,000.

American auction galleries have also attracted representatives of newly formed foreign investor-consortiums, organized to acquire artworks and antiques, jewelry, other valuables. These agents of firms domiciled in Hong Kong, the Middle East, and Europe have been aggressive buyers of the rapidly dwindling store of "collectibles." Even the staid British Rail Pension Fund has diversified into rare instruments in its search for investments that might appreciate more rapidly than the rate of inflation (the Pension Fund recently bought an old Italian cello for $30,000).

With rare instruments quickly disappearing into investors' hands, a booming market has developed for old bows fashioned by reputable bow makers. Some of these have been selling at $25,000 apiece. According to a chart recently plotted by Sotheby's, prices of bows have advanced at the rate of 25 percent to 35 percent a year since 1968, with the larger gains registered in the past several years.

A teeming demand—increased year after year by the growing tide of investable money and the climb of the consumer price index —has also driven up the price of other antiques. Last year $2.2 million was paid for a twelfth-century enameled medallion at a Sotheby Parke Bernet auction. At the same establishment an eleventh-century ivory relief was sold for $1.1 million, and a single twelfth-century candlestick brought $1 million. In Sotheby's of London, $371,000 was bid for a dressing table made in 1769 for the Elector of Saxony. An American businessman, Ronald Lauder, paid $196,000 in December 1978 for a Chippendale desk.* Another American executive, Malcolm Forbes, paid $100,000—a peak

*See article "Record-Setting Auction Stars of 1978," written by Rita Reif (January 25, 1979) in *The New York Times*.

price—for a twentieth-century airmail stamp (issued in 1918).

Highly regarded Japanese prints have attracted a growing amount of ready cash. In June 1975, Sotheby Parke Bernet was the scene of spirited bidding for a set of nineteen Japanese prints that brought $315,550, an increase of 75 percent over the $179,500 for which they were acquired at the end of 1972.

Diamonds—historically used as a "safety-net" against falling currency values—have recently surged in price as a growing number of investors and speculators have scooped up the carefully controlled supply.* In the New York retail market a one-carat flawless stone tripled in price—from $6,000 to $18,000—in the space of one year (1977 to 1978). The rise in less perfect stones, while not as sensational, has far outstripped the gains registered by other *Sachwerte.* The trend was described in a recent issue of *Jewelers' Circulation Keystone,* the leading publication of the retail jewelry trade: "Consider this fact: In 1972 a retail jeweler paid a major New York gem supplier $1,775 for a one-carat diamond. In April of 1978, he paid $7,665 for the same stone."† According to the magazine, this condition has been brought about by "the avid buying of investors of every kind, from small businessmen to wealthy professionals . . . gem dealers, appraisers, pension fund managers with money to invest, and banks looking for novel premiums to offer depositors." An unsuspecting public, stirred by planted newspaper accounts and television pitchmen in the guise of "expert diamond dealers," have been ordering gemstones—frequently of low quality—by the bagful. A similar craze has been noted in Japan and Germany (in recent years the United States, Germany, and Japan have accounted for approximately 80 percent of all gemstones purchased). Rampant buying and speculation finally impelled Tiffany and Company to sound a sharp note of warning. In an advertisement carried in *The New York Times* of March 17, 1978, the firm announced: "Diamonds are too high! This may be an unusual statement for an organization like Tiffany and Company. But some speculators have driven prices too high. We suggest you look before you leap!"

---

*De Beers Consolidated, which supplies between 80 percent and 85 percent of the world's diamonds, substantially—and admittedly—controls wholesale prices.

†On the basis of data of retail prices charted by Dun & Bradstreet in *Diamond Registry Bulletin* (now discontinued), a similar stone would have sold at $800 in 1953. The rise in price during the past quarter-century would have amounted to about 860 percent.

Such warnings may temporarily deter some speculation in collectibles but well intended admonitions are not likely to stem the pell-mell buying of consumer necessities such as houses, autos, furniture, household appliances, and clothing. A great deal of purchasing of such items would take place even in a noninflationary era by a population exceeding 216 million individuals, but a growing portion of buying has recently been generated in the race to "keep ahead of inflation." This is especially true in the housing area.

Expenditures for new houses reached an all-time high in 1978 despite the fact that the cost of the average new house almost quadrupled in the past fifteen years (from $18,000 in 1963 to $67,000 at the end of 1978*), while the median family income grew less than threefold ($6,250 in 1963 and approximately $17,000 in 1978).

Instead of impeding the acquisition of new houses, escalating prices have actually accelerated the process. "We finally saved enough for the down payment and with prices rising, we thought it was better to buy now than next year," Karen Lando of La Grange, Illinois, recently told a reporter concerning her reasons for buying a new home.† She and her husband bought their new house for $90,000, with a down payment of only $18,000.

"Last year I bought a house on waterfront property," recounted Arthur Britten. "I had a condominium, but I feel the value of the land will appreciate and the pool and the tennis court will give me luxurious living and offer good resale possibilities. I'm not depriving myself of anything."††

When asked by the *Wall Street Journal* in mid-1978 to explain the surge in buying of homes and cars, Jay Schmiedenkamp, director of the Gallup Consumer Survey, replied, "No one—unless they are nuts—believes prices will go down."

And Mary Gottschalk, assistant vice-president and economist at Citibank, explained the breakneck pace in the buying up of houses and other durables as follows: "Consumers tend to be rational, to make judgments about expenditures in the same way

*Based on figures released by Federal Home Loan Board.
†See article, "Housing—It Shelters More Than the Family" by Alan Osier, *The New York Times,* January 7, 1979.
††"Consumers Pile up Debt to Buy Homes, Furs, Autos" by Barbara Ettorre (article in January 7, 1979, edition of *The New York Times*).

as corporations. . . . The consumer has been saying that it is far more rational in a world of high or rising inflation to save in the form of real assets—real estate or durable goods—than in the form of financial assets."

Gottschalk might well have added that most buyers of homes or other durables require more than the wish to protect themselves against the ravages of inflation and more than a rational approach; they must be able to secure the very substantial financing (borrowing) that makes their purchases possible.

Consumers—availing themselves of billions of dollars continually created by the Federal Reserve System—have gone into debt at an unprecedented rate.

TABLE 3.

OUTSTANDING PERSONAL DEBTS

	Mortgage Debt*	Consumer Debt†	Total Debt	Per Capita Debt
1952	$ 58.5 billion	$ 32.5 billion	$ 91.0 billion	$ 578
1962	169.3	74.0	243.3	1,304
1972	372.2	177.6	549.8	2,632
1977	656.6	289.4	946.0	4,361
1978	762.0 (est.)	340.0 (est.)	1,102.0 (est.)	5,039
1979	875.0 (est.)	382.0 (est.)	1,267.0 (est.)	5,682

*Mortgages on private (one to four family) dwellings.
†Consumer debt consists of installment debt (75% to 80% of total) and noninstallment debt.

A continuation of the pace experienced since 1972 will push total outstanding personal debt beyond $1.6 trillion by 1982.

A similar trend has occurred in corporate debt. Having risen moderately from $171 billion in 1952 to $348 billion in 1962,* it shot up to $975 billion by 1972.† But in the next five years (by 1977) it had streaked to an estimated $1,500 billion. It is likely that corporate indebtedness will approach $2 trillion by 1981 if present trends prevail.

Like consumers, corporations have attempted to protect themselves against inflation by "building now." With prices of machinery and brick and mortar headed only one way—upward—company officials have been impelled to carry out expansion plans, whether their treasuries contained the funds or not. More often

*Source: *Economic Report of the President* (1980).
†Source: United States Bureau of Economics.

the money was not available, but for "preferred risk accounts" it could be had at a high-interest rate from the banks. And so the plants—and the mountains of debt—were erected.

Considerable amounts were also borrowed for the acquisition of other corporations. With the cost of constructing plants and equipment sky-high, the merger route frequently proved to be the most economical way of obtaining additional production facilities. In the eight years from 1970 through 1977, approximately $15 billion of assets were acquired through mergers,* an amount greater than all the assets transferred through acquisitions during the quarter-century prior to 1970.

(4) The rapid transfer of wealth to persons of power and influence.
During past inflationary episodes, accelerated agglomeration of wealth was unmistakable but its precise extent was carefully hidden. Elaborately staged ex post facto "investigations" somehow always failed to reveal the exact size of fortunes accumulated. Several "commissions of inquiry" were convoked in France after the assignat era and a few minor speculators were induced to go through a ceremonial expiation before they were assessed the heavy fines that should have been levied on more successful profiteers. A handful of petty foreign-exchange dabblers were led, kicking and screaming, to a central square in Paris where—to the unrestrained delight of assembled crowds—they were literally forced to bare their chests so that the word "gambler" could be branded into their skins. But these diversions only served to deflect the public's attention from the true facts. Similarly, after the German hyperinflation, the Committee on the Fall of the Mark and other "investigative" bodies planfully failed to secure enough information about the exact personal wealth-holdings of the beneficiaries of inflation.

We are more fortunate. Despite a persistent effort by government officials to keep the facts about personal wealth well hidden, the information has finally been divulged, largely as the result of

---

*Refers solely to mergers in the manufacturing and mining industries (in those industries fixed assets represented a major share of all assets transferred). Source: *Statistical Abstract* (p. 580), published by U.S. Printing Office.

the efforts of a handful of dogged and gifted economists who refused to be sidetracked. An insight into the struggle that has been waged may be obtained from the remarks made by one of these economists (James D. Smith) when he testified, on September 26 and September 27, 1977, before the Task Force on Distributive Impacts of Budgets and Economic Policies (established by the Committee on the Budget—a committee of the House of Representatives).* Professor Smith told the Task Force:

I would like to note here that most of what we have learned about the distribution of wealth—certainly most of what I have learned—has come about through the support of the National Science Foundation . . . in opposition to a rather enormous effort of the Internal Revenue Service to prevent such studies and—I might add—[of] some other agencies of government. . . . It took seven years in a more favorable climate than this for me to get access to the Federal estate tax returns on computer tapes without any names associated with individuals' information. During those seven years the IRS put up every conceivable argument how detrimental it would be to people if that information was available. The information was finally made available to me with the support of a number of members of Congress and some members of the Administration—and the Republic still stands! In fact, the IRS now distributes the data to anybody who wants that information. Nothing has come about that I know of that has been injurious to anyone.

By using the macrostatistics contained in the national balance sheets on wealth (total value of stocks, bonds, municipals, bank deposits, established value of real estate, miscellaneous personal possessions, etc.) and then comparing these facts with the information derived from estate filings with the Internal Revenue Service, Smith (and a few other economists) have been able to illuminate what the government—until recently—had been able to keep dark. By analyzing the filed estate returns† and employing them as a "stratified sample" of the whole living population, the dead have been made "to speak trumpet tongued" about the extent, distribution, and movement of wealth among the living.

*See "Data On the Distribution of Wealth in the United States," published by the U.S. Government Printing Office, September 26, 1977.
†Returns on estates of $60,000 or more.

The plethora of facts revealed through the use of the "estate multiplier" technique—so illuminating and so striking—is beyond the scope of our effort here. But some of the data needs to be considered so that we can trace the rapidity with which wealth has been amassed by the privileged during the present inflation.

What are some of the facts about the accumulation and distribution of personal wealth in these United States? In 1972 one-fourth of all individual wealth-holders had net personal wealth of under $1,000, and one-half owned less than $3,000. The lower half of the population owned less than 6 percent of all personal wealth held in the nation. Over 14 percent—according to the Bureau of the Census—lived in poverty. Furthermore, 70 percent of individual wealth-holders possessed less than $10,000 each, and only 10 percent achieved a net worth of $30,000. The level at which estates become taxable—$60,000—was attained by only 6 percent of the adult population. These figures, it should be noted, do not refer merely to cash and deposits; they take in, also, all other financial assets as well as such tangibles as houses, land, jewelry, cars, and so forth—in short, almost every important possession.

In sharp contrast are the facts about the small minority of the rich who occupy the top of the wealth structure. The accounting furnished by Professor James D. Smith before the Task Force on Distributive Impacts speaks for itself.

If you ask what share of the personally held wealth is owned by the richest one percent of the population, then I would respond to you: about one-quarter. If you took even a more rarified group—the upper one-half of one percent—they own about one-fifth of the personally held wealth in the United States. . . . If we ask what type of assets are held by this top wealth group—this top one percent of the population—they own about half of the corporate stock in America. One can say that the top one percent of the population literally controls all corporate assets in the United States via that half of the value of corporate shares. Now consider trust assets—a particularly beneficial way for the rich to transfer wealth from one generation to another—the top one percent of wealth-holders have 91 percent, we estimate, of the total trust assets in the United States. The richest one percent hold over one-third of all bonds. They own essentially 100 percent of municipals.

It is worth noting that none of the facts presented by Professor Smith were refuted or challenged by representatives of the Internal Revenue Service and other government agencies who appeared as expert witnesses before the Task Force of the Budget Committee.

An additional observation is required. One should resist any notion that the figures of wealth distribution in 1972 represent an anomaly. Other studies conducted over a period of time show that since 1945 there has been very little change—year after year—in the share of wealth held. The top 1 percent continues to own 21 percent to 27 percent, while the lower half of the entire population continues to hold only from 5 percent to 6 percent of all personal (net) wealth, regardless of changes in the economy and regardless of the time when the sampling is taken.*

Having obtained an insight into the maldistribution of wealth, we can now address ourselves to the question: exactly what has the ongoing inflation achieved for the very rich and the very powerful in the United States? As Table 4 readily reveals, it has made them enormously more wealthy in a short period of time.

By the end of 1953, the richest 1 percent of the country's wealth owners had been able to accumulate $305.7 billion of the nation's store of personal assets. Although there were some newcomers among the roster of the "super-rich," a considerable portion of the wealth then owned by the 1 percent elite had been built up over decades as legatees of large estates—using their inherited riches as a base—gradually erected new wealth on top of old holdings.

By the end of the idyllic decade (by 1962), the total assets of the top 1 percent were increased by $243 billion to a level of $548.3 billion. But during the next ten years of escalating inflation (1963–1972), the super-rich succeeded in amassing one-half trillion dollars of additional wealth, driving up their total holdings to $1,046,900,000,000 (1 trillion 46 billion 900 million). During the ten-year period the "old rich" were benefited substantially, and they were joined, in increasing numbers, by the newly created entrepreneurial "nabobs." In 1958, there were 47,000 multimillionaires in the nation, and in 1962 there were 71,000.

---

*See Dorothy S. Projector and Gertrude S. Weiss, *Survey of Financial Characteristics of Consumers,* Federal Reserve Board, 1966. See also Robert Lampman, *The Share of Top Wealth-Holders in National Wealth.*

TABLE 4.
SHARES OF RICHEST 0.5 PERCENT AND 1 PERCENT OF PERSONS IN NATIONAL WEALTH

(dollar amounts in billions)

Asset	1953					1962					1972				
	Value held by richest (%)			Share held by richest (%)		Value held by richest (%)			Share held by richest (%)		Value held by richest (%)			Share held by richest (%)	
	100.0	0.5	1.0	0.5	1.0	100.0	0.5	1.0	0.5	1.0	100.0	0.5	1.0	0.5	1.0
Real Estate	$439.0	$45.0	$68.0	10.3	15.5	$770.0	$79.6	$117.8	10.3	15.3	$1,492.6	$150.9	$225.0	10.1	15.1
Corporate stock	151.5	116.6	130.8	77.0	86.3	426.4	227.3	264.4	53.3	62.0	870.9	429.3	491.7	49.3	56.5
Bonds	72.8	33.0	38.3	45.3	52.6	94.5	33.2	38.4	35.1	40.0	158.0	82.5	94.8	52.2	60.0
Cash	160.1	20.9	28.8	13.1	18.0	278.3	28.9	42.5	10.4	15.3	748.8	63.6	101.2	8.5	13.5
Debt instruments	34.0	8.2	10.9	24.1	32.1	51.5	16.5	21.8	32.0	42.3	77.5	30.3	40.8	39.1	52.7
Life insurance (CSV)	64.5	6.6	9.1	10.2	14.1	93.8	7.1	10.7	7.6	11.4	143.0	6.2	10.0	4.3	7.0
Trusts	20.5	17.5	18.8	85.4	91.7	46.1	NA	NA	...	...	99.4	80.3	89.4	80.8	89.9
Miscellaneous	222.8	12.5	19.8	5.6	8.9	379.4	39.8	52.7	10.5	13.9	853.6	59.5	83.3	6.8	9.8
Total Assets	1,144.7	242.8	305.7	21.2	26.7	2,093.9	432.4	548.3	20.7	26.2	4,344.4	822.4	1,046.9	18.9	24.1
Liabilities	140.0	21.3	29.0	15.2	20.7	314.0	47.8	61.0	15.2	19.4	808.5	100.7	131.0	12.5	16.2
Net worth	1,004.7	221.5	276.7	22.0	27.5	1,779.9	384.6	487.3	21.6	27.4	3535.9	721.7	915.9	20.4	25.8
Number of persons (millions)	...	0.80	1.60	...	...	...	0.93	1.87	...	...	...	1.04	2.09	...	...

Source: Task Force on Distributive Impacts of Budget and Economic Policies (House of Representatives Budget Committee), published by U.S. Government Printing Office, 1977.

But by the end of 1972, their ranks had swelled to 218,000.*

It was a repetition of the phenomenon witnessed in all rapid inflations: the powerful and the advantageously situated had utilized the benefits that flowed from rapid money creation and inflation. In a single decade they had been able to transfer into their control an amount of assets almost equal to all the assets the "richest 1 percent" had been able to gather up in all the years prior to that time. Of the half-trillion dollars of wealth added in the 1963–1972 decade, approximately \$270 billion represented new assets acquired; the remainder constituted an inflation-induced increase in the worth of old assets.†

The extent to which a greatly expanded money supply facilitated rapid wealth acquisition by the "elite 1 percent" can be seen in the following: at the beginning of 1963 the nation's store of money (M^2) stood at \$243 billion and the average wealth-holding of each person included in the elite group amounted to around \$293,200 (while the average personal worth of each of the 87.5 million individuals comprising the bottom half of the nation's wealth owners came to less than \$1,200). By 1972—with the money stock having been expanded by an additional \$282 billion—the assets of each super-rich†† individual promptly soared, on average, to around \$500,960. But the average individual in the lower 50 percent saw his so-called wealth inch up to only \$2,000.§ The speeded-up conveyor of assets (the combination of excessive money creation and inflation) had added a mere \$800 to the assets of the individuals comprising one-half of the country's population, but it had delivered an additional \$207,760 (on average) to the wealth of each of the super-rich during a period of only ten years.

If we consider a still more privileged group—the top one-half of 1 percent of asset-owners—who, as a group, habitually possess around 20 percent of the country's personally owned assets, we find that the instrument of inflation delivered wealth to them even more rapidly. Each of the "superelite one-half percenters" owned, on average, assets amounting to around \$462,000 at the end of

*Source: Internal Revenue Service (Statistics of Income and Supplemental Report on Personal Wealth).

†Approximate figures derived by applying GNP implicit price deflator to figures contained in Table 3 (with 1972=100).

††The 1 percent of top wealth-holders.

§Approximate figures derived from exhibits presented before the Task Force on Distributive Impacts of Budget and Economic Policies (House of Representatives Budget Committee, September 27 to September 29, 1977).

1962. But by 1972, the average wealth of each had vaulted to more than $790,000.

This amount of wealth agglomeration may not seem very impressive in an age that has become accustomed to $3 million villas, second-hand Rolls-Royces priced at $79,000,* $30,000 mink bedspreads,† and $1 billion annual sales of cat food. We must keep in mind, however, that the growth in assets was expressed in "average" terms and reflected a highly disparate rate of wealth aggrandizement experienced by over 1 million individuals, with the holdings of some advancing from a base of "only" $100,000 (at the beginning of the period) to a level of $500,000 (at the end of the period), while the assets of others vaulted from a level of a million dollars to several hundred million dollars.

Since the "estate multiplier" method does not attempt to identify asset-holders by name, we must look to other sources to determine the scope of wealth-stripping by individual multimillionaires. During the 1963–1972 period, the very rich—as might be expected—had done their very best to thwart the inquiries of skilled and tenacious investigators. Consequently, even the revelations produced by the most diligent delvers must be regarded as incomplete. Nevertheless, their disclosures have uncovered considerable information about the extent of property-piling by the successful aggrandizers, information that has validated the general conclusions reached through the estate multiplier method.

An article in the September 1973 issue of *Fortune* magazine by Arthur M. Louis sheds a good deal of light despite the author's purposive exclusion of some efficient agglomerators. From his roster of multimillionaires, Louis had eliminated all the powerful "old rich"—many of whom had inherited their wealth. In addition, he eliminated those who had failed to reach his minimum criterion for inclusion: a net worth of at least $50 million (this meant, of course, that thousands of lower-level multimillionaires escaped his net). Finally, he came up with thirty-eight candidates, almost all of whom had possessed only very modest means prior to 1962.

Leonard N. Stern, president of Hartz Mountain Corporation (by 1973, one of the nation's leading purveyors of pets and pet foods), led the list. In 1959 his company "was on the skids" and

---

*See *The New York Times* of January 22, 1979, "Rolls Royce asks Price Rise."
†See *The New York Times* of December 14, 1978, "Glittering Stores for Sheiks, Stars," by Pamela G. Hollie.

was heavily in debt. But in 1962 it "went public" and its fortunes
and those of its struggling president were changed. Stern borrowed to expand, borrowed to engage heavily in real estate ventures, sold tons of pet food, and—by the time the article appeared
—was able to show a personal worth of between $500 million and
$700 million, at the age of thirty-five.

Following closely came H. Ross Perot (founder of Electronic
Data Systems, self-styled soldier of fortune, and former salesman
of electronic components), who was able—by raising millions of
dollars from a bulging money supply—to launch a highly successful company in the booming computer field. Worth very little in
1962, his personal holdings in 1972 came to around $400 million.
Before a breaking market (1969) reduced the value of his stockholdings, he was worth $1.5 billion.

Next came Edwin C. Whitehead, chairman and founder of
Technicon, Inc., one of the country's most profitable manufacturers of medical equipment. He, too, was disadvantaged by a plung-
ing stock market that substantially reduced the $1.1 billion fortune
he had erected in a brief period. But he managed to hold onto from
$300 million to $400 million.

Roy J. Carver, who had founded Bandag (retreading materials) in 1957, began making "real" money in the early 1960s. By
1968 he had put together about $10 million, but by 1972 his per-
sonal worth had soared from $200 million to $300 million. At
the age of sixty-three (when the article appeared), Carver
demonstrated the benefits of being egregiously wealthy. He
owned four apartment "homes," a large villa in Cannes, and a
$2 million jet plane that seated thirteen. A 70-foot yacht evi-
dently proved inadequate and the retreading mogul had ordered
a new aluminum 125-footer. For land transportation, he possessed one Rolls-Royce and four Mercedes-Benzes. Among his
other accoutrements, there appeared to be two attractive associates who were visible in a picture taken by a *Fortune* photogra-
pher.

The article then went on to deal, a bit more summarily, with
thirty-four other members of the new financial royalty who were
ranked in an order based on the number of multimillions they had
acquired. At the bottom were twenty-odd, each of whom had been
able to pile up somewhere between $50 million and $100 million.
The combined worth of the thirty-eight new multimillionaires

surpassed $5 billion—almost all of which had been amassed during the 1963–1972 inflation.

Louis came back to the lists again in February 1979.* Once again his roster included only those who had been able to collect at least $50 million and once again he had purposefully omitted the "old rich" such as the Rockefellers, the Murchisons, the Hunts, J. Paul Getty, Howard Hughes, the Bechtel family, the Du Ponts, Daniel Ludwig, the Mellons, and others. Since a rise of about $300 billion in the money supply and an advance of almost 50 percent in the cost of living had occurred in the five years subsequent to the publication of his previous article, it was only logical to assume that his new list would be longer and would contain a larger quantity of assembled assets. This time there were sixty-two new potentates identified, and their combined assets ranged between $7 billion and $8 billion. Moreover —as Louis indicated—he "had not found every last one of the Private Rich." Hundreds—perhaps thousands—may have eluded him. "The identities of many big real estate operators, for example," he stated, "remained effectively shrouded from scrutiny."

According to Louis†, not a single wealth-gatherer among the many he interviewed had attributed his recently amassed riches to the existence of inflation; in fact, the subject was never mentioned during his interviews. Present agglomerators—like their counterparts of the past—have no desire to disturb the goose that is laying their golden eggs.

Having noted some of the common manifestations present in previous periods of pervasive inflation, can we assume that today —as in the past—there exists a "net of interests vested in the maintenance and continuation of inflation"?

We *cannot* make such an assumption—if we are prepared to accept the opinion held by the great majority of economists, financial commentators, government spokesmen, and Federal Reserve officials. According to these sources, persistent inflation is a fortuitous phenomenon—a condition brought about, by and

---

*See *Fortune* magazine of that date for his article, "In Search of the Elusive Big Rich." This article concentrated on entrepreneurs whose fortunes were rooted in the privately owned companies they had established or acquired.

†This information was obtained in a conversation with Louis in March 1979.

large, by random, "unmotivated" events. Essentially it is a malfunctioning of the economy produced by the "miscalculations" of government or by the erroneous execution of fiscal and monetary policies or by the spontaneous creation of pressures, such as those generated by the "demand-pull effect" or the "cost-push" syndrome, and other autogenous factors. Occasionally, there is a fleeting reference to the cost-raising effects produced by self-serving actions such as the "enforcement" of inordinate wage rises by labor leaders or the "administered pricing" of dominant corporations in their quest for maximum profits. But in the final analysis, pernicious inflation is a creature of circumstance; it is *not* a creature of contrivance.

And so, in 1966 we find Arthur F. Burns writing, "It is unrealistic to expect the 'new economics' to protect government officials from making mistakes in their efforts to manage prosperity. In fact, by helping to bend government policy toward inflation, the new fiscal theory will at times promote mistakes."*

In his 1968 Economic Report of the President, Lyndon Johnson said, "Most economists believe that the rate of price increases would be significantly lower than it is now if we had attained the present level of unemployment more gradually." (More "errors.")

Richard Nixon, addressing the nation in his Economic Report (1970), stated, "The inflation unleashed after mid-1965 had gathered powerful momentum by the time this Administration took office a year ago. The expectation of inflation was widespread, as was skepticism of the determination of government to control it. Businesses anticipating rising prices and costs were eager to invest as early as possible and were willing to incur high interest charges that they would pay later in presumably cheaper dollars" (the anticipation mechanism).

"Workers demanded large wage increases," he continued, "to catch up with past increases in the cost of living and to keep up with future increases. Prices were being boosted to catch up with past cost increases and to keep up with the future" (the cost-push effect).

---

*See *The Management of Prosperity* (Pittsburgh University Press, 1966), written after Burns had completed his service as Chairman of the Council of Economic Advisers during the Eisenhower administration.

"In 1970," he went on, "we are feeling the postponed pinch of the late sixties. If responsible policies had been followed then, the problems of 1970 would be much easier. But we cannot undo the errors of the past. We have no choice now but to correct them, and to avoid repeating them." (Errors and more errors.)

Nowhere is the ascribing of inflation to miscalculation and error more evident than in the comments on Federal Reserve Board action. In a wide-ranging and informative article, "What's Wrong at Fed?" that appeared in the August 29, 1973, issue of *Financial World,* John F. Lyons wrote:

Now the Fed [the Federal Reserve Board] is under attack, as never before in its sixty-eight-year history for expanding credit too rapidly and too recklessly at the very time the nation's economy was gathering a powerful head of steam. . . . Perhaps the tone and focus of the debate can be gauged best by the comments of an economic expert close to the House Committee on Banking and Currency who says, "Inflation is of primary importance to people today and it's going to be of growing importance." I have no doubt that the Fed is one of the main contributors to today's inflation. Remember that the Fed has in its power the ability to change this environment from one of inflation to one of recession in a very short period of time. . . . Who would have thought in March [1973] that the money supply was going to rise at an annual rate of 11 percent for even as much as the next four months? But, in fact, it has. Who would have predicted in January 1972 that you would have had an 8-percent average annual increase for a period of eighteen months? But you did. The contribution to inflation is obvious.

What had caused "the contribution to inflation?" The answer was the usual one. "The Treasury Department," a major source of U.S. economic policy, the article continued, "is also casting a critical eye at the Federal Reserve. Says one economic expert at the Treasury, 'Looking back, it's clear that errors were made.'

"Even sources at the Fed itself," Lyons went on, "quietly concede that something has gone wrong. One expert who prefers to remain anonymous says, 'It would have been preferable to have begun slowing down the money supply much sooner, but nobody perceived the strength of the economic expansion that took place.'

"By midsummer," Lyons wrote, "the miscalculation had become so serious and so self-evident that Arthur Burns, Chairman of the Federal Reserve System, publicly confessed to the errors of the system's ways. . . . In early August Burns said somewhat grudgingly, 'Both monetary and fiscal policy moved in the right direction last year. In retrospect it appears, however, that restraint should have been somewhat greater.' " (Later in the article Burns is quoted as admitting, "As events turned out, the growth of the currency and demand deposits during the second quarter exceeded our expectations.")

After noting "the Fed . . . fell prey to major economic miscalculations . . . which caused monetary authorities to act much too little and too late for the U.S. economy," Lyons concludes with the following: "The real question . . . is whether the Federal Reserve has proven itself impotent to curb the tremendous expansion of credit and inflationary pressures. . . . As long as there remains a serious doubt about the ability and competence of the world's largest central bank to control its destinies, there will be disorder in the marketplace; in all marketplaces."

Lyons's article had referred, in the main, to the inflationary climate that had been created by "miscalculations" during 1972 and the first half of 1973, but in mid-1975 "errors," once again, became the assigned cause for overexpansionary decisions. Once again Arthur Burns—who for years had managed to convince financial commentators that he was an arch conservative on money matters while he went on pumping up the money supply—attributed his inflation-provoking policy to new "mistakes."[*] Appearing before the Senate Banking Committee, he declared, "The May–June–July [1975] bulge in the monetary aggregates did not come as a surprise, but it was larger than we had expected, and very much larger than we desired."

Two years later economists were attributing a new burst of inflation to the same old cause. According to a Reuters report of October 21, 1977, Robert Reid, appearing before the Institutional Investor Bond Club on the previous day, had "placed the blame for the current excessive growth on a fundamental mistake by the Fed in conducting policy in the second quarter."

In 1978, shortly before he left his post, Burns was forced once again to raise the shield of "error" against the charge of inflation-incurrence. Although some newspapers praised the dour, didactic

_____
[*]Burns was Chairman of the Federal Reserve Board from 1970 to 1978.

Chairman for his "policy of restraint," others belatedly pointed out that under his stewardship banking credit had expanded by 35 percent in 1976 and by over 25 percent in 1977. When asked to assess his own performance in the "unsuccessful fight against inflation," he replied flatly that he was "not aware of any serious mistakes" but he conceded that there had been "numerous minor ones."

Evidently his interrogator—like almost every economist in the nation, like the members of Congress before whom Burns had testified on many occasions, and like the numerous financial writers who, for years, had reported his decisions and actions—failed to ask two key questions: How was it possible for a man of such proven monetary expertise to go on repeating identical "errors" for almost a decade (under Burns's leadership, the Federal Reserve Board's "mistakes" almost invariably stemmed from an inflationary bias; almost no disinflationary "miscalculations" were made).*

And if errors and autogenous "pressures" were, indeed, the causes of pernicious inflation, why did not these causes—which existed during many previous eras—produce long-run inflation in the past? Those individuals (members of the Federal Reserve Board and the President's Council of Economic Advisers) who have exerted the greatest overt influence on economic policy since 1962 have been at least as able, diligent, and well informed as their predecessors. It could not be argued, therefore, that persevering inflation had not developed during the long-term past because of a superior ability of predecessor central bankers and government economists to avoid "errors" and to cope more effectively with demand-induced pressures.

Have these rather obvious questions not been raised during the past seventeen years of rapidly rising living costs because of the widespread and almost automatic acceptance of the dogma of "fortuitous inflation"? And were they not raised—even by those who privately admitted that inflation could be the creature of "purpose"—because of a desire to avoid the difficulties usually experienced by the espousers of a "minority" opinion?

It is time to face a reality we have long sought to avoid. "With-

---

*The same tendencies were evident during the closing years of McChesney Martin's tenure (Martin was Burns's predecessor at the Federal Reserve Board).

out making the exaggerated statement that the inflation is due to a conspiracy," we should, at last, recognize that—essentially—it persists because it "is favored in many ways by people who make a large profit from it."

The View From the Fed: The Triumph of Fiat Money

A "net of interests vested in the maintenance and continuation of money depreciation" (to which Bresciani-Turroni alluded a half-century ago) is present today. The most influential nucleus in the "network of self-interests" is currently represented by the "top 1 percent" of wealth-holders. This elite minority contains the nation's several hundred thousand multimillionaires, as well as the top-ranking officers and directors of the country's important commercial and industrial establishments and the leading officials and board members of the nation's banks.* Despite their publicly

---

*The "nucleus" also contains many rich professionals, important government officials of considerable means, and numerous successful entrepreneurs, each of whom possesses total assets of less than $1 million. (The one-percenters have risen to the apex of power, not only through their financial and political clout, but also because of their de facto control of the nation's business enterprises through their ownership of more than 50 percent of all corporate stock outstanding.)

avowed opposition to "inflationary programs," the one-percenters
have been among the leading behind-the-scene advocates of those
highly expansionary monetary policies that have assured the continued presence of massive amounts of lendable funds in the banking system—funds that could be borrowed by influential individuals to facilitate their accumulation of a growing portion of
inflation-hedging assets.

Since each asset accumulator has assiduously concealed the
extent of his loans and since government agencies and the media
have not demonstrated any special zeal to publicize the facts, the
relentless demand for credit by the one-percenters has—for a long
time—gone unnoticed by the general public. But some of the facts
have leaked out during the past two years. Verbal and supplemental written evidence presented in September 1977 to the Task Force
of the House Budget Committee revealed the insatiable appetite
of "especially creditworthy" borrowers.

The data in Table 5 (extrapolated from testimony presented to
the Task Force) shows that the faster the store of money rose, the
more rapidly did the one-percenters deplete it.

TABLE 5.

Year	M² Money Supply	Borrowing of Top One Percent Wealth Holders
1953	$174 billion	$ 20.7 billion
1962	242 "	61.0 "
1972	525 "	131.0 "
1975	664 "	169.1 "

During the twenty-two years from 1953 to 1975, the money
supply almost quadrupled but the borrowing of the one-percenters
surged by more than eight times. In the 1953–1962 span when the
money stock rose modestly, borrowing increased by $40.3 billion.
But during the expansionary ten years from 1963 through 1972,
when the reservoir of money was swelled by an additional $283
billion, borrowing spurted by $71 billion. In that single decade the
loans of the elite one-percenters soared by an amount that exceeded all the personal debts they had accumulated until 1962.

In the three-year interval between 1972 and 1975—with the
print-up of money proceeding at a record pace—borrowing by the
super-rich also rose to historical heights. During the three years,

their loans rose by over $38 billion, or at an average annual rate approaching $13 billion; this compares with a $7 billion average annual rate recorded during the 1963–1972 decade. At the end of 1975 the one-percenters had been able to secure an amount of loans that equaled 25 percent of the entire money supply outstanding.

No definitive statistics regarding asset accumulation and debt incurrence have yet been developed for the period beyond 1975, but certain fragmentary—although reliable—evidence suggests that the one-percenters pushed their demands for credit to new heights during 1976 and 1977.

On September 20, 1977, Senator William Proxmire, Chairman of the Senate Banking Committee, revealed that certain individuals in the top 1-percent nucleus had piled up bank loans to a point where "they comprised about 23 percent of all bank capital." Subsequent evidence presented to the Banking Committee* by witnesses from the three bank regulatory agencies (the Federal Reserve Board, the Federal Deposit Insurance Corporation, and the Comptroller of the Currency) reflected a sharply rising trend of borrowing during 1976 and 1977 on the part of a particular group of "one-percenters," namely, officers, directors of banks, and their close business associates. Senator Proxmire estimated that "bank insiders," through a credit draining operation, had extracted loans totaling $16.6 billion by June 30, 1977.† "This level of insider lending," Proxmire announced, "is far too high for a safe and fair banking system. . . . One of the most flagrant abuses in banking today is the practice of making loans to powerful insiders, who, because of their position with a bank, are able to gain preferential access to credit. . . . Perhaps the most serious problem in bank regulation is the cozy relationship between the three bank regulatory agencies and the banks they regulate. A single unified bank regulatory agency free of banking industry ties could curb most of the abuses in banking today."

Although the combined loans of "bank insiders" represented only a fraction of the total credit extracted by all one-percenters, (most top wealth-holders, of course, were not officers or directors of banks) they were sufficiently diverse and representative to be

---

*Hearings were held by the Senate Banking Committee in September 1977 and May 1978.
†Proxmire's figures were an extrapolation from a survey conducted in 1977 by the Federal Reserve Board, at the request of the Senator.

used as an index of all "top wealth-holder" borrowing. From the data revealed at the hearings, it is safe to assume that the total borrowing of all "top 1-percent of wealth-holders" had surpassed $200 billion by the end of 1977 and had maintained the 25-percent ratio to M^2 money outstanding at that time.

Testimony presented before the Banking Committee showed that bank insiders were willing to engage in questionable—and even illegal—practices in order to siphon off a maximum amount of credit from the banks in which they wielded influence. Chronic overdrafts were incurred, frequently with no interest charged; huge loans were secured with inadequate collateral or no collateral; loans were stretched out and were "repaid" by "kiting"—by replacing the overdue loan with a larger loan; insiders induced large correspondent banks to make questionable personal loans to them after the smaller bank they controlled made a token deposit at the correspondent bank; identical collateral was pledged simultaneously with several banks, without the borrower's revealing that he had already put up his collateral elsewhere, so that he could secure funds from various sources.

During the hearings the activities of Bert Lance—probably the most prominent bank-insider recently charged with credit-stripping (and with some more serious misdemeanors)*—were extensively discussed. But there was no mention of the fact that Lance, while serving as head of the Office of Management and Budget, continued to issue repeated assurances about his commitment to "sound economic policies in the struggle against inflation" at the same time as he was kiting loans running into millions of dollars, thereby abetting additional money fabrication.

The officers and managers of the nation's major corporations comprise another important nucleus in the "net of interests."

*After several years of glaring revelations about the prodigious loans Lance had secured for himself, his family, and his friends over a long period of time he was finally brought to trial on numerous charges of fraud. But a jury, though disapproving of the bank-capital depletions his loans had caused, found him innocent on April 30, 1980, of any fraudulent acts. But along the way the publicity about his multimillion-dollar loan "arrangements" secured some benefits. Spurred on by public clamor arising from the revelations, Congress in 1978 passed what is known as the Safe Banking Act. That piece of legislation to some extent restricted certain loan practices by bank-insiders and their associates (particularly in the area of chronic overdrafts) but nevertheless left open various loopholes which in the future will permit officers, directors, and important shareholders of banks to draw upon a considerable amount of available bank capital through preferential loans.

Although most members of the managerial elite are to be found among the top 1 percent of wealth-holders, they must be considered a special entity because their economic interests are determined almost exclusively by the results achieved in the companies they serve and direct. Those executives who can produce "rapid growth" for their corporations are rewarded by soaring salaries, an increasing amount of valuable stock options, and important fringe benefits whose value frequently exceeds their high "base" pay. Those who fail to achieve what has come to be regarded as the quintessential desideratum of modern corporate existence—rapid and continually escalating earnings—are summarily replaced and their "rewards" are abruptly terminated.

The enormity of some of these rewards was recently revealed in the proxy material submitted to shareholders by the nation's three leading automakers. In 1978 Henry Ford II, chairman of Ford Motor Company, received $375,000 in salary and $682,000 in bonuses and benefits for a total of $1,057,000, and Philip Caldwell, the corporation's president, received $1,040,128 (of which benefits amounted to $680,128); the firm's executive vice-president, J. Edward Lundy took down $1,000,928 (with benefits amounting to about 66 percent). Thomas A. Murphy, chairman of General Motors, got $975,000 (benefits came to $625,000) and Richard L. Terrell, board vice-chairman of the firm obtained a total of $925,000 (benefits amounted to $625,000). Rewards at the considerably less successful Chrysler Corporation were much lower; the two ranking officers—John J. Riccardo and Eugene A. Cafiero—received $360,191 and $323,554 respectively (their combined benefits came to less than $32,000). But Lee A. Iacocca, who had been second in command at Ford Motor until he was lured by Chrysler (in the hope that he could obtain for the "poor" cousin of the "big three" some of the superlative results he had secured for Ford), was the recipient of a bonus amounting to $1.5 million and a $360,000 salary. He will also receive a pension of $178,500 annually from Ford Motors for the next ten years and, thereafter, $175,000 yearly for the rest of his life. In addition, he will get a six-figure annual dividend on his Ford stockholdings, most of which he secured through attractively priced option arrangements.

In a stream of articles, business-oriented magazines have repeatedly commented on the egregiously successful results produced by the carrot-and-stick method (the carrot being the promise of high rewards available to successful company executives, and the stick being the relentless drive for ever-mounting company profits). These publications have not mentioned, however, that while managerial skill has played some role in the inordinate amount of corporate profits recently produced, a far greater factor has been the ceaseless creation of great amounts of new money by the Federal Reserve Board. The piling up of mountains of additional money and banking credit has enabled corporations (as well as federal and local governments) to pay its workers the progressively higher wages and salaries that have been translated into greatly expanded consumer purchasing power and, in turn, into burgeoning sales and rapidly rising profits for companies. The linkage between expanding money supplies and escalating profits can be seen in the following:

TABLE 6.
(Figures are in billions of dollars)

Year	M^2 Money Supply	Wages and Salaries*	Personal Consumption Expenditures	Corporate Post Tax† Profits
1952	$168.5	$ 270.4	$ 217.1	$ 39.8
1962	242.9	440.7	355.2	53.7
1972	525.3	942.5	731.0	89.5
1977	806.5	1,536.1	1,210.1	162.0
1978	879.0	1,717.4	1,350.8	180.8
1979	952.6	2,000.0 (est.)	1,510.0 (est.)	195.2

Source: Department of Commerce, Bureau of Economic Analysis and Economic Report of the President (1978).
*Approximately from 80 percent to 85 percent of all salaries and wages come from the private sector, with the remainder derived from the government sector.
†Profits after inventory adjustment but before depreciation and depletion charges.

In seventeen years of accelerating inflation (1963–1979), an unprecedented infusion of approximately 710 billion additional dollars into the money supply has helped stimulate a fourfold rise in annual consumer expenditures and a $141 billion increase in the level of annual corporate profits.

A bloated money supply has brought about a sharp rise in profits not only because it has laid the base for higher sales but also because it has enabled strategically situated corporations to hike prices repeatedly, even when goods were in ample supply. Of course, business managers have always been eager to maximize net income by pushing up prices by as much as the traffic could bear, but during the long-term past—when monetary policy was usually conservative and money supplies grew slowly (precluding a constant stream of wage increases)—employees would be "restrained" from buying progressively marked-up goods and services and would ultimately be forced out of the demand market as prices went beyond their reach. However, in recent years—with the money presses working around the clock and endlessly providing the means for constantly escalating wages—"reward-hungry" corporate managers have been impelled to push prices to their utmost limits at all times.

In the August 22, 1975, edition of the *Wall Street Journal,* there appeared an article ("Price-Rise Resurgence Despite Idle Capacity Stirs Debate on Causes") that dealt extensively with the desire by managers to increase prices at every opportunity, and particularly when slack demand threatened to reduce profits. In "Old Theories Don't Explain Spread of Boosts" readers were advised, and then they were asked a question seldom raised by the "free enterprise"-oriented *Wall Street Journal:* "Could Oligopoly Be the Answer?"

"Whatever happened to Adam Smith's law?" the writer of the piece—Harry B. Anderson—wanted to know. "That question," he continued, "has been raised repeatedly over the past two years as a severe drop in demand for goods during the recession has failed to bring a corresponding drop in prices. Now with evidence accumulating that the recession is ending, price rises are picking up at a faster pace than would be expected at the end of a recession.

"Although businesses traditionally try to increase prices at the first hint of rising demand at the end of a recession, this time— some analysts suggest—they seem to be outdoing themselves. The jolting government price statistics for July [the C.P.I. shot upward at a 14 percent annualized rate during the month], for example, don't even reflect the full effect of grain sales to Russia, aluminum price rises, and scheduled steel price rises." (The article later commented that "aluminum, steel, tires, autos, and synthetic fibers—all industries running far below capacity levels"—were "announcing price increases.")

"Some businessmen seem to be turning consciously away from

traditional economics—at least for the time being. Dow Chemical was one of the first concerns 'to do something about the suicidal* course the chemical industry had taken during the 1950s and 1960s in a quest for high volume and low price,' boasts a company publication. Since 1968, it says, 'Dow has been making an all-out effort to keep prices high and thus has aggressively seized control of its pricing destiny, rather than being a pawn 'of the market place.'

"In many cases, buyers," Anderson continued, "seem surprisingly willing to go along with higher prices. . . . A company will suddenly start painting its widgets green to justify its prices on the basis of the cost of green paint. . . . Sometimes even sellers are surprised at how much they can get away with. An official of one Eastern capital goods maker recalls one product that just wasn't paying its way. The company didn't want to abandon the product altogether for fear of alienating its customers, so it decided to price it out of the market. 'We raised our price,' the executive says, 'and then we raised it again. But the customers kept buying. Now the product is selling for 40 percent more than it did at the beginning of the year, and it's "a real star" in the marketplace.' "

Management's compulsion to keep boosting prices—even at the risk of going to jail—was reflected in a *Forbes* magazine article entitled, "The Boss in the Slammer."† Readers were told that "businessmen spent more time in jail for price-fixing in 1978 than in the previous eighty-nine years. It amounts to a new occupational hazard. . . . Altogether, thirty-one people were sentenced to jail in 1978 for antitrust violations, compared with twenty-six in 1977 and 9 in 1976. Total individual fines in antitrust crime were over \$1 million (up almost 40 percent from 1977) and total corporate fines rose fivefold to \$13 million."

Finally—in an apparent recognition that even the threat of incarceration may not deter unwarranted increasing and rigging of prices and other antitrust violations—the publication offered "a checklist†† of cautions to corporate officials, titled: "How to Stay Out of Court (Jail?)."

---

*The inference made by Dow's spokesman was unmistakable: business now regards "low prices" as "suicidal."

†February 5, 1979.

††According to *Forbes* magazine, the "checklist" was prepared by Joseph E. Johnson, chairman of the Practicing Law Institute's Seminar on Director and Officer Liability.

One can assume, however, that no amount of cautionary checklists will suppress the drive for quick profits that produce rich rewards, career advancements, social prestige, and a sense of power. This assumption is validated by recent revelations of illegal activities on the part of highly placed executives in the area of corporate bribery. The Securities and Exchange Commission recently charged that key officials of hundreds of the country's great corporations paid off foreign nationals and foreign governments with bribes running into many millions of dollars in an effort to secure contracts and sales. In almost every instance the case was settled with a plea of no contest by the defendants.

It is also safe to assume that executives who are willing to risk severe punishment to attain their goals will continue their advocacy of expansionary monetary policies, despite the destructive effects of those policies on many sections of society.

Another nucleus in the "network of interests vested in the maintenance" of rapid money fabrication is the federal bureaucracy—members of Congress, key figures in the executive branch, and highly placed personnel in government departments and agencies. Their influence, their career possibilities, and—ultimately—their economic interests are usually nurtured as federal budgets and expenditures grow. Expansion of governmental activities presents bureaucrats* with heightened opportunities to assist their constituents and to "benefit" those valuable "special interests" whom they favor (and who ultimately return "favors"). Big budgets create big opportunities for the granting of much appreciated dispensations; shrunken budgets bring complaints from the disgruntled mass electorate and—more important—they diminish the possibilities for favor-granting to "the right people." Woodrow Wilson, during a campaign speech made in 1912, gave a frank appraisal of the symbiotic relationship that exists between the center of power and influential legislators: "The masters of the government of the United States are the combined capitalists and manufacturers. . . . It is written over every intimate page of the record of Congress. . . . You will find that while you are politely listened to, the men really consulted are the men who have the biggest stake—the big bankers, the big manufacturers, the big

*The term "bureaucrats" is used here in its widest sense and includes all important members of the federal government.

masters of commerce. The government of the United States at present is a foster child of the special interests." To many members of Congress who regard government service as a revolving door to the business world, the loss of influence (brought on by shrunken budgets) is a regrettable development.

But constantly expanding budgets require progressively stepped-up revenue receipts or heightened budget deficits, or what has come to be the modus vivendi in modern fiscal affairs: a simultaneous presence of proliferating receipts and high deficits. However, the funding of great deficits and the securing of escalating revenues require a soaring money supply (rapid money creation helps to bridge the purposively created budget gap and stimulates increased individual and corporate earnings. And increased earnings—in turn—bring in higher taxes and a rise in other governmental receipts).

In recent years members of Congress and key officials involved in the budgetary process have—with rare exception—opted for rapid money fabrication which would support a high level of government spending.* As we have already observed, a substantial portion of such spending since 1962 has been financed through budget shortfalls (approximately $455 billion was met by deficits from 1963 through 1978). The funding of these deficiencies was accomplished by—and was, to an extent, responsible for—the inflation-begetting creation of additional money by the Federal Reserve System. In times of low industrial activity, high unemployment, and stable prices, such deficits could have been justified as a means by which the economy could be stimulated. But many of the shortfalls were tolerated in years of high activity, full or nearly full employment, and escalating prices. During the 1963–1972 decade when unemployment remained below 5-1/2 percent in all but three years and when the rate of inflation was accelerating sharply, persistent annual shortfalls were planfully and inexcusably countenanced. Their maintenance was especially unwarranted because high individual and corporate income presented a ready source for increased revenue through higher taxation—taxation that would have moderately (and beneficially) reduced demand in

---

*In addition to Congress, the most influential figures involved in the budgetary process are the high-ranking officials in the Office of Management and Budget, the Treasury Department, the Council of Economic Advisers, and—of course—the President.

an overheated economy and thereby would have blunted the rise in prices.* Of course, there were some legislators and other government officials who sincerely opposed the fiscal policies that abetted inflation, but they were rendered ineffective by a majority whose self-interest lay elsewhere, a majority whose publicly stated resolve to "wage war against inflation" and to "restore a balanced budget with all appropriate speed" was an exercise in obfuscating rhetoric.

Many economists have ascribed considerable blame for the persistence of inflation to the "undisciplined buying of consumers." Undoubtedly, the conspicuous consumption and the hectic buying of properties and "collectibles" by the wealthy and the increasingly opulent middle class have propelled prices upward. But the charge leveled against the "average" consumer is—to a considerable extent—unwarranted.

Evidence does not substantiate the notion that the country's 175 million "typical consumers" have a "discretionary power to bring inflation to a quick end at any time they choose—simply by refusing to chase after high-priced goods." Of all family units in the United States 80 percent spend 75 percent of their disposable income on four basic necessities: food, housing, utilities, and medical costs. A considerable part of the remaining 25 percent of take-home pay is expended on clothing, automobile maintenance, or other transportation, insurance, and other "basics." Less than 7 percent is expended on luxuries (and even some of these outlays —such as those devoted to cosmetics and grooming aids—may fall into the necessities category). Almost nothing goes into savings.† Virtually no reserves are set aside for the purchase of major items

---

*Moreover, the bountiful supply of money would have precluded the phenomenon of "crowding out" of borrowers.

†Only the families who are classified as belonging to "the upper one-fourth of income-earning units" are able to accumulate any meaningful savings. Family income, in 1977, was distributed as follows: top 5 percent obtained 15.7 percent of total national family income; the top fifth obtained 41.5 percent of total national income; the second fifth obtained 24 percent; the third fifth obtained 17.5 percent; the fourth fifth obtained 11.6 percent and the lowest fifth obtained 5.4 percent. The 14.5 million families who were in the upper one-fourth of all income earners—and obtained approximately 50 percent of total pretax national family income—were, with rare exceptions, the sole accumulators of substantial savings. Those families who had a total pretax income of under $15,000 (they represented 44 percent of all families) had almost no savings and were substantially in debt. An additional 18.4 percent (with income ranging between $15,000 and $19,000) had savings that came to well under $3,000 per family.

such as houses, autos, refrigerators, or TV sets; these are obtained only through an ever-increasing amount of borrowing. The great bulk of buying that emanates from the typical consumer is not indiscriminate and essentially is not based on discretionary decisions; it is almost entirely an automatic, unavoidable response to the dictates of necessity.

But the progressively stepped-up expenditures of 175 million individuals do exercise an inflationary impact—albeit an involuntary one. A massive work force that continually wrests higher wages and then strips the supermarkets and shopping centers of newly marked-up goods certainly exacerbates the very condition against which it inveighs: the constant rise in prices. However, when all is said and done, the average consumer must be viewed primarily as a pawn in a game whose rules he does not fashion, and as an involuntary victim who has been forced to participate in his own disadvantagement. In assigning responsibility for the continued depreciation of money, his or her role must be ranked considerably below that of the top wealth-accumulators, the profit-piling corporate managers, and the compliant federal bureaucrats—all of whom have considerable latitude to chose between those actions which abet inflation and those which diminish it.

But the major share of responsibility for any serious or persevering inflation must, in the final analysis, be assigned to the authority that possesses the power to control the supply of money. We have seen—again and again throughout history—that the authority over money fabrication—whether primitive village chief, ancient king, or modern central bank—could quickly turn inflation on or off by opening wide or closing the spigot of money and banking credit. In the United States, for the past sixty-five years, that power has been vested in the Federal Reserve System and notably in the Federal Reserve Board (more recently referred to as the Board of Governors).* Under existing laws the Board's authority

---

*The tool of money creation and money control is actually held by the twelve-man Federal Open Market Committee (FOMC), composed of seven members from the Board of Governors and five members who are presidents of Federal Reserve Banks. The remaining seven Federal Reserve Banks are also represented at the meetings by their respective presidents who attend in an advisory capacity but do not vote. In almost all of its decisions and actions, the FOMC has followed the direction of the Board of Governors, which controls seven of the twelve votes.

to determine the quantity of money is almost absolute. The provisions of the Glass–Owen Act of 1913 under which the Federal Reserve System operates has conferred a virtually veto-proof autonomy upon its officials. While it is true that Congress has the ability to modify the Board's power by adopting changes in the original act, it is also true that the important modifications Congress has enacted in sixty-five years have widened the Board's powers. At any rate, within the confines of the existing legislation the Board enjoys an unassailable hegemony in monetary matters; its decisions cannot be altered or reversed by any person or agency of the government, and they are not susceptible to appeal or to change by the courts. Nor can Federal Reserve officials be removed by any government authority—even for gross ineptness or unmistakable negligence.

But there is indisputable evidence that the Federal Reserve Board—despite its autonomy—has succumbed to a confluence of pressures. The proof lies in the creation of a staggering $629 billion of additional money and banking credit* during the 1963–1978 period, and especially in the fabrication of $260 billion from 1975 through 1978, when the economy was already awash in dollars and the Board was serially publishing pledges about its intention "to foster monetary and price stability" (the $260 billion fabricated in the four-year 1975–1978 interval was greater than the total money supply accumulated until 1963).

The Board had succumbed to a demand for money to fund the federal government's purposively incurred budget shortfalls; it had accommodated to the demands exerted for additional bank credit by powerful individuals who were voracious buyers of vast amounts of "inflation-hedging" assets; it had acceded to the pressure of influential managers and directors of major corporations who were seeking the monetary means by which they could continue to achieve exponential "growth"; and it had accommodated to the pressure for substantial amounts of new money that would fund an ever-escalating disposable income for the nation's work force and a continually mounting volume of consumer-credit purchases.

Even before the Federal Reserve System was established, prescient observers warned that a central bank might become "overre-

*M² money.

sponsive to the demands of influential entrepreneurs" and would yield to the requests of "powerful financial interests."

So strong was public sentiment against the creation of a central reserve system that "the small band of Wall Street plotters" who attempted to draw up a plan for a central banking organization were forced to meet in secret.* In fact, the institution now known as the Federal Reserve System was conceived and born in an elaborate intrigue. The existence of the collusion remained hidden until 1916 when it received a little-noticed reference in Frank C. Leslie's magazine. Seventeen years later, Professor James Laurence Laughlin, in his informative opus *The Federal Reserve Act, Its Origins and Problems,* wrote of a group that met secretly at Jekyl Island for about two weeks and concentrated on the preparation of a bill "that became the model for the subsequent Glass–Owen legislation [the Federal Reserve Act]." Laughlin mentioned Frank A. Vanderlip, president of the nation's largest bank (National City Bank), as a "secret participant." Vanderlip brought the cabal into the full view of the public in a series of autobiographical articles published in the *Saturday Evening Post* in 1934 and 1935,† twenty-four years after the "clandestine rendezvous" had occurred. He began his disclosures with the following:

There was an occasion near the end of 1910 when I was as secretive—indeed as furtive—as any conspirator. None of us who participated felt that we were conspirators; on the contrary, we felt we were engaged in a patriotic work. We were trying to plan a mechanism that would correct the weakness of our banking system as revealed under the strains and pressures of the panic of 1907. I do not feel it is any exaggeration to speak of our secret expedition to Jekyl Island as the occasion of the actual conception of what eventually became the Federal Reserve System.

Vanderlip then recounted how "our particular group" (consisting of several officials of some of the nation's major banks, a partner in one of the country's most prestigious securities firms, an Undersecretary of the Treasury who had previously been an officer of a

---

*Unlike most advanced nations the United States had functioned without a central bank since 1836, when Andrew Jackson concluded a successful campaign to force the Second Bank of the United States out of existence.

†See page 291 of Appendix for more extensive excerpts from Vanderlip's revelations regarding the secret genesis of the Federal Reserve System.

leading bank, and Senator Nelson Wilmarth Aldrich—multimillionaire father-in-law of John D. Rockefeller, Jr., leading exponent of legislation favoring power and privilege, and known as "J. P. Morgan's floor-broker in the Senate") had come in stealth to the "privately hired and curtained" railroad car that was to take them to their rendezvous at the exclusive Jekyl Island Club. Once aboard the "private car" Vanderlip felt a deep sense of relief because he and his "patriotic" group had escaped detection. "Discovery," he wrote, "would have made our mysterious journey significant in Washington, in Wall Street, even in London. Discovery, we knew, simply must not happen or else all our time and effort would be wasted. If it were to be exposed publicly that our particular group had got together and written a banking bill, that bill would have no chance of passage by Congress."

For about ten days the Jekyl Island "duck hunters"* met in their retreat and hammered out the provisions and legislative details of what later became known as the Aldrich Plan. Their task was accomplished only after repeated altercation between Senator Aldrich and Paul Moritz Warburg, partner in the securities firm of Kuhn, Loeb and Company. Warburg (who had had wide experience in European banking before emigrating to the United States and was an expert in central banking procedures) repeatedly clashed with Aldrich, warning him against openly recommending the establishment of a central bank and against attaching his (Aldrich's) name to the proposed bill. Any piece of legislation "tainted by association with the money trust," Warburg admonished, would be immediately rejected. But Aldrich persisted and won the others over; Warburg then devoted his efforts to introducing some camouflaging compromises. The completed draft (prepared mostly by Warburg) provided for the equivalent of a central bank to be known as the National Reserve Association. Headquartered in Washington and containing fifteen branches located in

---

*Vanderlip's account contained a curious omission. Somehow he forgot to mention that reporters, who evidently had gotten wind of something brewing, were waiting at the Hoboken, New Jersey, railroad station where the curtained car was ready. As each member of "the particular group" approached the car, he was accosted by a reporter and asked about "a secret mission." A stock answer was given in each case: "Just going duck hunting." Several pointed to their leather encased hunting guns. The reporters—who either were unusually gullible or had been bought off—accepted the explanation. Subsequently the group became known as the "Jekyl Island duck hunters."

various parts of the country, the Association would hold a portion of the reserves of those commercial banks that joined it, would provide the reserves in "time of need," and would determine reserve requirements. The member banks would issue currency backed primarily by commercial paper and gold; the money created would be a liability of the Association's member banks (rather than that of the federal government). A board of forty-six directors would manage the Association, with forty-two directors elected by the member banks and four appointed by the government. The Association would be owned outright by the commercial banks which would purchase 100 percent of its outstanding stock.

After the finishing touches were put on the plan, the duck hunters held a farewell dinner consisting of grouse, quail, venison, and "several rich desserts and many libations." (But there was no duck on the menu.) On the following day the celebrants quickly headed northward to their individual destinations.

Aldrich—who as head of the Congress-appointed National Monetary Commission had been assigned the task of presenting a plan "for banking reform"—was deprived of the pleasures of ceremony when he suddenly became ill in January 1911 and could not present his bill in person. The Aldrich Plan (after some last-minute, behind-the-scene consultations between leading Chicago bankers and the four duck hunters who were not indisposed by illness) was released to the nation in a pamphlet on January 16, 1911, entitled "A Suggested Plan for Monetary Legislation."

The proposal was immediately endorsed by those bankers who understood it since it would deliver the power to create and control money exclusively into the domain of the commercial banks, and it would greatly enhance their lending capacity and their profits through the use of commercial paper. Heretofore—in accordance with the provisions of the National Banking Act of 1863 under which most major banks still operated—the amount of money and credit a bank could issue was determined largely by the amount of gold and United States government bonds it owned among its assets. Since gold and government bonds were in short supply (the interest-bearing debt of the government stood at a mere $894 million in 1910), banks had encountered difficulty in creating substantial amounts of additional currency and credit.

But under the Aldrich Plan, commercial bills (IOUs and notes executed by favored borrowers) could be used as an "asset" base for money fabrication. Since the supply of commercial bills would be virtually inexhaustible, the supply of money could be greatly expanded at all times.

A secret $5 million fund was rapidly created by banking institutions to drum up public support for the new money bill. Newspapers and magazines were immediately filled with articles lauding Aldrich's plan and dozens of economists quickly enumerated all the financial advantages that would "flow from the far-sighted legislation." The *Wall Street Journal,* in what must surely have been a spell of purblindness, editorialized,* "To the surprise of everyone who has followed Mr. Aldrich's course on the subject of monetary reform, the plan does not involve a central bank of issue. Perhaps the Rhode Island Senator saw that the country was not prepared for such an institution. Mr. Aldrich has worked hard to meet the objections that the reserve machinery—no matter how constituted—would get into the control, ultimately, of a little clique in Wall Street."

Although the *Wall Street Journal* had difficulty seeing what was plainly visible, others were not similarly afflicted. In Congress, a vocal coalition representing populism, agrarianism, and progressivism bitterly assailed the bill as "a scheme for a central bank in disguise." Charles A. Lindbergh, Sr. announced, "The Aldrich Plan is the Wall Street Plan. It is a broad challenge to the government by the champion of the Money Trust." William Jennings Bryan and—to a lesser extent—Robert LaFollette also castigated the bill. But the most outspoken criticism came from the common people in every walk of life and in every section of the nation.

Events proved Warburg correct: the bill was "stopped dead in its tracks," never to be voted out of committee, although opponents continued to speak out against it on the floor of the House and the Senate long after Aldrich's retirement in 1911.

There now began the long campaign of drafting a "suitable" substitute bill whose purpose was cogently described by Ferdinand Lundberg in his book *America's Sixty Families* (published

*On January 17, 1911.

in 1937). "The task of the Wilson administration was to place essentially the Jekyl Island measure on the statute books, but in an eccentric disguise. Warburg collaborated with the big financiers, as his memoirs reveal, and when administration views were needed he conferred with Colonel Edward M. House, Wilson's roving commissioner. The Warburg–Wall Street draft (known to posterity as the Federal Reserve Act), superficially revised by Wilson and Carter Glass of Virginia, was simply the Jekyl Island duck hunters' scheme for a central bank dressed in fancy toggery."

No one knows the exact number of drafts drawn up in the attempt to "place essentially the Jekyl Island measure on the statute books." Separate and secret documents were prepared by economists laboring on behalf of the government and by economists covertly engaged by the banking interests, and there were different versions prepared surreptitiously and simultaneously by several congressmen. All of these had one central aim: to erect a new money-creating system that would be completely owned and controlled by the commercial banks. All of these efforts took on a new urgency after Woodrow Wilson—who professed little interest in monetary affairs while energetically pushing for a central bank—moved into the White House in 1913.

The new President—a man of pince-nez rectitude and evangelical appearance—was also a man of contradictions. On the one hand he could announce in public: "The control of credit has become dangerously centralized . . . the financial resources of the country are controlled by small groups of capitalists . . . the great monopoly of this country is the monopoly of big credits . . . our system of credit is greatly concentrated . . . the growth of our nation, therefore, and all our activities are in the hands of a few men. This Money Trust . . . is not a myth."* But on other occasions—especially during secret conversations—he could take a completely opposite line. Once, having been asked in a private meeting by Henry Parker Willis (an economist who collaborated with Carter Glass in drawing up various versions of the Glass–Owen bill) whether he (Wilson) believed that the Federal Reserve legislation would ever see the light of day and whether its regulations could be enforced, the Great Idealist replied, "We must rely

*See *The Federal Reserve and Our Manipulated Dollar* by Martin A. Larson.

on American business idealism."* About five years before that meeting—while discussing the traumatic events of the banker-fomented panic of 1907—he had asserted, "All this trouble [the panic] could be averted if we appointed a committee of six or seven public-spirited men like J. P. Morgan to handle the affairs of our country."†

Spurred on by Wilson, Carter Glass (then Chairman of the House Subcommittee on Banking and Legislation), by late spring of 1913, had made considerable progress in drafting the legislation that was to be contained in the final version of the Glass–Owen Act. Following the outlines of the Aldrich Plan, Carter's bill provided for the establishment of a "Federal Reserve System" that was to be comprised of twelve regional Federal Reserve Banks, each of which was to be owned exclusively by the commercial banks that had bought stock in it. The affairs of each Reserve Bank were to be run by its officers and a board of nine directors, a majority of whom were to be either officers or directors of commercial banks or individuals "active in commerce, business, or 'industrial pursuit.' "†† The Federal Reserve Banks were vested with the power to set interest rates and reserve requirements and were assigned the responsibility of "inspecting and regulating" the banking practices of member banks (the "regulators" and "inspectors"—in effect—were required to "monitor" the entities which they represented). Each Reserve Bank was to carry the reserves of the member banks in its district and make these available in "time of need," and to maintain check-clearance facilities.

But the crucial function and purpose of the Federal Reserve Banks was to "create an elastic currency and provide for the credit instruments of commerce an instant sale." This somewhat abstruse terminology requires some elucidation: in essence the Federal Reserve Banks were endowed with the power to fabricate great amounts of money or banking credit at the request of their

---

*See May 1929 issue of *North American Review*.
†See *Adventures in Constructive Finance* by Carter Glass.
††The final Glass–Owen draft stipulated that three directors should be representatives of the member banks while three should be active in business, agriculture, or commerce but not in banking. These six directors were to be elected by the commercial banks. In addition, the Federal Reserve Board would designate three directors not engaged in banking.

member banks or on their own initiative. If a commercial bank belonging to the Federal Reserve System wished to create lendable funds (in the form of either cash or deposits), it could do so simply by going through the following procedure: it could "accept" an IOU (otherwise referred to as a "commercial bill" or an "acceptance" or a "bankers acceptance") executed by a "creditworthy" commercial borrower. After having created a deposit in favor of the borrower in an amount equal to the loan less a small discount, the bank could immediately sell the commercial bill to its district Reserve Bank or could borrow against it from the Reserve Bank by pledging it as an asset. The Federal Reserve Bank would then issue a check or cash to the commercial bank for the amount of the commercial bill it took in, less a small rediscount charge. By using this mechanism a loan could be converted into money "out of thin air," and by a constant repetition of that mechanism money and bank deposits could be created "out of thin air" in virtually limitless amounts through the limitless "printing" facilities of the Federal Reserve Banks. A similar procedure could create money or banking credit whenever the Reserve Banks wished to add to the money supply through open-market operations. A Reserve Bank could purchase government bonds in the open market and immediately issue a check to the seller (or in some unlikely instance present cash to the seller if he requested it). In either case the seller would deposit the proceeds at a commercial bank and this deposit would enable that commercial bank to lend additional funds to someone else.* (Representative Wright Patman, a frequent and acerbic critic of the Federal Reserve System, explained the procedure in his book, *A Primer on Money:* "Where does the Federal Reserve get the money with which to create bank reserves? Answer: it doesn't 'get' the money, it creates it . . . it creates money purely and simply by writing a check. And if the recipient of the check wants cash, then the Federal Reserve can oblige him by printing the cash—federal reserve notes—which the check receiver's commercial bank can hand over to him. The Federal

---

*The above description deals only with the initial step in a complex money-creation process. In our fractional-reserve system of banking an initial deposit creates a "falling-domino" or "multiplier" effect, as the first deposit sets off a string of deposits. For every $1.00 injected into the commercial banks by the Fed, $6.00 of new deposits in various commercial banks are usually created. For a more detailed description, see Patman's *A Primer on Money* and Peter L. Bernstein's *A Primer on Money, Banking and Gold.*

Reserve, in short, is a total money-making machine. . . . It never has any problem making its checks good because, of course, it can itself print the $5 and $10 bills necessary to cover the check.")

By June 1913, all the highly complicated provisions of the Federal Reserve Act had been drafted, and after months of countless revisions, the heretofore secret legislation was ready for the perusal of Congress. But a sudden hitch occurred.

Bryan—now Secretary of State and a leading voice in the liberal wing of the Democratic party—having suddenly obtained one of the yet secret copies of the bill, announced that he would block it if it were not revised in two respects. He insisted that a Federal Reserve Board be established, as a "capstone on the whole structure"—a Board consisting of governors each of whom was to be appointed by the President and approved by the Senate. The Board would assume some of the more important functions that had been vested in the Federal Reserve Banks in Glass's original proposals. He insisted also that the notes (money) to be issued should appear to be "Treasury currency, issued, payable and guaranteed by the Government."*

When Wilson spoke to Glass about the required revisions, the Congressman accepted the first readily but balked at the second. He tried to alert the President to the danger of permitting banks to create money that the government might later be asked to pay for in gold (the banks could create a limitless debt but the "government would be asked to stand behind it at all times" even though it might not have sufficient gold on hand). But Wilson—who had already decided to accede to the "Great Commoner's" (Bryan's) demagogic demands—stood his ground and the exchange between the two men became more tense. Carter Glass has recorded the concluding section of the highly revealing colloquy:†

His [Wilson's] good sense told him the notes [money] should be issued by the banks and not by the government but some of his advisors had told him Mr. Bryan could not be induced to give support to any bill that did not provide for a "government" issue. . . . With all the earnestness of my being I remonstrated: . . .

"There is not, in truth, any government obligation here, Mr. Presi-

*See *The Federal Reserve and Our Manipulated Dollar* by Martin A. Larson.
†See *Adventures in Constructive Finance* by Carter Glass.

dent," I exclaimed! "It would be a pretense on its face! Was there ever a government note based primarily on the property [assets] of a banking institution? Was there [ever] a government issue not one dollar of which could be put out except by demand of a bank? The suggested government obligation is so remote it could never be discerned," I concluded, out of breath.

"Exactly so, Glass," earnestly said the President. "Every word you say is true; the government liability is a mere thought. And so if we can hold to the substance of the thing and give the other fellow the shadow, why not do it if thereby we save our bill?"

Glass left the conference and dutifully rewrote the bill to include the "shadow" revisions that established the seven-member Federal Reserve Board of Governors (with each governor appointed by the President to a fourteen-year term and confirmed by the Senate). Some of the more important powers and duties formerly vested in the officers and directors of the Federal Reserve Banks were shifted to the Reserve Board, but the crucial money-fabricating mechanism of the Federal Reserve System was maintained intact, despite the inclusion of Bryan's "reform" that saddled the government with the responsibility of converting Federal Reserve notes into gold, upon demand. The House and Senate overwhelmingly passed the revised bill on December 22, 1913, and Wilson signed it a day later.

The covert architect of the original plan on which the bill was modeled (Paul Moritz Warburg) immediately sent Glass a letter of congratulations. A short while later he was appointed to the Board of Governors of the Federal Reserve. Another member of the "duck hunters" who represented the banking and business interests at the Jekyl Island meeting was also elevated into high office in the Reserve system. Benjamin Strong, president of J. P. Morgan's Bankers Trust, became president of the powerful Reserve Bank of New York, although he had been exposed as "a Morgan lieutenant" who had participated in some of the clandestine maneuverings that precipitated several bank failures during the panic of 1907.

The opening of Federal Reserve Banks in 1914 triggered an unprecedented money print-up and a rapid inflation. As soon as the "money-making machine" was in place, the commercial banks that owned it outright through their 100-percent stockholdings insisted that it be put to work in their behalf. The few doubts that may have existed as to whether their demands would be met were soon lifted. In his 1915 Treasurer's Report, William G. McAdoo, then Secretary of the Treasury and Wilson's son-in-law, announced, "The primary purpose of the Federal Reserve Act was to alter and strengthen our banking system [so] that the *enlarged credit resources demanded by the needs of business and agricultural enterprises will come almost automatically into existence* and at rates of interest low enough to stimulate, protect, and prosper all kinds of legitimate business." (Italics supplied.)

This official clarion call to the Federal Reserve System to create whatever money and banking credit was required by business and agriculture and to bring it "automatically into existence" was immediately echoed by officers and directors of several Reserve Banks. In 1916 the governors of the Reserve Board urged commercial banks to "discount commercial bills at Reserve Banks and thereby extend credit to enterprises," and in the same year Comptroller of the Currency John Skilton Williams encouraged farmers to withhold crops from market for a higher price and "hold out" by borrowing the funds "the Federal Reserve Banks will provide." He announced that "sufficient funds could be made available through "existing sources" and through the "rediscounting" of commercial bills and acceptances "to carry the entire cotton crop and half—if not all—the wheat crop and the tobacco crop and also to finance a billion of exports."*

In 1921 the Federal Reserve Board promised that it would extend "whatever amounts were legitimately required" for harvesting and marketing of agricultural crops. At the same time Andrew Mellon (who was Secretary of the Treasury in 1921 and owned the controlling interest in several banks and dozens of corporations including the nation's leading aluminum concern) privately urged the Reserve Board and some of his friends in the banking community to "stimulate business" by inducing the creation of "an abundant supply of money that would be available at low-interest rates."

But the most candid and most revealing admission by the Fed-

---

*A considerable portion of the money fabricated during the 1915–1927 period was used to finance our exports to Europe. During 1928 and 1929, most of the money created went into fueling a stock market boom. Almost $4 billion was used in those years for margin loans.

eral Reserve Board that it stood ready at all times to fabricate whatever additional money was needed by the commercial banks and business enterprises was contained in its Annual Report for 1923 (published in 1924). The Report stated, "The Federal Reserve Banks are the . . . source to which the member banks turn when the demands of the business community have outrun their own unaided resources. The Federal Reserve supplies the *needed addition to credit* in times of business expansion and takes up the slack in times of business recession." (Italics supplied.) (In short, the Fed is ready to create money at any time at the request of entrepreneurial interests.)

One does not require clairvoyance to see that a monetary policy that "supplies additional credit" in periods when business is already booming as well as in weak periods is a policy that must— in the long run—produce inflation.*

Inflation is what the country got immediately after the Reserve Banks began operating. In the seven-year interval between 1914 and 1920, the Federal Reserve System, through a variety of devices (the creation of money and credit via purchases and rediscounting commercial bills, notes and acceptances, the lowering of reserve requirements, and the "bending" of gold-reserve requirements), doubled the money supply. The rise of $18 billion in M^2 money supply—from $16.5 billion in 1914 to $34.5 billion in 1920†—was the sharpest in the history of the nation until that time (in seven years the "money-making machine" had produced more money than the country had acquired in its long history before the machine had been created).

The inevitable surge in prices followed; the consumer price index doubled, leaping from 30.1 to 60.0. This represented an annual compounded 12-percent rate of inflation. (In the ninety-five years before the Reserve Banks opened, consumer prices in the United States had risen by an annual compounded rate of less than one-half of 1 percent.) With the pace of money print-up less rapid during the 1921–1929 interval, prices declined moderately and then plunged during the Depression of the 1930s.

---

*See *America's Great Depression* by Murray Rothbard, published by University Press Syndicate. The book presents a similar view on the Fed's statement.
†Note: of the $18 billion bulge in the money supply, only $4 billion occurred during the nineteen-month period when we were involved in World War I.

In 1933 another restraint on the creation of money was suddenly removed when Congress—at the instigation of Franklin Roosevelt —took the nation off the gold standard. The Glass–Owen Act had stipulated, "They [the paper money notes issued by the Federal Reserve] shall be redeemable in gold on demand at the Treasury of the United States . . . or for gold or lawful money at any Reserve Bank." While in force these provisions, to some extent, had limited the fabrication of money and banking credit out of fear that the government might not have sufficient gold on hand to meet the expanded demands for conversion. But in a series of emergency enactments in the early part of 1933, these provisions were swept away. The presses that could grind out paper dollars and the Fed's "open checkbook" were now unencumbered.

For about six years after the revocation of convertibility, the presses and the checkbook were used somewhat sparingly as the nation lay quagmired in the Great Depression. But, of course, the lull proved temporary and the demands to speed up the creation of money soon asserted themselves and became too hard to resist.

Nor have similar demands been resisted during the past two years although two new chairmen—each of whom promised to wage "a vigorous battle" against inflation—were appointed in rapid succession to head the Federal Reserve Board. In March 1978 Arthur Burns was replaced by G. William Miller, who assured the Senate during confirmation hearings that he "would pursue a highly conservative monetary policy." The press and numerous friendly economists praised the new nominee, asserting that his successful career as the head of Textron, Incorporated had given him the experience and expertise to carry out a restrictive monetary program. Miller promptly emulated his predecessor as he swelled the money supply and banking credit at a pace twice his announced "target" rate. According to the new measures of money instituted early in 1980 by the Fed, the annual growth rate in the "L" money supply ("L" is the widest measure of money) came to 10.4 percent in the first quarter and 13.1 percent in the second quarter of 1979. (Most conservative economists estimate that the "L" growth would need to be reduced to 4 percent or 5 percent annually before inflation could be brought down to a "tolerable" level.)

And despite the fanfare that greeted the elevation of Paul Volcker (Miller's successor) to the chairmanship in August 1979, the "L" rate dipped down only modestly to 11.7 percent during the third quarter. In the fourth quarter of 1979 and the first two months of 1980 the M1A money stock (the newly created, narrowest measure of money) did decline after the new chairman instituted a full-point rise in the discount rate and several minor "tightenings" on October 6, 1979. But the "L" money supply continued to race ahead at a double-digit pace, impelling a keen Fed watcher to comment that Volcker was a "hard-nosed, tight-fisted man when it came to words, but a soft-money man when it came to actions."* And Henry Kaufman, an astute and conservative monetary analyst and partner in the prestigious banking house of Salomon Brothers, commented that "the recent increase of the broad money aggregates" had at last convinced people that the Fed was not using its powers to bring inflation to a halt; its recent actions, he asserted, "have evoked a growing skepticism." On the same day (February 11, 1980) economist Leif Olsen of Citibank commented that the money-supply figures of January 1980 raised serious questions whether the Reserve Board had "again dropped the reins and is once again on an overly expansionary track."

Such doubts were resolved several weeks later when banking credit figures (total bank loans outstanding) climbed sharply. Total loans—the greatest volume outstanding in the history of the nation—were 15 percent greater than a year ago.

On March 15, 1980, in an illuminating article that once again revealed the Fed's ready acquiescence whenever member banks exerted pressure for new funds, *The New York Times* said, "Taking advantage of bargain rates offered by the Federal Reserve System, the nation's banks increased their borrowings from the central bank in the week ended March 12 by almost $1 billion to a daily average of $3.3 billion, the highest level in more than five years. The Federal Reserve discount rate at which the central

---

*In one of its weekly *Research Reports* (August 6, 1979), "Volcker—Just Another Unsound Money Man," the highly conservative American Institute for Economic Research stated that "Paul Volcker is from the same mold as the unsound money men who have misguided the monetary actions of this nation for the past five decades." The publication then mentioned that Volcker is a member of the semisecret Trilateral Commission (a group of world capitalists, who—like Volcker himself—have continually recommended the demonetization of gold and the elimination of gold as soon as possible from the world scene as "a monetary vehicle" (note: when you eliminate gold you insure the unlimited print-up of irredeemable money).

bank lends [creates money] to its member commercial banks was at 13 percent in the week [it had been running at a 13-percent rate since October 6, 1979]. Banks have been paying as much as 18 percent from other sources.

"The Federal Reserve discourages banks from borrowing from its loan window but when the discount rate is so much cheaper than market rates, banks tend to borrow from the Fed despite the central bank's displeasure." (Note: the article did not indicate that the Fed's "displeasure" is more cosmetic than real, since the central bank is not required by the Federal Reserve Act to extend credit to member banks when they wish to borrow.)

"The Fed tried to block this borrowing," the *Times* article continued, "announcing yesterday that the nation's largest banks would have to pay a 3 percentage point surcharge to borrow from the Fed. That brought the effective discount rate to 16 percent." (History has shown that raising the discount rate is frequently an exercise in futility; the commercial banks, in turn, increase their own prime rate and raise the interest they are willing to pay for new funds borrowed from non-Fed sources. This game of leapfrog results in an exacerbation of inflation but does not stop the creation of money achieved through "borrowing" from the Fed.)

Had the Fed wished to put a quick end to rapid money fabrication and speeded-up banking-credit creation, it would not have resorted to raising the discount rate but would have sharply increased reserve requirements. This would have thwarted monetary expansion (and price rises) immediately.

The creation of great amounts of new money and banking credit, of course, produced the inevitable consequences. When the January 1980 consumer price index was made public in February, it revealed that living costs had shot up at an annualized, compounded rate of 18 percent.* The sudden announcement of an 18-percent rate of inflation sent a shock wave across the nation, and President Carter, for the first time, admitted that we had entered a "crisis" stage. On the same day (February 25, 1980) *Business Week,* the staid publication that could usually be counted

---

*About one-third of the rise was attributed by administration sources to the sharp run-up in the price of petroleum products. A similar explanation was offered one month later when the February CPI was released; it, too, showed inflation running at an annualized 18-percent rate.

on to take up the cudgels for entrepreneurial interests and conservative policies, inferentially advocated the enactment of wage-price controls in an article headlined "Controls Gain Backing as the Only Alternative." It then mentioned Bruce K. MacLaury (former president of the Minneapolis Reserve Bank), Senator Edward Kennedy, Thomas Juster (director of the Institute for Social Research of the University of Michigan), Barry P. Bosworth (former director of the Council on Wage and Price Stability), and Felix Rohatyn (director of the Municipal Assistance Corporation and director of Lazard, Freres & Co.) as "new supporters of controls." A week later the publication came out unequivocally for a six-month wage-price freeze as part of a five-point "anti-inflation program." In a long editorial titled "Shock Treatment for Inflation," *Business Week* asserted, "For fifteen years government has simultaneously deplored and fueled inflation. Its actions to fight it have been aimed mostly at making it tolerable." These illuminating sentences implied strongly that the long-running American inflation, to a considerable extent, had been unnecessarily abetted and extended.

But *Business Week*'s urgent call for controls over wages and prices as well as a rising public clamor for an immediate freeze had already been preempted by Jimmy Carter on February 27. On that day the President voiced his unreserved opposition to controls and asserted that "the basic policies we have espoused suit me fine!"

And what were these basic policies that pleased the chief executive although they had produced an 18-percent rate of inflation? For about two weeks the nation waited for elucidation while a specially appointed congressional advisory committee toiled over a much publicized "anti-inflation package" the White House had promised. When the package was finally unwrapped in mid-March, the nation was informed that there would be severe cuts in federal expenditures in 1981 and that the budget for that fiscal year would be brought into balance. Senator Robert Byrd, a prominent member of the advisory committee, pointed out that a balanced budget would probably reduce the rate of inflation by two-tenths of 1 percent—eighteen months later. The only other recommendation was the imposition of a 10-cents-per-gallon tax on gasoline purchased (a levy that was insufficient to deter petroleum consumption but one that would increase its price to the consumer). Obviously there were no other "basic policies" in President Carter's "package" worth mentioning since he failed to divulge them.

The shocking 18-percent rate of inflation that disturbed President Carter galvanized the Federal Reserve Board into action. In April and May 1980 the Fed rigorously tightened up on new money creation; during those two months the M1A supply actually registered a dramatic net decline. Simultaneously in April, the Fed's restrictive consumer credit controls (put into force in mid-March) began to make their effects felt. These two "tightening" measures—the draining of money from the banking system and the clamp-down on financial institutions' granting of loans for consumer time payments—suddenly cooled the overheated economy. With money tight in the banking system the prime rate shot up, reaching a heretofore unheard-of 20 percent; mortgage rates on private dwellings soared to 19 percent. The housing industry, already beginning to register some deterioration in February, now slumped badly as prospective buyers of homes were priced out of the market by the exorbitant interest rates. And the new consumer credit strictures made it progressively difficult for buyers to obtain loans for the purchase of "big ticket items." Automobile sales slumped. Unemployment spread throughout the construction industry, the automobile industry, and in steel manufacturing (whose output goes chiefly into auto-making and construction). By the end of April the unemployment rate climbed close to 8 percent, having been barely over 6 percent at the end of 1979. And the rate of inflation, as might be expected, moderated; the CPI advanced at a nine-tenths-of-one-percent rate in April and May (or at an 11.4-percent annualized compounded rate, which was meaningfully less than the 18.3-percent annualized rate of February and March).

But in the third week of May, the Federal Reserve Board gave way to the pressure exerted by the banks and industry; it dismantled a part of the credit controls it had erected and at the same time began to loosen its grip on the money supply. In June, the rate of new money fabrication surged upward, and M1A supply bulged by 11 percent. As money became "easier," and some corporations began deferring expansion plans because of the gathering recession, there were few borrowers among the major companies who were willing to borrow from the banks even though loans were becoming available at an 11½-percent prime rate at the end of June.

Then, in the early part of July, the Federal Reserve Board announced that by the third week of the month it would remove the remaining restraints contained in its credit controls program. On July 14, the *Wall Street Journal* hinted that having paid "his political debt" to Mr. Carter who had appointed him, Paul Volcker (who had supposedly opposed the imposition of the credit controls but had erected them at Mr. Carter's request for their obvious political implications in a presidential election year was, by the beginning of July, "free" to announce their demise.

And a few days later, in confidential interviews, the administration admitted that a tax cut would be put into effect early in 1981 which would result in a budget deficit. Some members of the Department of the Treasury, insisting on anonymity, estimated that the much heralded "balancing of the budget in 1981" had gone by the boards, and that actually there might be a $50 billion deficit incurred that year, a deficit that would be met in the usual way —by printing up new money.

The Federal Reserve Board and the government—disregarding the evidence of history—after "deploring inflation," were "simultaneously fuelling it" and, once more, their "actions were aimed mostly at making it tolerable."

Evidently the Fed (and all those whom it represented) as well as the government had paid very little attention to the leading editorial that had appeared in *Business Week* on May 5, 1980. The editorial had stated: "When economists write the history of the great inflation that has distorted the U.S. economy for the past ten years, they will record the Spring of 1980 as a crucial point. . . . The question now is whether the U.S. can stick with strong anti-inflation policies. If it cannot, it may throw away its last chance to avoid a total collapse of its monetary and credit structure."

EIGHT

The Summing Up:
The Edge of
the Abyss

In each of the four past inflation eras we have reviewed (the Roman, the French, the American Civil War, and the hyperinflation of the Weimar Republic), there was a replay of the same scenario. There were some differences in such minor matters as places, dates, and the cast of characters, but in the more important aspects—such as the cause-and-effect relationships, the unfolding of economic events, and final denouements—there was a striking similarity.

In each period inflation was triggered after the outbreak of a war that threatened the safety and life of the state.* The sudden

---

*During the assignat era the exigency of war was preceded by the threat of national bankruptcy and revolution; the solutions of those problems required the sudden outpouring of prodigious amounts of money, which the government sorely lacked. And during the Weimar episode the need for funds—once the war emergency was over—was, for a brief period exacerbated by the demands brought on by cash reparations.

exigency required immediate and monumental expenditures, but in each instance the government—lacking the means to fund the immense outlays—proceeded to create those means through the use of the printing press.* In each episode the government—or the central bank—was well aware (although it pretended not to know) of the dangerous inflation that might be unleashed by the precipitous introduction into the economy of massive amounts of newly created money, but the consequences that might be brought on by inflation—no matter how onerous—were correctly viewed to be a lesser danger than the mortal danger posed to the State by war.

Once having renounced a conservative approach in managing the monetary supply, the money printers could not resist the temptation to run the presses at greater speed and with greater frequency. And as the supply of new money mounted the expectable transpired: money began chasing goods and services, sparking a rise in prices. Workers now demanded and obtained wage rises to offset their heightened living costs and employers—in turn—raised prices to offset their newly increased expenses. The accelerating inflation, in turn, adversely affected the budgets of the government as the cost of conducting military and civilian affairs climbed, requiring still greater fabrication of denarii, francs, greenbacks, or marks. These new money infusions triggered yet another round of price rises as the purchasing power of the monetary unit continued to sink.

Then—in each of the four eras—the inflation passed into a more threatening, secondary phase. Whereas prices had risen steadily but with relative moderation during the initial stage of the inflation, they now began vaulting upward in sudden, great unpredictable jumps. As time passed each new price leap exceeded the one that had preceded it, disrupting the pricing structure and the production and distribution of goods and services; the growing chaos that invariably accompanies inflation in its advanced stages progressively enveloped more and more of the economy.†

Several other distinct phenomena began to appear during the second stage of the inflation (they were encountered in each of the

---

*In the Roman era, when paper money was not in use, the government systematically expanded its money supply by reducing the metallic content of its coins.

†In the greenback era there had been only a sixfold increase in the money supply; consequently, the disruption encountered in the Roman, French, and German episodes was substantially avoided by the North during the American Civil War.

episodes we have reviewed). The first of these was a refusal by the government to create and implement an adequate and efficient taxing system that would have obviated a considerable amount of additional money fabrication and its by-product: more inflation. But at the behest of powerful individuals, governments kept taxes low for a considerable period, and finally—when an adequate levy was at last reluctantly imposed—the tax-gathering system somehow "broke down" and did not gather the taxes due from the rich although levies against the poor, the working class, and the rentier middle classes were somehow most diligently and efficiently collected.

Another phenomenon was the overcreation of money in favor of the rich classes. Money that exceeded actual governmental budgetary needs was fabricated so that it could be made available to "creditworthy" borrowers. Such "excess" fabrications were resolutely pushed by governments (or central bankers) despite their highly adverse effect on already inflated prices.*

The rapid accumulation of inflation-resisting assets through the use of borrowed funds was another manifestation observable in each "secondary" phase. Business enterprises and "successful individual borrowers" were able to pile up assets whose worth rose at a pace higher than the rate of inflation—assets that would retain their value long after the inflation had run its course. That the powerful rich should have been able to amass great wealth in a relatively brief period was not surprising. More startling was their continued success during the secondary phase of each inflationary era in influencing governments to adopt those generally deleterious fiscal and monetary policies that created havoc for the great majority of the population while it transferred wealth quickly to a few.

Still another phenomenon unmistakably evident in the "secondary" stage of inflation was the unqualified insistence by "the estab-

---

*The destruction of records of the Roman Empire after the third century A.D. prevents a completely accurate discussion of excess money fabrication (financial data regarding the needs of the Roman government after the second century, budget requirements and government income, the amount of money fabricated, as well as the amount of money borrowed by the privileged classes of Rome for asset accumulation—all have disappeared with the passage of time and with the distruction of records by the invading Vandals). Scattered and partial historical evidence does, to some extent, reveal that excess money creation (fabrication of money beyond actual governmental needs) occurred in post-third-century Rome and was used for asset accumulation by the Roman privileged classes.

lishment" (government officials, central bankers, economists, historians, financial commentators, the press, etc.) that the runaway rise in prices and the destruction of the currency was due entirely to "uncontrollable" causes—that is, to "exigency" (after the exigency had passed), or to "errors of policy," or to "reparations" after reparations were terminated, or to the supposed need for more money creation long after past money outpourings had already inundated the economy. But there was never a hint from establishment sources—despite all the abundant contrary evidence—that the depreciation of money was being abetted and maintained by a "net of vested interests." And the small group of revisionist commentators who tried to expose the situation were soon hooted down and were silenced. It was through such methods that the "advantageously situated" were able to nurture the inflation after the "emergency" that had triggered the inflation had ended.

They nurtured it until its tertiary or "final" stage. In the third stage*—with money being slammed out of the presses in a lunatic fury, prices roared upward in mad, quantum leaps. Then as money became virtually worthless, economic paralysis set in, with producers refusing to accept payment in irredeemable paper—at any price. Ultimately—with the monetary unit completely destroyed—barter became the last result. In a final act, the government was forced into introducing a completely new monetary unit that maintained its value because it was issued in very modest quantities.

It is easier to see the shape of the past than to perceive the yet incomplete form of the present. The inflation that has lasted for almost two decades in the United States has not yet run its full course and it is, therefore, not possible to make a final assessment of it. We may readily conclude, however, that we have entered the critical "secondary" phase; the leaps in the cost-of-living index during the early months of 1980 are clear, telltale signs of an accelerating economic disorder.

Are we—like the Romans, the French, the Germans, and the numerous other nations that were finally overwhelmed by superinflation—likely to fall into the abyss? Or will we draw back (as the

---

*In the greenback era, with its more restrained money creation, the third stage was never reached.

North did during the Civil War) by putting an end, while there is yet time, to excessive money creation? As these words were being written in July 1980, there were few indications that we would suddenly take the route of monetary restraint. We cannot logically count on those individuals who have benefited most from inflation (the top wealth-holders and especially the leading officers and directors of the nation's major corporations and banks) to precipitously renounce the program that has produced such egregious rewards for them. Swollen monetary supplies have produced constantly increasing sales and profits for the nation's important companies. This rapid growth, in turn, has brought career advancement for corporate officials, peer approval, high financial rewards, and a growing sense of power. Other symbols of executive success—the erection of extensive plants, the acquisition of additional corporations, the rapid piling of new corporate assets on old assets—have been derived, to a considerable extent, by newly printed, borrowed money. It would be the height of optimism to expect present-day industrialists who (like their counterparts of the past) have "acquired one domain after another by using the weapon of inflation" to suddenly throw away that winning weapon in the midst of a seemingly successful campaign.

Nor can we expect key government officials to recommend willingly those monetary and fiscal policies that would precipitate a lessening of Big Government's role—a diminution that would attenuate each bureaucrat's influence, power, and opportunity to confer favors on important constituents (notably, the influential members of the banking-industrial complex).

And certainly, in a period of vaulting living costs, we cannot hold out much hope that workers and their union leaders will endorse those conservative economic policies that would immediately put a stop to the endless round of wage rises (secured through bulging money supplies).

What could possibly put an end to the dangerous drift? It is to be hoped that—after the inflation becomes more menacing and more disruptive—responsible leaders in the corporate community and in government will finally react to what, at last, they perceive to be a mortal threat to our society. That recognition should illuminate the real peril: the possible destruction of capitalist society by Communism. For far more than the dollar as a monetary unit and the abundant economy of the United States would be wiped out by a raging hyperinflation: the entire free world—so dependent on the leadership and protection of this nation—would be in ruins. Both Marx and Lenin in their dissertations on "finance capitalism" prophesied "imperialism's end" after inflation wrecked free-enterprise societies; both forecast that under such circumstances capitalism would have "sown the seeds of its own destruction." Perhaps the belated recognition that this prophecy might be fulfilled will, at last, stir leaders at the center of power to appropriate action.

Swift and decisive action would then be required. A rigid, across-the-board program of wage and price controls (covering salaries and "benefits," wholesale and retail prices, service costs, dividends, and interest) should immediately be enacted. This program should be accompanied by a government announcement that the controls would be kept in force for several years and that they would be accompanied by cuts in federal expenditures that would result in budget surpluses. The government would need—at last—to convince the nation (and particularly the business community) that it will no longer tolerate inflation. At the same time, drastic measures to curtail the supply of money would need to be implemented by the Federal Reserve System, including a meaningful rise in reserve requirements. This three-pronged program—(1) rigid controls, (2) steep cuts in federal expenditures resulting in budget surpluses, and (3) the throttling down of the Fed's money-making machine—must be kept in force until we return, for an extended period, to an annual inflation rate of between 3 percent and 4 percent.

But the centerpiece of this new approach would be the comprehensive, long-range wage and price control system. Such a system would undoubtedly result in some rigidities and inequities; it would create mountains of paper work for corporations; it would produce resentment and charges of bureaucracy, as well as opportunities for a few black marketeers. But these onerous by-products would be egregiously preferable to the chaos that hyperinflation would inevitably bring.

If only we had the time to create a less rigid and less exacting program that would bring the inflation to a swift end! Under such circumstances we would proceed—given the willingness of international leaders—to reerect a worldwide monetary structure based on gold convertibility. Such a system—rooted in voluntary self-restraint—would completely choke off the immense amounts of money being printed up by almost every advanced capitalist nation in the world—a print-up that is feeding every nation's inflation. But the erection of such a worldwide monetary order would take years to accomplish by which time it would be far too late for the United States as well as for other nations suffering from advanced inflation. Perhaps the creation of such a system can be attempted during the several years after a comprehensive wage-price control plan is put into place.

For years we have been told by administration after administration and by central banker after central banker that a "fight against inflation" was being waged. Such assurances have turned out to be illusory, to say the least. But there is no time left for illusions. We must act promptly and resolutely; otherwise, we may soon (like Lotte Hendlich) see an envelope on which there has been affixed a canceled postage stamp costing $250,000.

A P P E N D I X

EXCERPTS FROM PRIVATE DIARY OF HUGO STINNES (JUNE 23, 1923) REGARDING THE USE OF INFLATION AS A "POLICY" AND A "WEAPON"

Just as Mr. Bemmelmans and I parted I was telephoned at 10:15 by Dr. Rathenau from the American Embassy and asked to come to the American Embassy as soon as possible for a thorough discussion of the coal problem with the American ambassador and the American representative on the Reparations Commission: for it was Dr. Rathenau's opinion that this would be more effective than for him to describe the situation. . . .

At the request of Dr. Rathenau and of the two other gentlemen, I analyzed the situation in all its details. . . .

The greater part of the conversation dealt with the reparations

From *The German Inflation of 1923*, Fritz K. Ringer, ed., reprinted by permission of Oxford University Press.

problem, rather than with the coal situation. At Dr. Rathenau's request I expressed my views on the several aspects of the reparations problem. Usually, Dr. Rathenau then stated his own position on these things, and thus the whole problem was discussed.

First the reasons why Germany carried on the inflation policy which it did after the war were established. I pointed out that after the lost war it had been absolutely necessary for Germany to bring four million men then in the field, out of the habit of regular work, back into the regular routines of useful activity; and for that raw materials and employment were necessary. To get the raw materials and obtain the markets for production, it was necessary to sacrifice some capital for the purpose of sustaining the life of the nation, if it could not be avoided; for if the masses had remained unemployed, then doubtless Bolshevism would have seized Germany. And however dreadful the ravages of Bolshevism had already been in Russia, there is no doubt they would have been even worse in Germany, because in Germany it was a matter of a predominantly industrial country, where the effects of food shortages, caused notably by the maintenance of the blockade, would have brought a far worse manifestation of Bolshevism than in agrarian Russia.

I also informed the gentlemen that the weapon of inflation would have to be used in the future too, without regard to the resulting extraordinary capital losses, because only that made it possible to give the population orderly and regular activity, which was necessary to preserve the life of the nation.

It was further established in the discussion that the American gentlemen had been told not only by Germans but especially by the French that I deliberately aimed at growing inflation as something economically desirable, whereas in their view the growing inflation meant an extraordinary loss in national wealth.

I called the gentlemen who had expressed views like that to the American gentlemen fools; and Dr. Rathenau, who in all respects took the same positions I did, compared the situation of Germany to that of an army which is completely surrounded, and which to preserve its existence must break through, however great its losses, so as to get air and a chance at life for the whole.

Dr. Rathenau also pointed out that a people grown so poor as the Germans could not support wealth, unearned income or pensions for large groups of the population—a position the Americans did not believe they could follow, on the grounds that a population that could support large groups of rich profiteers could also support larger bodies of decent people. It was on this question that the single instance of differing views among the four persons present arose that evening.

Beyond that, the Americans did agree that lives were worth more than money, and that from this standpoint they understood why Germany followed a policy of inflation, if that was the only way the life of the nation could be sustained. . . .

For the rest, we were also in agreement that simultaneously with the granting and accepting of a loan, the currency problem would have to be solved in such a way that debts would be converted into gold debts. The Americans were highly satisfied to hear that both Dr. Rathenau and I would rather undertake the stabilization of the mark today than tomorrow and tomorrow than the day after, and that we would also have the courage to convert paper debts into gold debts. Following the consideration of these problems, which lasted until about one o'clock, we left, after I had promised the American ambassador to discuss the Russian problem and other similar matters with him in the near future.

Dr. Rathenau brought me to the Hotel Esplanade, where we parted after one o'clock, about ten hours before he was murdered.

GROWTH IN MONEY SUPPLY (M^2)
OF SEVEN LEADING CAPITALIST NATIONS

	Canada	France	Germany	Italy	Japan	United Kingdom	United States
1952	9.1	42.8	33.8	3,452	3,952	4.2	168.6
1962	16.8	167.8	135.3	17,749	17,668	10.4	250.3
1967	25.4	255.6	245.3	32,213	34,097	14.8	369.5
1972	42.2	493.8	469.3	65,808	84,040	26.0	570.0
1973	51.0	567.6	522.9	81,240	98,188	33.1	634.0
1974	60.5	670.2	572.5	94,020	109,493	37.4	693.6
1975	69.5	777.0	650.2	117,001	125,329	40.1	738.8
1976	83.2	875.1	707.6	141,599	142,248	44.6	796.6
1977	94.9	998.1	778.7	172,606	158,034	45.8	874.7

Above figures in billions. Amounts indicated are in terms of each nation's monetary unit (those of Canada are in Canadian dollars; those of France are in French francs; those of Japan are in Japanese yen, etc.). Each figure is a total of money, plus quasi-money, and conforms approximately to the term M^2, as used in the United States.
Source: International Financial Statistics Supplement (May, 1978), published by International Monetary Fund.

PERSISTANCE OF INFLATION (1953–1977)
AMONG LEADING CAPITALIST NATIONS

	Canada	France	Germany	Italy	Japan	United Kingdom	United States
1952	48.6	33.6	52.4	33.9	27.1	30.1	49.3
1953	48.4	33.0	51.5	34.4	29.2	31.1	49.7
1954	48.7	33.2	51.6	35.4	31.1	31.6	49.9
1955	48.8	33.5	52.5	36.2	30.8	32.7	49.8
1956	49.5	34.9	53.8	37.4	30.8	34.1	50.5
1957	51.0	34.7	54.9	37.9	31.8	35.2	52.3
1958	52.4	40.0	56.1	39.0	31.7	36.2	53.7
1959	53.0	42.3	56.7	38.8	32.0	36.4	54.2
1960	53.6	44.0	57.5	39.7	33.2	36.8	55.0
1961	54.2	45.1	58.9	40.5	35.0	37.8	55.6
1962	54.8	47.4	60.6	42.4	37.3	39.3	56.2
1963	55.7	49.9	62.4	45.6	40.2	40.1	56.9
1964	56.8	51.4	63.8	48.3	41.7	41.4	57.6
1965	58.1	52.8	65.9	50.4	44.5	43.2	58.5
1966	60.3	54.2	68.2	51.6	46.7	45.0	60.4
1967	62.5	55.7	69.3	53.5	48.6	46.2	62.0
1968	65.0	58.2	70.5	54.3	51.2	48.3	54.6
1969	67.9	61.8	71.8	55.7	53.9	51.0	68.1
1970	70.2	65.4	74.2	58.4	58.0	54.2	72.1
1971	72.2	69.0	78.2	61.3	61.6	59.3	75.2
1972	75.7	73.3	82.5	64.8	64.3	63.6	77.7
1973	81.4	78.7	88.2	71.8	71.9	69.4	82.6
1974	90.3	89.5	94.4	85.5	89.4	80.5	91.6
1975	100.0	100.0	100.0	100.0	100.0	100.0	100.0
1976	107.5	109.2	104.5	116.8	109.3	116.6	107.7
1977	116.1	119.6	108.6	136.6	118.1	135.0	117.0

| Rise in Consumer Price Index (%) 1953–1977 | 238% | 355% | 207% | 403% | 436% | 441% | 237% |

Above figures reflect the rise in Consumer Price Index of each of the seven nations. Figures are obtained from International Financial Statistics published by The International Monetary Fund (5/1978). In above Table 1975 = 100. Figures for United States are slightly at variance with those published by Bureau of Labor Statistics (CPI).

THE CLANDESTINE GENESIS OF THE FEDERAL RESERVE ACT, AS
REVEALED BY FRANK A. VANDERLIP IN HIS AUTOBIOGRAPHY,
"FROM FARM BOY TO FINANCIER"

A Secret Expedition to Jekyl Island

Despite my views about the value to society of greater publicity
for the affairs of corporations, there was an occasion, near the
close of 1910, when I was as secretive—indeed, as furtive—as any
conspirator. None of us who participated felt that we were conspirators; on the contrary, we felt we were engaged in a patriotic
work. We were trying to plan a mechanism that would correct the
weaknesses of our banking system as revealed under the strains
and pressures of the panic of 1907. I do not feel it is any exaggeration to speak of our secret expedition to Jekyl Island as the occasion of the actual conception of what eventually became the Federal Reserve System.

Congress, after 1907, had realized that something had to be done
to strengthen our banking system. To provide itself with a better
understanding of the problem, there had been appointed a joint
commission of twenty-five members of both houses, under the
chairmanship of Senator Aldrich, who was, on the whole, the
best-informed and the most dominant man in Congress on financial measures. This group had gone to Europe, had interviewed
bankers and the heads of the central banks, and then, after a
pleasant summer, they had returned to the United States without
a definite idea of what they ought to do. Senator Aldrich did not
know what they ought to do, either, although he really had been
working hard for two years.

For me the beginning of the adventure, I should think, was a
letter that came from Mr. Stillman in Paris. He said he had just
had a long conference with Senator Nelson Aldrich—Zivil in our
code—who was very keen to get to work on banking and currency
revision. Aldrich, Mr. Stillman reported, regretted that Henry
Davison, of J. P. Morgan & Co., and I had been unable to join him
in Europe during the summer; he felt that over there we might
have had plenty of time for our discussions, and been free from
interruptions. In a moment of entire candor he would have said,

"free from reporters." Mr. Stillman said he had told Mr. Aldrich that freedom from interruptions was essential, but that it could be accomplished by getting Davison and me down to Warwick—his place in Rhode Island—without anyone's knowing of it. That was Mr. Aldrich's plan as he left Paris. Mr. Stillman wrote me that I should make everything else subservient to giving my whole time and thought to a thorough consideration of the subject. He said that Aldrich was persuaded that he could accomplish more by getting out of the Senate, so as to put the work of revision on a nonpartisan basis. Mr. Stillman expressed to me a fear that after revision "the banks might not be so well off. He wrote that from that time on Davison and I ought to follow the matter very closely, and keep in touch with Aldrich. Aldrich, I was informed, believed in some sort of centralization, but not in the establishment of a central bank such as France had. Mr. Stillman also reported to me that in his talk with Senator Aldrich he himself had not expressed any views, except as he had impressed on the senator his belief in the necessity of not being too much influenced by "our Wall Street point of view."

But would the electorate have believed that? I question their ability to do so. Just to give you a faint idea: Senator Aldrich was the father-in-law of John D. Rockefeller, Jr., and himself a very rich man. Once I had written to Woodrow Wilson at Princeton, inviting him to speak at a dinner. Wishing to impress him with the importance of the occasion, I had mentioned that Senator Aldrich also had been invited to speak. My friend Doctor Wilson had astonished me by replying that he could not bring himself to speak on the same platform with Senator Aldrich. He did come and make a speech, however, after I had reported that Mr. Aldrich's health would prevent him from appearing. Now then, fancy what sort of headlines might have appeared over a story that Aldrich was conferring about new money legislation with a Morgan partner and the president of the biggest bank.

On October 28, 1910, I wrote to Mr. Stillman in Paris: "Senator Aldrich met with what came very near being a severe, if not fatal, automobile accident. You probably have seen the report of it in the papers. He was pretty well bruised, having cuts on each side of his face. He is very much better now, but the accident has naturally postponed the conference that was in mind. He will be about in a few days, and Mrs. John D., Jr., tells me that they do not think there will be any serious effect from the accident."

As the time for the assembling of Congress drew near, Senator Aldrich became increasingly concerned about the report he must write on behalf of the joint monetary commission; likewise, there ought to be, he knew, a bill to present to the new Congress, and none had been drafted. This was how it happened that a group of us went with him to the Jekyl Island Club on the coast of Georgia.

Since it would be fatal to Senator Aldrich's plan to have it known that he was calling on anybody from Wall Street to help him in preparing his report and bill, precautions were taken that would have delighted the heart of James Stillman. Those who had been asked to go were Henry Davison, Paul Warburg, Ben Strong, and myself. From Washington came A. Piatt Andrew, Jr., who was then an Assistant Secretary of the Treasury, and who now is a member of Congress from Massachusetts. We were told to leave our last names behind us. We were told, further, that we should avoid dining together on the night of our departure. We were instructed to come one at a time and as unobtrusively as possible to the railway terminal on the New Jersey littoral of the Hudson, where Senator Aldrich's private car would be in readiness, attached to the rear end of a train for the South.

When I came to that car the blinds were down and only slender threads of amber light showed the shape of the windows. Once aboard the private car we began to observe the taboo that had been fixed on last names. We addressed one another as "Ben," "Paul," "Nelson," "Abe"—it is Abram Piatt Andrew. Davison and I adopted even deeper disguises, abandoning our own first names. On the theory that we were always right, he became Wilbur and I became Orville, after those two aviation pioneers, the Wright Brothers. Incidentally, for years afterward Davison and I continued the practice in communications, and when we were together.

Secret Meeting on Jekyl Island

The servants and the train crew may have known the identities of one or two of us, but they did not know all, and it was the names of all printed together that would have made our mysterious journey significant in Washington, in Wall Street, even in London. Discovery, we knew, simply must not happen, or else all our time and effort would be wasted. If it were to be exposed publicly that our particular group had got together and written a banking bill, that bill would have no chance whatever of passage by Congress. Yet who was there in Congress who might have drafted a sound piece of legislation dealing with the technical banking problem with which we were concerned? . . .

We were taken by boat from the mainland to Jekyl Island and for a week or ten days were completely secluded, without any contact by telephone or telegraph with the outside. We had disappeared from the world onto a deserted island. There were plenty of colored servants, but they had no idea who Ben and Paul and Nelson were; even Vanderlip, or Davison, or Andrew, would have meant less than nothing to them. There we worked in a clubhouse built for people with a taste for luxury. The live-oak trees wear fantastic beards of Spanish moss on Jekyl Island; in November brown leaves make its forests utterly charming. Without our ever stopping to hunt, deer, turkey and quail appeared on the table; there were pans of oysters not an hour old when they were scalloped; there were country hams with that incomparable flavor that is given to them in the South. We were working so hard that we ate enormously. We worked morning, noon and night. . . .

As we dealt with questions I recorded our agreements in that shorthand I had first practiced with chalk on the tail stock of my lathe back in Aurora. If it was to be a central bank, how was it to be owned—by the banks, by the Government, or jointly? When we had fixed upon bank ownership and joint control, we took up the political problem of whether it should be a number of institutions or only one. Should the rate of interest be the same for the whole nation, or should it be higher in a community that was expanding too fast and lower in another that was lagging? Should it restrict its services to banks? What open-market operations should be engaged in? That was the sort of questions we dealt with, and finally, at the end of our week, we had whipped into shape a bill that we felt, pridefully, should be presented to Congress. As I recall it Warburg had some objections, but we were in substantial agreement on the measure we had created. We returned to the North as secretly as we had gone South. It was agreed that Senator Aldrich would present the bill we had drafted to the Senate. It became known to the country as the Aldrich Plan.

Aldrich and Andrew left us at Washington, and Warburg, Davison, Strong and I returned to New York.

Congress was about to meet, but on a Saturday we got word in New York that Senator Aldrich was ill—too ill to write an appropriate document to accompany his plan. Ben Strong and I went on to Washington and together we prepared that report. If what we had done then had been made known publicly, the effort would have been denounced as a piece of Wall Street chicanery, which it certainly was not. Aldrich never was a man to be a mere servant of the so-called money interests. He was a conscientious, public-spirited man. He had called on the four of us who had Wall Street addresses because he knew that we had for years been studying aspects of the problem with which it was his public duty to deal.

As is now well known, the bill we drafted did not get through Congress. Aldrich retired from the Senate, and then a Democratic majority came down to Washington along with Woodrow Wilson, who had defeated President Taft. The platform on which he was elected contained a statement expressing the opposition of the Democratic Party to the Aldrich Plan, or a central bank. There was a good deal of discussion about that. It was contended that originally the platform committee had agreed upon the statement: "We are opposed to the Aldrich Plan for a central bank."

Now, although the Aldrich Federal Reserve plan was defeated when it bore the name of Aldrich, nevertheless its essential points were all contained in the plan that finally was adopted. It provided an organization to hold the reserves of all member banks and arranged that they would always be ready to relieve a member bank under pressure by rediscounting loans that it held. The law as enacted provided for twelve banks instead of the one which the Aldrich Plan would have created; but the intent of the law was to coordinate the twelve through the Federal Reserve Board in Washington, so that in effect they would operate as a central bank. There can be no question about it: Aldrich undoubtedly laid the essential, fundamental lines which finally took the form of the Federal Reserve Law.

Index

Index